THE IMPACT OF THE FIRST WORLD WAR ON THE BASQUE COUNTRY

THE IMPACT OF THE FIRST WORLD WAR ON THE BASQUE COUNTRY

BY

Eneko Bidegain

This book was published with generous financial support from the Basque Government.

Center for Basque Studies
University of Nevada, Reno
1664 North Virginia St.
Reno, Nevada 89557 USA
http://basque.unr.edu

Copyright © 2024 by the Center for Basque Studies and the University of Nevada, Reno

ISBN-13: 978-1-949805-92-5

All rights reserved.

Library of Congress Cataloging-in-Publication Data

Names: Bidegain, Eneko, author.

Title: The impact of the First World War on the Basque country / Eneko Bidegain.

Other titles: Lehen Mundu Gerra eta Euskal Herria. English

Description: Reno, Nevada : Basque Studies Press, [2024] |

Series: Basque politics ; 28 | Includes bibliographical references and index. | Summary: "This book tells the story of the First World War from the perspective of the Basque Country. It recounts the background to the First World War, to set context, and talks about how this war was experienced in the Basque Country including the after-effects it left behind, especially the human devastation wrought by the war. The social, economic, and political consequences it had in the Basque Country are discussed in this work, as it is clear that this conflict had a decisive influence on the future of the Northern Basque Country and its ties with France"— Provided by publisher.

Identifiers: LCCN 2024032495 (print) | LCCN 2024032496 (ebook) | ISBN 9781949805925 (paperback) | ISBN 9781949805932 (epub)

Subjects: LCSH: World War, 1914–1918—Influence. | World War, 1914–1918—France—Pays Basque. | Nationalism—France. | World War, 1914–1918—Spain—País Vasco. | World War, 1914–1918—Participation, Basque.

Classification: LCC D762.P34 B5313 2024 (print) | LCC D762.P34 (ebook) | DDC 940.3/4475—dc23/eng/20240829

LC record available at https://lccn.loc.gov/2024032495

LC ebook record available at https://lccn.loc.gov/2024032496

Printed in the United States of America

Basque Politics #28

TABLE OF CONTENTS

1 INTRODUCTION

PART ONE
3 THE SPARK

ONE
5 Franco-Prussian War (1870)

TWO
13 The Awakening of Nationalisms

THREE
24 From Deep Division to Sacred Union

FOUR
31 The Spark of Sarajevo

FIVE
42 The Position of the Southern Basque Country

PART TWO
49 THE FIRE

SIX
51 The Massacre of Fonteny and Gozée

SEVEN
56 In the Heart of the Quagmire

EIGHT
64 The Deserters

NINE
74 Life in the Basque Country

TEN
87 The Position of the Basque "Intelligentsia"

ELEVEN
96 Off to Salonika

TWELVE
101 Verdun and the Somme

THIRTEEN
107 The Chemin des Dames

PART THREE
113 THE SMOKE

FOURTEEN
115 Basques and France

FIFTEEN
128 The Final Showdown

SIXTEEN
139 Counting the Dead

SEVENTEEN
154 The Consequences

161 Bibliography

171 Index

LIST OF FIGURES AND TABLES

FIGURE 16.1
149 Basques killed in war per year

FIGURE 16.2
151 Basque soldiers killed by French département or country

FIGURE 16.3
152 Basque soldiers killed by cause

TABLE 16.1
142 Basque soldiers killed by home village

TABLE 16.2
148 Basque soldiers killed by age

TABLE 16.3
149 Basque soldiers killed by month

Introduction

A decade after the commemoration of the centenary of the First World War, this book aims to analyze the consequences of this war in the Basque Country. It is important to note that the Southern Basque Country did not experience the war in the same way as the Northern Basque Country did, and thus the commemoration did not have the same echo on one side of the border as on the other, as Spain was not involved in the war.

In the Southern Basque Country, history lovers know what most of Europe celebrates on November 11. The rest of the Basques, for the most part, have no idea. How could they? For the Southern Basque Country, the First World War is remote in both time and distance. Although it is not much further away for the citizens of the Southern Basque Country than it is for those in the North, differences between Basques on either side of the Bidasoa exist. On the one hand, the population has continued to live as before; the war had no real impact on society and left no deep wounds. On the other hand, there isn't a village that doesn't have its own war memorial and doesn't remember, every year, those who died in the war or who took part in it. Every year, wreaths of flowers are laid around the French flag. In the Northern Basque Country, these symbols perpetuate the memory of the First World War—from a French point of view.

The aim of this book is to tell the story of the First World War from the perspective of the Basque Country. To set the context, I recount the background to the First World War. I also examine how the Basque Country experienced this war and its aftereffects, whatever they may have been, with the most tragic obviously being the deaths the war caused. This book often mentions the Basque Country deaths. Note that the list of soldiers officially considered to have died in the war can be consulted on the French Ministry of Defense's *Mémoire des Hommes* website, which has been a useful resource for the number of deaths and related information presented in this book. These figures do not always tally with the lists on the war memorials erected in almost every community. These monuments list the names of those who were considered members of the community when they died. However, in the case of the list compiled for this book, the classification is based on place of birth, not on place of residence. In other words, here a reference to the day on which forty-seven Basques died means that forty-seven men born in the Basque Country died on that date, though perhaps some of them had not lived in the Basque Country for a long time. Conversely, those who had lived in the Basque Country but were not born there are not included in this list.

In addition to the human devastation wrought by the war, its social, economic, and political consequences in the Basque Country are discussed in this work, as it is clear that this conflict had a decisive influence on the future of the Northern Basque Country and its ties with France. To better understand this aspect, this work has not been limited only to the war. The course of events and the fighting are briefly recounted, of course, but the book also takes a close look at the periods leading up to the war, nationalism, and political debates.

To better understand the differences between the political situations in the Southern Basque Country and the Northern Basque Country, it is essential to understand what happened not only between 1914 and 1918 but also between 1870 and 1914. The relationship between the inhabitants of the Northern Basque Country and France was quite different from the relationship between the inhabitants of the Southern Basque Country and Spain, particularly because the Northern Basques went to war with and for France, and this had a considerable impact.

This book is organized in three parts. The first analyzes the decades leading up to the war, setting out the international and social context of the late nineteenth century. This context had obvious consequences in the Basque Country, especially in terms of the Basques' relationship with the French language and nation. The second part is dedicated to the war itself. Although the events directly linked to the war are explained, the focus here is on the social consequences in the Basque Country, whether seen in the daily life of the villages of the Northern Basque Country or in the economic activity of the Southern Basque Country. The third part looks at the consequences of the war. Here, this book shows the human toll among the Basques, presenting a precise census of the dead, village by village, month by month—a detailed analysis that has not existed before now. But beyond this census are the political consequences whose analysis shows how the war changed the Basques' cultural and political vision.

PART ONE

The Spark

CHAPTER ONE

Franco-Prussian War (1870)

On the threshold of the twentieth century, the major event that was to cause the 1914 war had already happened. Europe was to enter a war that would later become global and that crystallized within it many other conflicts, latent or manifest during the previous decades. Fires happen in many places, finally causing the explosion of the powder keg. France and Germany knew that the slightest spark was a threat. The two neighboring countries were sworn enemies and not only during the two great conflicts of the twentieth century in which they were opposed—namely, the First World War (1914–1918) and the Second World War (1939–1945). The main protagonists of these two conflicts, they had been devoted to mutual hatred for a long time. The spark that caused the conflagration in the summer 1914 sprang from still embers, smoldering in a state of lethargy since 1870 and yet alive, waiting only for the bellows of one or the other of the two enemies to be fanned again.[1] Precisely this, a war between France and Prussia happened between July 1870 and September 1871. The Prussian kingdom was the winner while France lost Alsace and Lorraine and, with these two territories, the French Empire and its honor. At the same time, the German Empire was born. Since then, France was aiming for revenge.

In 1870, the French army was very vulnerable. Indeed, Frenchmen were not obliged to do military service, and, considering the reservists, only 238,487 men were likely to be mobilized in addition to the 316,907 professional soldiers.[2] The army was disorganized, the command was ill-prepared, and the combatants arrived late to the scene of the conflict. The Prussian army was more powerful and better organized. It had 500,000 soldiers ready to serve and more than 150,000 reservists.

No one expected a long war.[3] The conflicts of previous years had been settled in a few weeks, notably the war between Austria and Prussia, which had begun in June 1866 and ended in July of that year. The war between France and Austria in northern Italy, by contrast, had lasted from April to July 1859, and Napoleon III had emerged victorious even though his army had suffered heavy losses. The French went to war, therefore, with the conviction that everything would happen as in previous conflicts, that they would emerge the winners. The official documents were very optimistic—they showed no doubt that the war would be very quick, which would result in the victory of the French. This is what the population was led to believe. On August 2, for example, if one is to believe the newspapers of the following days, the French army won a huge victory on Prussian soil. If the newspapers boasted, it was because of the news that was reaching them. The French army had not, in fact, taken the border town of Saarbrücken, as reported. It had entered the town, fired to make itself known, and then turned back without destroying the bridges in its path. Since this village was not in the hands of the Prussian army, the French army achieved no exploit to boast of.[4] But the news spread nonetheless, which benefited the Prussian army. Later, the press would be reproached for having spread false news and providing the enemy with valuable information. This was a key reason to justify the lack of information available to the public during the First World War.

Four days after this operation, the Prussian army won a victory at the battle of Woerth, and the following day, they won in Alsace-Lorraine. The French had not been expecting such news. The prevailing optimism suddenly cooled, but the newspapers continued to say that the situation could again turn in favor of the French. The farther away they were from Prussia, the more the inhabitants south of the Loire, especially the peasants, remained unaware of Prussia and therefore took what they were told at face value. However, on September 2, less than one and a half months after the beginning of the war, Napoleon III was forced to capitulate at the battle of Sedan and taken prisoner by the Prussian army. Thus ended the Second Empire. However, the war continued for several months. On January 29, 1871, France signed the armistice and ceded the territories of Alsace and Lorraine to Germany. In reaction to the situation caused by this war, uprisings took place in Paris between March and May 1871 as part of the insurrectionist movement of the Paris Commune.

"Wounded" France

The war met with little response in the Northern Basque Country, where the only region somewhat affected by the conflict was Baiona (Bayonne).[5]

Basically, the inhabitants did not feel as concerned by this war as they would be, later, by the First World War. At least eighty-four Basques died during the conflict.[6] Not until the First World War did the counting of losses become exact.

Among the Basques who took part in the Prussian war was Jean-Baptiste Elissamburu, a native of Sara (Sare) and an author of songs, poems, and a short novel. In 1849, he joined the army for two years and took part in several campaigns, including the war of 1870,[7] first as an officer, then as a captain. On October 29 of that year, he was arrested when the army surrendered in Metz. He remained a prisoner until April 6 of the following year in the village of Soest, in the region of Westphalia.

Elissamburu also left some verses about this war, written a few years later under the title "Biba Frantzia!" ("Long live France!").[8] He expresses the pain he felt on seeing how France seemed wounded during the postwar period in the following verses:

> How to say today, France
> Our joy, that of your children?
> You, our motherland
> Left for dead by the enemies.
> All the blood they have sucked
> Left you on the ground, weakened.
> Now your people have risen,
> Long live! Long live! Long live France!
>
> A few years ago, on a dark night,
> As he slept in his nest,
> An eagle was attacked
> By two hundred crows at once.
> They defeated him; impossible to resist
> In the face of so many dark enemies.
> Even though they tore off one of his wings
> He continues to fly.

Original version:

> Nola guk erran egun, Franzia.
> Gu hire haurren alegrantzia?
> Ama ginian hitan heria
> Etsaiek hiltzat utzia;

Hek xurgaturik odol guzia
Apal hindagon eroria;
Xutitu bait haiz orai, Herria,
Biba! Biba! Franzia!

Urte guti du, gau ilhun batez,
Lo zagolarik bere ohatzean,
Arrano bati lotu zirela
Berreun bele batean.
Bentzutu zuten; ezin atxiki
Hoinbertze etsai beltzen artean.
Hegal bat ere kendurik utzi...
Halare dabil airean.

The following verses about the glory of France were written by someone who would become one of the most famous Basque authors of the nineteenth century. He was not the only one to take this position. The author of the song "Agur Euskal Herriari"—"Zazpi Euskal Herriek bat egin dezagun" (Let's unite the seven Basque provinces)—Gratien Adema Zaldubi also wrote verses in which he asks for protection for France[9]:

The Church and France
implore you with their sobs
They need so much
Of your help

Help the Church
By your power
May this same power
Allow France to rise again

Original version:

Eliz'eta Frantzia
Dagotzu nigarrez,
Zure ganik Maria
Laguntza beharrez

Lagun zazu Eliza
Zure bothereaz

Bothere berak beza
Frantzia altxaraz

These verses convey the atmosphere reigning in the Northern Basque Country during the decades following the war. The wounds of France evoked by Elissamburu and Zaldubi illustrate that the defeat of 1870 not only left superficial scratches but also, in fact, deeply bruised the country.

Immediately after the beginning of hostilities, the French Empire was to disappear, following the arrest of Napoleon. A few days later, with France still at war, the Third Republic—the longest that France has known to date—was proclaimed. Meanwhile, in Germany, the dream of uniting all the states into a single empire became a reality with the birth of the German Empire. As the Kingdom of Prussia was the largest of the territories making up the empire, it was Prussia's king, William I, who became emperor of Germany. France, as the loser, and Germany, with its new empire, constituted two sides of the same coin. By 1914, Germany was one of the greatest powers in Europe.[10]

One of the most important wounds inflicted on France was the loss of Alsace and Lorraine, the ceding of which to Germany constituted the most wounding part of the armistice. Since 1859, Prussia had had its sights set on these two territories because for Germany they were Germanic regions.[11] Alsace had been a territory of the Holy Roman Empire since the birth of that empire. It had become part of France only in the seventeenth century.

However, the loss of Alsace-Lorraine to the Germans was damaging for the French. The obligation to pay 5 billion francs to Germany, along with the loss of the Alsace-Lorraine territory, constituted an immense dishonor for the French. Furthermore, clearly the French had been unprepared militarily.[12] This humiliation was a "trauma for the French,"[13] who realized that their supposed military, cultural, and economic superiority was a myth. The French no longer considered their country to be among the most powerful states. This situation, unacceptable to the French people, led to the awakening of a strong patriotism. This French nationalism had its roots in the French Revolution, but with the loss of Alsace and Lorraine, it took on a new face.[14]

The memory of the defeat of 1871 inevitably led to a demonstration of loyalty to the two lost territories and to praise for the French army.[15] This topic occupied a considerable place (not always with the same intensity) in French politics during the five decades preceding the end of the First World War, even if it was often only a pretext for easy demagoguery. Basically, the loss of these territories symbolized a deeper malaise affecting France, and the demand for repossession of the lands served to achieve another aim—that of awakening nationalism in a weakened France.

While this new situation was earth-shattering for France, Europe, for its part, continued to evolve at its own steady pace without suffering any other repercussions and without modifying European stability. Clearly, apart from France, no other nation was shaken by the cession of Alsace and Lorraine to Germany.[16] The loss of Alsace and Lorraine did not affect the demography of France, however, nor its economic production, nor its army. France had no need to recover these territories to enable its army to equal that of Germany. Moreover, less than five years after the defeat, it had indeed reconstituted its army. France's problem lay elsewhere; as a defeated country, it would remain diplomatically isolated for twenty years, deprived of the support and assistance of other European states.

The manifestations of this nationalism were not demonstrated in a politically united France. Right and Left, supporters of the monarchy, Bonapartists, and Republicans were opposed to each other, some reproaching the others for their lack of patriotism.[17] At the end of the nineteenth century, Charles Maurras and Léon Daudet, members of the extreme right-wing group Action Française, put themselves forward as exemplary French nationalists.[18] This movement also had followers in the Northern Basque Country. Some Basques, especially those who were close to the Catholic Church (priests as well as political figures), were in favor of the return of either the monarchy or the Bonapartists, for they remained loyal to Napoleon Bonaparte. The founders of the weekly magazine *Eskualduna* (1887) belonged to such movements. They published several articles on the events of 1870 in order to attribute the responsibility for the defeat to the Republicans.

Forty-three years separated the two wars. During this period, the French never lost sight of their intention to take their revenge on Germany. This desire manifested itself more strongly at two specific moments—between 1879 and 1889, then after 1905—because the tensions that increased between the two states brought back to the French the trauma of 1871 and the feeling of dishonor that accompanied it.[19] As for the Germans, they knew, it seems, that the French had no intention of giving up and would, as soon as they had the opportunity, try to recover what they had lost in 1871.[20] To what extent this thirst for revenge was felt by the ordinary French citizen is another matter.[21] In any case, that this feeling repeatedly resurfaced illustrates that at some point a new war was going to confront France and Germany. The event that the French had been waiting so long for would break out in 1914.

The last two verses of Elissamburu's poem "Biba Frantzia!" perfectly reflect this preparation for revenge:

Seeing now that this eagle
Did not die under their blows
But that it flies higher and higher
The crows are afraid,
With time this eagle
Will know better days;
The hour of revenge will come
For you have children.

Soon the French people
Will stand up as before;
The children will bring back to their mother
The wing stolen by the crows.
By putting all our forces there
Who will say what our power can be?
By gathering all the French
May God hear me!

Elissamburu evokes France as having the features of an eagle (*arrano*) and the Germans as being crows (*beleak*). The author writes these verses while the eagle is recovering its strength, and he clearly suggests that when it is fully recovered, France will take back from the crows "the stolen wing"—namely, Alsace and Lorraine. These verses also reflect the way in which the Basques themselves idealized the image of France. These verses were written during the long process of French nation-building. By 1914, this long process would reached maturity.

NOTES

1. Becker and Audoin-Rouzeau, *La France, la nation, la guerre: 1850–1920*, 147.
2. Martinien, *La Guerre de 1870–1871—La Mobilistation de l'Armee—Mouvements des dépots*, 424.
3. Roth, *La guerre de 1870*, 15.
4. Wawro, *The Franco-Prussian War: The German Conquest of France in 1870–1871*, 94.
5. Darrigrand, "La guerre de 1870–1871 à Bayonne et dans les environs," 255.

6. Jourdan, "Noms des morts à la guerre ou des suites au Pays Basque et à Bayonne,"
7. Elosegi, "Jean-Baptiste Elizanbururen bizitza," 83.
8. Labaien, *Elizanburu bere bizitza ta lanak: Su vida y obras*, 202.
9. Adema, "Maria bekhaturik gabe kontzebitua," 4.
10. Fischer, *Les buts de guerre de l'Allemagne impériale, 1914–1918*, 27.
11. Caron and Vernus, *L'Europe au XIXe siècle*, 299.
12. Sohier, "L'enfant et la guerre à l'école primaire: En Bretagne 1871–1914," 16.
13. Thiesse, *Ils apprenaient la France: L'exaltation des régions dans le discours patriotique*, 3.
14. Girardet, *Le nationalisme français: Anthologie 1871–1914*, 14.
15. Joly, "Le souvenir de 1870 et la place de la Revanche," 110.
16. Roth, *La guerre de 1870*, 583.
17. Hereafter referred to as Republicans, these people supported the French Republic and its left-leaning ideology.
18. Weber, *L'Action française*.
19. Caron and Vernus, *L'Europe au XIXe siècle*.
20. Joly, "Le souvenir de 1870 et la place de la Revanche," 113.
21. Becker and Audoin-Rouzeau, *La France, la nation, la guerre*, 147.

CHAPTER TWO

The Awakening of Nationalisms

Whereas France felt wounded, Germany was proud of the 1871 victory. The Prussian chancellor Otto von Bismarck promoted the German Second Reich, where Prussia united with twenty-four other states, among them the Kingdom of Bavaria, Würtemberg, Sax, and Bad Duchy.[1] The first event that paved the way for this particular union was the Crimean War (1853–1856).[2]

The Russian Empire lost the Crimean War to the Ottoman Empire, along with control of the Crimean part of the Black Sea and southern Ukraine. In this conflict, England and Austria supported Turkey to prevent Russia from having access to the Black Sea. France joined them because Napoleon III saw the military opportunity to regain France's honor following his uncle's 1812 defeat in Russia. After the defeat of the great Russian Empire, it became clear that classical empires were obsolete. The principle of nationalities and the idea of nation-states was strengthened. This change was also at the root of the nation-state character the German Empire would exhibit fifteen years later.

Three years after the end of the Crimean War came the Italian War (1859–1861), initially between Austria and Spain, who fought over possession of Lombardy. It was at the end of this war, in 1861, that the Kingdom of Italy was established, uniting the Kingdom of Sardinia, the Kingdom of the Two Sicilies, and the Duchy of Italy. The Kingdom of Sardinia occupied most of northern Italy, whose sovereign, Victor Emmanuel II, acceded to the throne. The only territories that remained outside Italy were Veneto and the city of Rome; the first remained attached to Austria for another five years, the second remained under the authority of the Vatican until 1870.

After Italy had become a nation-state, the next step was to bring the disparate regions of Germany together as well. That each region had its own specificities posed some difficulties in the process of cohabitation. However, the German Empire recognized the identity of each region and set in motion a process of centralization that did not impose uniformity.[3] In addition, Germany's economic development facilitated these regions' acceptance of German unity.

The creation of the empire, as such, had a profound impact on the propagation of nationalist sentiment among Germans.[4] The message to young Germans was that the country was surrounded and that threats came from both east and west, from the Slavic countries as well as from France. German youth were concerned about Russia's intentions, England's strong economy, and France's thirst for revenge. It was against this background that an anti-Semitic, dynastic, militaristic, conservative, and racist nationalist movement emerged in German student circles in the 1880s and was further strengthened by the accession of Kaiser Wilhelm II (grandson of Wilhelm I) in 1888. In the years leading up to 1914, the main promoters of this expansionist nativism of the younger generation were to occupy important political positions.[5]

The young people who had grown up in the era of Chancellor Bismarck now constituted a strong power in terms of numbers. In the forty-four years following the establishment of the empire, the German population increased by 65 percent; in 1871 there were forty-one million Germans, and in 1915 there were sixty-eight million. Moreover, one in three inhabitants was under fifteen years of age. In addition to having a politically and demographically powerful empire, Chancellor Bethmann-Hollweg's objective beginning in 1909, when he came to power, was to control continental Europe economically.[6] The economic expansion was commensurate with this aim. In the industrial sector, Germany reached the same level of development as England—in other words, the level of a European economic power. French industry, by contrast, was aging.

Germany now demanded its place among the world's great powers, which did not fail to create tensions. Indeed, compared with the countries around it, Germany lacked a trapping of empire in that it had no colonies or had, at least, very few. As a result, it experienced difficulty in obtaining products at good prices and in meeting the needs of a growing population. The only territories in its possession were Cameroon, Togo, German East Africa (present-day Rwanda, Burundi, and part of Tanzania), Southwest Africa (present-day Namibia), and the Bismarck Archipelago (several islands in northern New Guinea).

At the end of the nineteenth century, economic issues were stirring up nationalism, including in other European states. With the Industrial Revolution and the development of capitalism, the economic system had been transformed and each country had to compete with the whole world. In the second half of the nineteenth century, England's agriculture and France's industry were confronted with unprecedented international competition, particularly from the rapidly industrializing United States and Germany. The crisis threatening these countries led to a rise in nationalism.[7] Driven by economic development, the French and English were forced to compete.

Likewise driven by economic development, Russia proceeded, through its officials, to a Russification of its entire territory. In the Baltic States and in Ukraine in particular, the Russian presence was reinforced, especially by means of language. If until then there had been no particular aversion between these regions and old Russia, the obligation to speak Russian awoke regionalist sentiments, although this Russian policy was, overall, considered by many to be more beneficial than prejudicial to national unity.[8]

A vigorous Frenchification process

France also turned to its civil servants to develop national unity on its territory. The pain caused by the defeat of 1871 did not affect all the inhabitants of French territory with the same intensity. Most of the population, being illiterate peasants, were largely unaware of the nationhood of France and its political and cultural life.[9] In 1860 a large number of the inhabitants (22 percent) still did not know French,[10] even though most of the regional languages shared similarities with French and therefore regional peoples had no problem understanding French.[11] The situation in the Basque Country was different, however, because Euskara (the Basque language) and French lack this linguistic proximity. At that time, there were many small villages where only Basque was spoken. Most of the inhabitants did not go to school, so those who did not know French were in the majority.[12]

The French authorities of the Third Republic wanted to radically change this situation. Jules Ferry was the main instigator of the policy of building French identity. He devoted all his efforts to spreading the French language and to excluding the regional languages and making them minority languages. School was the main tool that made it possible for him to achieve these goals, and it was Jules Ferry who established free and compulsory education. This not only would result in the schooling and better education of all citizens but also would lead them to learn French and, later, to forget their own language. The process was "painful and violent" for the children of the time.[13] In the classroom first and then during recess, the children began to speak more and more in French, until the language penetrated even into their homes.[14] During the interwar period the literacy of most children was a direct result of Jules Ferry's law on compulsory schooling. In 1914 in France, only 4 percent of the population could not read.[15]

In addition to encouraging learning to read, another message was also delivered to the children of this era. Schools praised the city dweller, which was to cause a feeling of inferiority among the inhabitants of the rural world and directly influence the language spoken in the countryside. More and more people refused to speak in their local language, and young people who were also learning French tended to choose this language over their regional one.[16]

In any case, the process was not immediate; it took more than one generation. Those who went to school at the beginning of the 1880s had barely learned French, whereas those who followed them ten years later—in other words, the war generation—mastered the language very well.[17] Until 1880, only boys were required to attend school. While the girls did not go to school, once they became mothers, they passed on their language to their children, and it was a language other than French. As soon as girls were required to attend school, they learned French and, once they became mothers, began to speak French with their children.[18]

According to some testimonies collected in Brittany, relentless campaigns were carried out against the Breton language in order to spread French, resulting in punishments for children who spoke Breton at school.[19] In the Basque Country, similar accounts circulated: a stick was given to any child who spoke Basque, and if children heard another child speaking in Basque, they would give the stick to that child. In this way, the one who had the stick at the end of the day was punished. Testimonies to this effect date mainly from the twentieth century. The problem for the teachers in the nineteenth century was that their students had difficulty following lessons presented in French. It was therefore necessary to appoint teachers who knew Basque so that they could teach in it.[20]

In the case of Brittany and the Basque Country, the objective of this action against the local languages was to establish a secular state. For the Republicans, Basque and Breton were tools for transmitting the Christian faith. The Catholic Church used the language of the local inhabitants to spread its message, and in the Basque Country this language was Euskara. Therefore, if the Basque language was harshly attacked, it was with the aim of weakening the influence of the Catholic Church by prohibiting, among other things, catechism in this language.[21]

In this process of Frenchification of Basque society, some deeper and less visible changes had a considerable impact. Not all was limited to the politics of France and to the school. As a result of economic developments, increasing numbers of people were moving to the city. However, the process of urbanization had begun much earlier. The concept of civilization has its roots in the eighteenth century, when courtiers, bourgeois, and other elites were considered civilized and the little people, the "barbarians," were thought to still be in the process of becoming civilized, according to this view.[22] For city dwellers, peasants were little more than animals who lived with other animals: they were poor, backward, ignorant, and savage.[23] Leaving one's village to live in the city became a sign of progress in the process of "civilization." This view of society had more impact on the decline of regional languages than all the efforts made by the administration. The regional language (which the French call *patois*) was the language of the dominated, whereas French was the language of the dominant. The regional languages thus became used by the dominated to communicate among themselves in their daily relations. French was the language that allowed for contact with the outside world, that of the administration, of the authorities. Not knowing French or not mastering it properly meant being oppressed.[24] The way to escape this oppression was, therefore, to learn and use French.

In this way, shamefulness at being a peasant was surreptitiously introduced into the peasants' self-concept. Rural people began to admire the Parisians, for example, and to resemble those they admired they had no other solution than to learn their language.[25] In the same way, when they left their villages to live in the city, the peasants made a point of speaking French. Thus, the very people who spoke their regional languages ended up despising them.[26] Only the official language, French, made it possible to move up the social ladder through urbanization.[27] In addition, it was difficult to halt the process of migration to cities, since remaining in the village meant accepting rural overcrowding and misery.

With the rural exodus and the development of transportation, people left their regions and began to cross paths with those from other places. Witnessed at the same time as the decline of the rural world was the development of cities, which resulted in distancing the inhabitants from their roots. The destruction of these rural roots forced people to turn to another solidarity network. This network was to be the nation, and the nation was France.[28] These changes were also accompanied by cultural evolution, for as people learned to read, the dissemination of information spread, which contributed greatly to the spread of

French nationalism. Finally, with the development of democracy and universal suffrage, citizens began to take part in political debate and to feel that they belonged to the nation-state. Leaving one's village also meant detaching oneself from religion and becoming secular.[29] Those who left their villages no longer had to work as much as they had done on the farm, had more time and opportunities for leisure, did not go to Mass as often as they had done when they lived in the countryside, and could, moreover, live anonymously. Nationalism was now taking over the function that religion had previously occupied. When those who had gone to the city returned to visit their native village, they were admired. In the countryside, contempt for the peasantry grew as the prestige of the city increased.[30]

While this trend developed in the rural world throughout France, the urbanization of the coast of the Northern Basque Country came later.[31] Moreover, the Catholics and the devout disapproved of this movement toward the city, which they considered a path to perdition for the heartlands of the country and for religion.[32] In contrast with regional languages in the rest of France, the Basque language faced fewer threats, although the rural exodus did lead to a negation of Euskara. France attached great importance to the integration of the countryside within the process of nation-building.[33] It did not want to pit the countryside against the city, nor did it want to pit the countryside against the French nation. On the contrary, the French nation was legitimized by the rural world because that was where its roots lay.

In some places however, notably in Brittany, this centralism was not readily accepted. Regionalist movements appeared, driven by the desire to defend a regional language in the face of the so-called national language.[34] Most often, the motivation of these movements was not political. The parish priests of the Basque Country, Brittany, and Occitania knew that the peasants did not use French. If the priests wanted to be understood, they therefore had to express themselves in the language of the countryside around them. Along with the local language, they promoted the traditions and folklore of the villages. In other words, they acted in favor of the values of a traditional society in Basque, Breton, and Occitan.[35] Although the influence of the priests was fundamental to the survival of the Basque language, their efforts were primarily focused on religion. The regionalism of this period was conservative. In Brittany, though, a regionalism of a political nature was born in 1911, and certain movements also appeared in northern Catalonia and Occitania.[36]

From 1789 onward, there were two models for France: those who favored an interregional federation, and the Jacobins, who demanded centralism. The latter feared that the federal model would undermine the gains of 1789. Yet, the political figures who criticized centralism and demanded that the regions be strengthened were right-wing, such as members of the extreme right-wing movement Action Française. Left-wing politicians were opposed to such ideas because they saw centralism as guaranteeing France's unity, and they feared that federalism would lead to division that would benefit the Germans.[37]

However, the proponents of French unity found a way to "naturally" integrate Brittany, Corsica, Occitania, Catalonia, and the Basque Country into the French nation, claiming that these local identities were part of a more general identity.[38] Here, then, appeared the concepts of the small homeland and the large homeland. At the end of the nineteenth century, these regions had strong identities, and France considered it preferable to integrate them into its midst (while hindering the languages of the regions and setting them aside) than to resort to confrontation. In order to characterize the small homeland, one mentions not language but landscapes, geography, famous men, folklore, and *terroir*,[39] or "products of the land."[40] All these things still have a strong impact on the French definition of local identity, especially *terroir*. There is no doubt that the term is related to *terre* (land), not to the Basque word *erro* (root), even though both sound similar. The word *terroir* has as much to do with land as with roots. It demonstrates, in fact, an attachment to the land and to local roots, limiting itself principally to gastronomic culture and presenting these local roots as a fundamental element of the large homeland. France was depicted as the sum of all these regions in order to undervalue the identity and language of these regions and to praise the French. French nationalism promoted in schools (lay and Catholics).[41] Thus, the message that France was the union of all these territories was disseminated in schools, starting from the local region's position in it, in order to make people aware of what the full territory of France was, including Alsace and Lorraine, which the French expected to recover one day.[42]

In the Basque Country, too, the notions of small homeland and large homeland were making their appearance with phrases like "pure Basques, unreservedly French" or "the more Basque you are, the better French person you will be."[43] However, this attachment to France did not remove the fact that the presence of the Basque language was extremely important. Even if the inhabitants were learning French gradually, the Basque language remained the language spoken at the hearth, the mother tongue. Furthermore, the priests knew that it was in this language, linked to affection, that they should address the people.[44] Indeed, by communicating in Basque, parish priests managed to save the language.[45] In the Northern Basque Country, the priests were the elite in the Basque culture of the time.[46] The priests' influence was great, and the inhabitants of the interior of the country were highly religious. For these reasons, secular civil servants and teachers were not well received in the Basque Country.[47] The Basque language became an instrument to fight against secularism,[48] but this attachment to the language did not trigger Basque patriotism.[49] In fact, the Basque language was the instrument that allowed the faith to be strongly maintained in the Northern Basque Country.[50] Defending Euskara was a matter of preserving the tradition, the way of life, and the social organization of the past.[51] The consequence of this was that Basques and speakers of minority languages were reproached for being reactionary.[52]

In the Southern Basque Country, too, the attachment to the Basque language was linked to faith and traditional society, but it also had a political flavor. By founding the Basque Nationalist Party (Euzko Alderdi Jeltzalea), Sabino Arana Goiri created a political party that claimed statehood for the Basque Country. Like the nationalisms that were developing in Europe, Basque patriotism was also emerging in the Southern Basque Country. In the Northern Basque Country, by contrast, there was no Basque national consciousness despite the presence, at the end of the nineteenth century, of *abertzale* (patriotic) politicians, notably Albert Goyenetche, mayor of Donibane Lohizune,[53] or Pierre Broussain, mayor of Hazparne.[54] However, led by Manex Hiriart-Urruty, director of the weekly *Eskualduna*, most Basque writers did not support the idea of uniting the seven provinces of the Basque Country into a single state.

Although it had cultivated an attachment to the Basque language, the Basque Catholic Church did not send out a message against the French nation. The schools, though, did everything possible to glorify France and did not help the Basque language. The pain of the loss of Alsace and Lorraine was integrated into the school programs. In all of France, the same lessons were given, whether in history, in geography, or in songs.[55] In schools, the concept of "our homeland" was constantly repeated with emphasis on France with the map of France occupying an important place in the classroom and in school textbooks.[56] The aim was to give children a precise territorial vision.

The propensity to tell the national history of France was built up both in and out of school, notably in the museums created for this purpose.[57] This was a trend that other European countries were also experiencing. Each state developed an attachment to its own country, particularly through sports.[58] The press also contributed to this phenomenon to a large extent by widely spreading the figure of the hero forged through sports. In addition to theoretical lessons favorable to France, children also received physical preparation. From 1880 onward, sports became a fundamental subject of instruction. Children had to be prepared to become future soldiers, ready to sacrifice themselves for the French motherland.[59] However, children were not taught *pelota*, soccer, or athletics; instead, the boys were required to do military exercises, including learning to use firearms. Girls were prepared to become mothers or wives of soldiers.[60] It was at school that those who were to go to war in 1914 learned to love France; it was also at school that they were trained, psychologically and physically, to wage war.

After leaving school (at that time, children did not continue their schooling beyond the age of fourteen), the further anchoring of a patriotic spirit and the continuation of the psychological and physical preparation for war took place during compulsory military service. The army was also a school for commitment to the French homeland. In the booklet distributed to conscripts, not only was it clearly stated that France was a father to them and should be loved as a mother, but it was explained that they should be ready to sacrifice themselves for this father and be proud of this sacrifice.[61]

NOTES

1. Kurtz, *The Second Reich: Kaiser Wilhelm II and His Germany*.
2. Kott, *L'Allemagne du XIXe siècle*.
3. Caron and Vernus, *L'Europe au XIXe siècle*, 298.
4. Prost and Winter, *Penser la Grande Guerre: Un essai d'historiographie*, 67.
5. Fischer, *Les buts de guerre de l'Allemagne impériale, 1914–1918*, 23.
6. Soutou and Duroselle, *L'or et le sang: Les buts de guerre économiques de la Première Guerre mondiale*, 45.
7. Ferro, *La Grande Guerre*, 24.
8. Ferro, *La Grande Guerre*, 36.
9. Sohier, "L'enfant et la guerre à l'école primaire: En Bretagne 1871–1914," 15.
10. Cabanel, *La question nationale au XIXe siècle*, 25.
11. Becker and Audoin-Rouzeau, *La France, la nation, la guerre: 1850–1920*, 128.
12. Cabanel, *La question nationale au XIXe siècle*, 27.
13. Sohier, "L'enfant et la guerre à l'école primaire: En Bretagne 1871–1914," 17.
14. Cabanel, "Sentiments nationaux et terre 'irredente,'" 39.
15. Feyel, *La presse en France des origines à 1944: Histoire politique et matérielle*, 82–83.
16. Moulin, *Les paysans dans la société française. De la Révolution à nos jours*, 150.
17. Weber, *La fin des terroirs, la modernisation de la France rurale, 1870–1914*, 121.

18. Weber, *La fin des terroirs, la modernisation de la France rurale, 1870–1914*, 453–454.
19. Brunel, "L'Académie bretonne au grand séminaire de Quimper," 31.
20. Weber, *La fin des terroirs, la modernisation de la France rurale, 1870–1914*, 450–452.
21. Orpustan, "Rôle et pouvoirs de l'Église," 139.
22. Elias, *La civilisation des mœurs*, 103.
23. Weber, *La fin des terroirs, la modernisation de la France rurale, 1870–1914*, 20.
24. Charle, "Région et conscience régionale: Questions à propos d'un colloque," 40.
25. Weber, *La fin des terroirs, la modernisation de la France rurale, 1870–1914*, 23.
26. Weber, *La fin des terroirs, la modernisation de la France rurale, 1870–1914*, 134.
27. Walter and Lagree, *Les parlers de la foi, religion et langues régionales*.
28. Caron and Vernus, *L'Europe au XIXe siècle: Des nations aux nationalismes, 1815–1914*, 434–435.
29. Girardet, *Le nationalisme français: Anthologie 1871–1914*, 28.
30. Weber, *La fin des terroirs, la modernisation de la France rurale, 1870–1914*, 413–415.
31. Goyhenetche, *Histoire générale du Pays Basque: Le XIXe siècle 1804–1914*, 78.
32. Camino, "Hitzaurrea," 12.
33. Thiesse, *La création des identités nationales: Europe, XVIIIe–XXe siècle*, 160.
34. Vigier, "Régions et régionalisme en France au XIXe siècle," 165.
35. Cholvy, "Régionalisme et clergé catholique au XIXe siècle," 194.
36. Guiomar, "Régionalisme, fédéralisme et minorités nationales en France entre 1919 et 1939," 89.
37. Guiomar, "Régionalisme, fédéralisme et minorités nationales en France entre 1919 et 1939," 91.
38. Thiesse, *Ils apprenaient la France: L'exaltation des régions dans le discours patriotique*, 1.
39. Here is what the TLFi (Le Trésor de la Langue Française informatisé) says on its website (http://atilf.atilf.fr/): "Region, province, country considered in its rural particularities, its traditions, its culture, its productions and from the point of view of the character of the people who live there or come from there."
40. Thiesse, *Ils apprenaient la France: L'exaltation des régions dans le discours patriotique*, 34.
41. Ott, *War, Judgment, and Memory in the Basque Borderlands, 1914–1945*, 33.
42. Sohier, "L'enfant et la guerre à l'école primaire: En Bretagne 1871–1914," 16.
43. Goyhenetche, "Les origines sociales de l'association Eskualzaleen Biltzarra," 5.
44. Lachaga, *Eglise particulière et minorités ethniques, jalons pour l'évangélisation des peuples minoritaires*, 128.
45. Urkiza, *Elizaren Historia Euskal Herrian*, 1:1074.

46. Casenave, *De l'article de presse à l'essai littéraire: Buruchkak (1910) de Jean Etchepare.*
47. Moulin, *Les paysans dans la société française: De la révolution à nos jours*, 165.
48. Goñi, "Interdiction du catéchisme en basque," 51.
49. Saly et al., *Nations et nationalismes en Europe: 1848–1914*, 206.
50. Fabas, "Aspects de la vie religieuse dans le diocèse de Bayonne (1905–1965)," 54.
51. Goyhenetche, "Les origines sociales de l'association Eskualzaleen Biltzarra," 5.
52. Lachaga, *Eglise particulière et minorités ethniques, jalons pour l'évangélisation des peuples minoritaires*, 262.
53. Altzibar, "Zazpiak bat gaia XIX. Mendean," 667–668.
54. Charriton, *Pierre Broussain, sa contribution aux études basques (1895–1920)*, 34.
55. Sohier, "L'enfant et la guerre à l'école primaire: En Bretagne 1871–1914," 18.
56. Thiesse, *Ils apprenaient la France: L'exaltation des régions dans le discours patriotique*, 238.
57. Thiesse, *La création des identités nationales: Europe, XVIIIe–XXe siècle*, 143.
58. Ferro, *La Grande Guerre*, 32.
59. Gerbod, "L'éthique héroïque en France (1870–1914)," 411.
60. Sohier, "L'enfant et la guerre à l'école primaire: en Bretagne 1871–1914," 23.
61. *Notes sur l'éducation morale du soldat:13e corps d'armée. 25e division. 49e brigade; 38e régiment d'infanterie*, 10.

CHAPTER THREE

From Deep Division to Sacred Union

This unity of France and adhesion to the French motherland did not happen without tumult. However, neither the question of identity nor that of language was at the origin of the struggles that took place in the Northern Basque Country. The roots of the conflict went back to the French Revolution of 1789. It was not only that the suppression of the Biltzar (Assembly) of Lapurdi, the states of Navarre (Nafarroa), and the court of order of Zuberoa (Soule) had deprived the provinces of the Northern Basque Country of their autonomy but also that the request for the creation of a Basque administration area to replace them had gone nowhere. In fact, at the end of the nineteenth century and the beginning of the twentieth, this demand no longer found an echo or place in the political life of the Northern Basque Country. It was the attempt to weaken the Catholic Church that left the deepest wounds. Even if at first the inhabitants of the Northern Basque Country favored the French Revolution, in 1794 the situation was quite different; the population did not agree with the clergy's civil constitution nor with compulsory conscription. To change this position, the French Republic appointed delegates whose mission was to propagate the love of the French motherland. In Sara, Itsasu, Azkaine, Ezpeleta, and in many other villages, these delegates failed in fulfilling their mission. At the time when France went to war with Spain, the inhabitants of these villages were accused of being deserters and of not loving France. Deemed responsible for this situation, the parish priests were accused of having campaigned against the Republic. With regards to this, the measures taken by the delegates of the French Republic caused serious trauma in that most of the inhabitants of these villages were deported to the Landes.

One hundred years later, traces of these events still lingered in the political atmosphere of the Northern Basque Country. The priests of the Northern Basque Country did not favor the Republic, and most of them were supporters of the monarchy or were partisans of Napoleon III and demanded the return of the empire.

During the elections of the first twenty years of the Third Republic and in the following decades, the priests campaigned wholeheartedly in favor of Bonapartist or monarchist candidates. In fact, in 1889 the elections of the electoral district that included Lower Navarre (Nafarroa Beherea in Basque, Basse-Navarre in French) and Zuberoa were canceled on the grounds that the Catholic Church had used too much influence in favor of the "white" candidate Louis Etcheverry.

The Republicans considered the priests a threat. In 1881, when Jules Ferry, France's minister of education, proposed his law on compulsory schooling, the influence and power of priests, monks, and nuns was weakened. Until then, monks and nuns had been teaching, but as a result of the law, public schools spread and the Catholic Church lost much of its power in education. For the Republicans, it was necessary to weaken the influence of the men and women of the Church; hence the creation of the secular school.[1] In their eyes, clericalism was a threat to the Republic, and they were convinced that it was the will of the Catholic Church to undermine or destroy the French state and national unity.[2] To cut out the evil at its root, they established the secular school, aiming to eliminate religious teachings, establish a separation between science and religion, and offer children a Republican education. They achieved this by excluding monks from schools in 1891 and nuns a little later. The parish priests feared that children would no longer have the opportunity to learn the catechism and would lose their faith.[3] So, in many villages of the Northern Basque Country, they created Catholic schools, but with a fee. In addition, they taught catechism outside school hours.

The parish priests did not go happily along with the French Republic, which appointed François-Antoine Jauffret bishop of Baiona. In 1892, he called on the priests of the Northern Basque Country to align themselves with the Republic. Although the churchmen reluctantly agreed, they persisted in their criticism of the Republic. This was a source of conflict, as the new bishop sanctioned some parish priests by sending them to other parishes. Although the latter won an appeal in Rome, the dispute left a legacy between the Republicans and the Church of the Northern Basque Country.

The culmination of this conflict occurred in 1905, just nine years before the First World War. At the end of the nineteenth century, the Dreyfus affair, in addition to the school law, divided the Right and the Left.[4] Conservatives (including Catholics in the Northern Basque Country) led a full-scale attack on the accused traitor, Alfred Dreyfus, which accelerated the passage of laws in the years that followed.[5] In 1901, an uproar arose from the promulgation of the law on associations because of the freedom it offered for the associations it created. In fact, religious associations and congregations had to ask for authorization, and in the Northern Basque Country many were refused. Monks were forced to leave the region, and they migrated to the Southern Basque Country.[6] Thus, the monks of Belloc left their abbey and were welcomed in the monastery of Lazkao.[7] In 1904, monks and nuns were banned from teaching, and the French government ordered the closure of their schools. The following year the law on the separation of church and state was passed, which allowed the state to get its hands on the Church's property after having inventoried it. Many parish priests in the Northern Basque Country lived in seclusion, aided by local inhabitants, a situation reminiscent of the conflicts that had occurred during the French Revolution.[8] By 1920, all the countryside in the Northern Basque Country was under the control of the state.

Until 1920, all the electoral campaigns had been marked by extremely lively political rivalry between secular society and conservative supporters of the Catholic Church. The main debates of the legislative elections of April 26, 1914, had also centered on the theme of the separation of society on religious grounds. A young candidate, the lawyer Jean Ybarnégaray, ran in the electoral district of the interior of the Basque Country.[9] At the time, he ran as an independent candidate, but at the end of the 1930s he joined the French Socialist Party, an extreme right-wing organization. Supported by the Church, he won the election hands down. It should be noted that those supporting the Republic had little influence in the interior of the Basque Country, where elections revolved around one person and did not involve the party structure that the Republican parties favored. The Republicans were grouped around the schoolteacher or the village officials, whereas the conservatives had the support of the priests. The elite and priests of the villages tended to be monarchists or Bonapartists, and their words were widely echoed among the villagers, who saw them as defenders of Basque tradition, language, and identity.[10] Even when emperor Napoleon III lost power, his supporters continued to be a force in the interior (in the 1870 elections, for instance, the Bonapartists received 75 percent of the votes in the Northern Basque Country[11]). After 1920, disputes between republicans and opponents of the Republic ceased, as the Catholic Church finally admitted that the separation decreed between it and the state had certain advantages.

On the eve of the war

In August 1914, when the First World War broke out, this divisive atmosphere subsided considerably, although it was not completely extinguished and sprang into flames subsequently. However, the days immediately leading up to the war were far from peaceful, and from the beginning of the war there was a freezing of political divisions. For a month the war had simmered on the fire ignited by the Sarajevo bombing. Yet in July 1914, public opinion was hardly preoccupied with international politics. Those who followed the news had a more interesting topic to focus on: the trial of Henriette Caillaux, wife of French finance minister Joseph Caillaux, accused of murdering Gaston Calmette, director of the daily newspaper Le Figaro.[12] The peasants, though, did not follow the political news, as in the Basque Country they were busy enough with their haymaking.

This situation does not imply that everyone was unaware of political events. Some were concerned by the risk of war, especially the trade unionists. The Confédération Générale du Travail, or General Confederation of Labor, sent pacifist messages; its militants were anti-militarists and opposed to nationalism. From July 12, 1914, onward, demonstrations and rallies were organized to protest the war. The most important ones took place on July 30 and 31, but at the end of the second day, this opposition movement suddenly deflated like a balloon.[13] Incidents also occurred between opponents and supporters of the war, notably in Baiona, where revolutionary syndicalists wishing to organize an assembly and opponents of the demonstrations had met.[14] The pacifist doctor Fernand Elosu, who was a member of the National Assembly of France, was one of the first to take part in this event. He had wanted to organize the rally in Saint-Esprit, but serious incidents occurred in this connection. Then on July 29, while Elosu and his friends were distributing leaflets, some of their opponents attacked them.[15] Although the prefect of the Basses-Pyrénées wanted to forbid the gathering, Joseph Garat, the mayor of Baiona, gave his approval for it to take place. After two hours, incidents broke out in front of Elosu's house between war supporters and pacifists while nearby the men of the 49th Infantry Regiment sang "La Marseillaise." Beginning August 2, the incidents in Baiona ceased. The fervent pacifist Georges Miremont took part in these events and was later to die in the war.

Since anti-militarism was widespread among the Left, the French minister of the interior elaborated Carnet B, a prewar plan to identify radicals and anti-militarists and, in the event of a declaration of war, to arrest them.[16] From 1911 onward, the General Confederation of Labor's position in relation to Carnet B became confused, and in the year before the war began, unionists did not clearly show whether a "defensive" war was to be faced. Worse, anti-militarist tendencies became increasingly muted in union general assemblies. In short, socialists did not support insubordination.

Even if paradoxical, the July 31, 1914, assassination of Jean Jaurès, a French socialist deputy and pacifist activist, by a fanatical Action Française activist, was the event that pushed the last pacifists to accept the war.[17] The very same people who had previously been rather hostile to the war wrote that day that the "Motherland is in danger" and, with Jaurès assassinated, headlined the next day that the "defense of the nation is a priority." This event symbolically marked France's entry into the war. The death of their pacifist leader left the militants weakened, and the Left ended up accepting the war. Basically, the explanation for the deactivation of the pacifist movement, with the death of Jaurès, is based on the weakness of the movement itself. It was a movement that was not as anti-nationalist as some would have liked and for whom the interest of the nation was a priority, including particularly these men from the Left, who constituted a minority within the population.[18] In the end, the French government decided not to launch a movement against those listed in Carnet B, which also led extreme left-wing activists to rally to the idea of war.[19]

In the days leading up to the outbreak of war, public opinion in Germany and France changed radically. In German society, initially favorable to the war, concern and fear emerged as the fateful hour approached.[20] In France, public opinion was favorable not only to the war but also to its outcome. Furthermore, the population felt that the country was in danger from a possible attack by Germany, and so the need to save the country took root in people's minds. Moreover, the time had come to quench the thirst for revenge accumulated in the previous decades, and with it came the possibility for "history being made." Faced with this, there was no room for political divisions, and wider political projects became irrelevant. The Left, the Republicans, and the Jacobins decided to accept the war in order to defend the values of the French Revolution and the French model born out of it. The Right, following another line of reasoning, supported the war in the name of the "old France" of the monarchs. In short, those who had been fervent opponents until then forgot their divisions and rallied around a common idea.[21] In reality, whether on the Left or the Right, nationalism existed in both camps, which shared the same point of view when it came to defending the French nation, a view that greatly facilitated the Union Sacrée.[22] For the French, there was no doubt that Germany bore full responsibility for the war. Therefore, it was obvious to all that France should retaliate against Germany's "attack."[23]

The Northern Basque Country also took onboard this logic of union. The Catholic Church took a position in favor of the war, even though there were some exceptions; in 1915, a monk and a priest were judged for having given sermons in favor of the Germans, and in 1917, another priest was judged for having helped deserters, an accusation from which he was later cleared.[24] Despite these few cases, the official message of the Church was of a different tone; the Basque-language magazine *Eskualduna*, a pro-Church publication, defended the war, France, and unity in no uncertain terms. Although the week before the outbreak of hostilities the magazine evoked the terror of the threat, after the war had broken out, the following headline appeared on its front page: "Gerla haste. Biba Frantzia" (The war has begun. Long live France). The defense of France in the face of Germany's attack was expressed entirely in Basque: "Is there, could there be anything more moving, more comforting, than to see, from one end of France to the other, the union of all the citizens concerning the war? No more whites, no more reds, no more divisions, all French in France; in the Basque Country, all Basques, all brothers. From Donibane Lohizune (Saint-Jean-de-Luz) to Atharratze (Tardets), everywhere, to the last border of the last villages, let us all be united behind France."[25]

This unitary atmosphere was firmly established for several months. Louis Malvy, minister of the interior, contributed to it by announcing the freezing of measures resulting from the 1905 law, those concerning the dissolution of congregations or the closing of Catholic schools.[26] However, the union was not unconditional. Even though everyone agreed to serve France, hatreds were not long in coming.

NOTES

1. Ozouf, *L'Ecole, l'Eglise et la République (1871–1914)*, 55.
2. Langlois, "Catholiques et laïcs," 2,330.
3. Bascans and Arbelbide, "Uztaritzeko seroren eskolen hestea," 32.
4. The Dreyfus affair was a political scandal that divided France from 1894 to 1906. In 1894 Alfred Dreyfus, a French artillery officer of Jewish descent, was convicted of treason and sentenced to life imprisonment for allegedly communicating military secrets to the German embassy in Paris. In 1899, under pressure, the army agreed to a retrial. Dreyfus was again found guilty, but with extenuating circumstances. He was pardoned by the president but not exonerated. It was not until

1906 that the French Supreme Court fully exonerated Dreyfus and ordered a new trial, in which he was acquitted.
5. Cabanel, *1905, la séparation des Églises et de l'État*, 10.
6. Cabanel, *1905, la séparation des Églises et de l'État*, 33.
7. Doucet, "Estadoaren eta Elizaren arteko borrokak 1900 inguruan: Fraide batzuen ihardespena Belokeko fraidetxean," 41–42.
8. Itçaina, *Les virtuoses de l'identité: Religion et politique en Pays Basque*, 72.
9. Bidegain and Gostin, "1914 ko hauteskundekanpaina Eskualduna astekarian," 27.
10. Orpustan, "Rôle et pouvoirs de l'Eglise," 152–153.
11. Micheu-Puyou, *Histoire électorale du département des Basses-Pyrénées sous la IIIe et la IVe République*, 126.
12. Becker, "La population française face à l'entrée en guerre," 35–38.
13. Becker, *1914: Comment les Français sont entrés dans la guerre*, 158.
14. Becker, *1914: Comment les Français sont entrés dans la guerre*, 163.
15. Garat, "Insoumissions et désertions en France pendant la Grande Guerre: Le cas des cantons basques," 32.
16. Cohen, "L'antimilitarisme des jeunesses avant 1914," 42.
17. Ferro, *La Grande Guerre*, 75.
18. Becker, *1914: Comment les Français sont entrés dans la guerre*, 249.
19. Becker, *1914: Comment les Français sont entrés dans la guerre*, 406.
20. Krumeich, "L'entrée en guerre de l'Allemagne," 65.
21. Jeissmann, *La patrie de l'ennemi, la notion de l'ennemi national et la représentation de la nation en Allemagne et en France de 1792 à 1918*, 296.
22. Caron and Vernus, *L'Europe au XIXe siècle: Des nations aux nationalismes, 1815–1914*, 350.
23. Becker, *1914: Comment les Français sont entrés dans la guerre*, 370.
24. Garat, "Insoumissions et désertions en France pendant la Grande Guerre: Le cas des cantons basques," 8–9.
25. "Orok bat," *Eskualduna*.
26. Delaunay, "La grande guerre ou la clé du retour," 347.

CHAPTER FOUR

The Spark of Sarajevo

At the start of the twentieth century, Europe was highly unstable, and even a small incident could have triggered a major conflict. This happened on June 28, 1914, in Sarajevo when a Serbian student shot the Austrian archduke Franz Ferdinand and his wife, Sophie, Duchess of Hohenberg, killing them both. Within a month, the uproar over the event had spread like wildfire. Of course, the background to the situation was complex, and the tensions between France and Germany were not unique in Europe.

As heir to the throne since 1896, Franz Ferdinand was destined to become the future ruler of Austria-Hungary. The attack on him was therefore a blow to the aging empire. Sarajevo was the capital of Bosnia-Herzegovina, whose population was mostly Serbian. Serbia had lost this territory in 1908 to Austria. The young Bosnians living there, as well as the Bosnians and Serbian refugees in Serbia, resented being under Austrian rule. At that time, there was unrest that resulted in several attacks. The announcement of the visit of Archduke Franz Ferdinand on Serbia's national holiday sparked a plan by young Serbs to attack, and one of them, a student named Gavrilo Princip, was the perpetrator.[1] He was arrested but escaped the death penalty because of his young age. He died in 1918 of illness as a result of the mistreatment he suffered in detention.

From this event unwound the thread that would lead to the outbreak of the First World War. Although the assassination shook Europe, people were far from imagining that it could initiate such a momentous conflict. Even the perpetrators of the attack saw it only as an episode in the struggle between a minority nation and the oppressor. In fact, Austria-Hungary, unlike Germany, had internal problems, and so for attacks to occur when a representative of Austria came to Serbia was quite common.[2] The unity of Austria-Hungary was already very weakened, however.

Founded in 1867, this new empire had been led by Emperor Franz Joseph of Austria. It was composed of many nations: some had state's rights, others did not.

There were also national minorities. The main difficulties came from the South Slavs and, above all, from the Serbs.[3] The occupation of Bosnia-Herzegovina by Austria-Hungary in 1878 irritated the Serbs of the region and created a major problem. When this territory officially came under Austro-Hungarian rule in 1908, the alliance signed by Serbia and Austria-Hungary in 1881 was invalidated, and relations between the two parties deteriorated considerably.[4]

However, even if the attack really aggravated relations between Serbia and Austria-Hungary, most people wanted to believe in a diplomatic solution. The Second International, whose objective was peace and socialism, did not perceive any threat of war during the whole month of July. The Second International, comprised of socialist and labor parties, had not yet reached agreement on how to respond to a possible war. In 1910, the parties still could not reach an agreement, and the organization's next congress was to be held in Vienna in August 1914. But war had broken out before then, and socialists in each country favored unity in their own nations over international union.

Unrest had previously occurred over Serbia. This unrest had never led to a full-scale war between Serbia's long-time ally Russia and Austria because Germany had counseled Austria-Hungary to remain calm, and France had done the same with Russia. In 1914, the idea that events would take the same course was fairly widespread. Nor was it envisaged that the United Kingdom would enter the war. Certainly Germany, for its part, did not expect the British to enter the war; nor did it seek conflict with them, for the Germans preferred to see the United Kingdom as a rival of France. The United Kingdom, for its part, wanted to see the same relationship of rivalry between France and Germany. The two most powerful states in Europe wanted to rule.

Until 1907, the United Kingdom was not an ally of France. It did not want to lose its position as the world's main economic power, which created some tension with France. However, its biggest rival was Germany, not France. In 1892, France signed a treaty of military cooperation with Russia, which stipulated that if either side was attacked by Germany or Austria-Hungary, the other would provide aid. This treaty ended the isolation from which France had suffered after the war of 1870, even if Russia's support was insufficient to recover the lost territories. The treaty of 1907 between the United Kingdom, France, and Russia sealed the Triple Entente. Europe was then divided into two large blocs: on the one hand, the United Kingdom, France, and Russia; on the other hand, Germany, Austria-Hungary, and Italy, as well as the Ottoman Empire.

Austria and Germany had not always been friends, as evidenced by the 1866 war between the two countries.[5] The 1879 alliance that brought them together was signed because both parties had an interest in helping each other.⁶ The fact that France wished to strengthen itself militarily encouraged Germany to look for allies.⁷ And Austria-Hungary, pushed by its internal conflicts with Serbia and the other southern Slavs, decided to make a pact with Germany.

The case of Italy was different insofar as the country did not feel at ease in its pact with Austria and Germany, which became known as the Triple Alliance. For a long time, Italy had been experiencing territorial conflicts with Austria-Hungary. The Ottoman Empire, with which Germany had just signed the alliance, had been weakened by the loss of many of its territories in previous decades. With the help of Greece and Bulgaria, it had won the First Balkan War against its historical enemies, Russia and Serbia, in 1912. Strengthened by this victory, Serbia then thought of demanding access to the Adriatic Sea, but Austria-Hungary did not accept this claim. Tensions between Serbia and Austria-Hungary could lead to more serious repercussion because neither of them was alone.

These tensions, combined with significant industrial development, had a direct impact on arms production. The war of 1870 clearly showed that it was quite possible for a European state to enter the lands of another state and appropriate that territory. The obvious consequence of this was that each state strengthened the protection of its borders. However, it turned out that guarding one's borders was not enough: each state had to ensure that its army was more powerful than that of the other state.⁸ France, for its part, had to ensure that its borders were protected. France also faced a serious demographic problem. Over the previous thirty years, the birth rate had fallen; fearing that it would not have enough soldiers to face the strengthening German army, France needed a solution to this problem. At first the army recruited "indigenous" Algerians, but in 1913 Germany had 850,000 soldiers, whereas France had only 480,000. For this reason, in 1913, the French government decided to extend the duration of military service from two to three years.⁹ This military preparation showed that tensions between Germany and France were growing and that the threat of war hung over them.

The crisis that occurred in the Agadir region of Morocco in 1911 is a case in point. This was the second incident between Germany and France over the issue of the control of Morocco. The first had occurred in 1905, when Germany had objected to France's free movement in Morocco. An agreement signed in 1906 authorized the French presence in Morocco as long as France did not infringe on the sovereignty of that country. In 1911, Germany sent the gunboat *Panther* to the port of Agadir with the aim of obtaining a settlement.

Finally, France ceded part of the Congo to Germany in exchange for free movement in Moroccan territory. These two crises, in 1905 and 1911, further strengthened the ties between France and the United Kingdom in their preparation for a possible war.[10] But England's primary intention was to avoid war, and Germany was convinced that this would be so. In any case, this was what Germany was betting on.

The United Kingdom did not look kindly on the rise of Germany, however, nor did it wish to lose its maritime supremacy to Germany.[11] Neither did it approve of certain projects initiated by William II in the Middle East, in particular the railroad to Baghdad. Germany intended to establish commercial relations with these regions, to the detriment of the United Kingdom and Russia, a move that was unlikely to guarantee the neutrality of London.

Serbia in the firing line

The scale of the attack in Sarajevo must be seen within this sensitive climate. For the Austro-Hungarian army, this attack represented an unprecedented opportunity to "definitively resolve its problem with Serbia by force of arms."[12] In Germany, too, some officials thought that the time was right to push Austria to war, even if this idea was not unanimous. On the one hand, Chancellor Bethmann-Hollweg feared Russia's retaliation. On the other hand, Kaiser Wilhelm II was convinced that Russia and France, which he believed to be too weakened, would not go to war. Consequently, he believed that the wisest thing to do was to engage in the war against Serbia as soon as possible. Germany, through the intermediary of its ambassador in Vienna, Heinrich von Tschirschky, put pressure on Austria to give Serbia an unacceptable ultimatum.[13] Indeed, Germany did not want the dispute between Serbia and Austria to be settled by a diplomatic agreement. It simply wanted the destruction of Serbia. Austria-Hungary, for its part, feared that the other small nations under its domination would in turn revolt, like Serbia. It was therefore necessary, from its point of view, to stop the revolt in Serbia at its roots.

Germany and Austria-Hungary blamed Russia for financing Slavic movements in order to encourage Pan-Slavism and thereby dismantle the Austro-Hungarian Empire over the long term. To easily overcome Serbia, it was necessary to state the ultimatum as quickly as possible. However, nothing was done before July 23, when Raymond Poincaré, president of the French Republic, made an official visit to St. Petersburg to meet with the Russian government. It was only at the end of this visit that the ultimatum was sent, so Russia and France did not have time to agree on the answer to be given. Nevertheless, Sergei Sazonov, the Russian minister of foreign affairs, informed the German ambassador in St. Petersburg, Count Pourtalès, that a conflict between Austria and Serbia could lead to a generalized war. Pourtalès made a report in which he explained that the United Kingdom would also disapprove of a possible attack by Austria. The German chancellor then sent a note in which he stated that Pourtalès was mistaken.

Assured of Germany's full support, Austria-Hungary issued an ultimatum to Serbia on July 23, 1914.[14] It demanded that the Serbian government disapprove of the propaganda carried out by the Serbs in Austria-Hungary, that it dissolve the Serbian organizations responsible for this propaganda, and that it take part in the fight led by Austro-Hungarian officials against these movements as well as in the investigation into the attack carried out by these same officials. Serbia refused to give in on this last point. It submitted to the other demands, but not to the one that would require it to give up its sovereignty and accept the presence of the Austrian administration on its territory.

The Germans succeeded in their aim. Germany's calculation was as follows: following Austria's attack on Serbia, France and Russia would come to its aid but would not be strong enough to resist the German army. Germany would subdue France first, within six weeks, and then make Russia bend. Germany therefore knew that a European war could break out, yet it was backing this project.[15] Its main objective was not to invade Serbia but to implement Bismarck's plan to make Germany the axis and leading power in Europe.[16] The German army wished to implement its plan in a way that would make it possible for Germany to become the leading European power.

The German army wanted to implement the Schlieffen plan, a strategy conceived in 1905 by Alfred von Schlieffen, a German soldier and strategist. It was later somewhat modified. Initially the idea was to concentrate all forces on the Western Front, to oppose France. Instead of going directly to Paris, the German forces would surround the French army. However, two conditions were necessary to achieve this: the Germans had to enter Belgium, thus violating its neutrality, and they had to do so without the United Kingdom entering the war; in addition, it was imperative to send nine tenths of the German military forces to the west and to leave only one tenth on the Russian front, knowing that the mobilization in Russia would be considerably more passive. Moreover, Germany hoped that Italy would also enter the war and therefore that France would have another front in the Alps, which would further weaken the French army.

After the Sarajevo attack, several diplomatic maneuvers were made to avoid war. Both sides tried to intervene to dissuade Austria-Hungary from going to war. The United Kingdom proposed mediation between Austria and Russia, but as soon as Serbia announced on July 25 that it had refused the last point of the ultimatum, Austria prepared for hostilities. It declared war on Serbia on July 28. While the United Kingdom persisted in its willingness to mediate and Russia was ready to ask Serbia to accept the ultimatum, Austria's final decision set Russia on the road to war.

One of the personalities working to avoid war was Karl Max, Prince Lichnowsky, the German ambassador to the United Kingdom. On the night of July 29–30, he sent a report to the ambassador in Vienna, Heinrich von Tschirschky. In this letter he informed the ambassador that if Austria refused mediation, the neutrality of England would no longer be assured and Italy and Romania would not join the German camp. Therefore, Germany had to push Austria not to declare war and had to sit down at the negotiating table to reach a diplomatic solution. Bethmann-Hollweg, the German chancellor, sent this note to Vienna to warn of the risk of starting a world war. In reality, the chancellor's real objective was not to avoid war but to ensure that Germany did not appear to be responsible for it and to blame Russia. On July 30, Bethmann-Hollweg informed the German emperor of this missive, presenting the situation in such a way that Russia would be considered responsible for the outbreak of war, as well as insisting that the United Kingdom's neutrality was not assured.[17] This presentation of the facts triggered the fury of the emperor, who denounced the encirclement of Germany and accused those who surrounded him of wanting his destruction.[18]

Did all these leaders and diplomatic officials imagine for a moment that they were in the process of unleashing a cataclysm that would cause millions of deaths and completely change the map of Europe? Germany is presented as the main culprit of the conflict because it pushed Austria to war and implemented the military plan against France and Russia. Germany's intention had been to end the Balkan problem, weakening Russia. This had a direct impact on the events of the following days, which did not take place according to Germany's calculations. However, the United Kingdom was also blamed for its share of responsibility. By giving the impression that it could remain neutral, in particular through its offers to serve as a mediator, it convinced Germany that it could carry out its attack calmly and that the British posed no threat. France and Russia were accused of having done nothing throughout the month of July to avoid the conflict. In the eyes of Germany and Austria, Russia also held responsibility: its support for the Slavic peoples would have led, in the medium term, to the dismantling of Austria-Hungary. Russia, the United Kingdom, and France, for their part, wanted to prevent Germany from becoming too powerful and overshadowing their own status as great nations.[19]

The first country to declare war was Austria-Hungary. On July 28, 1914, the empire declared war on Serbia and, using its artillery, attacked Serbia's capital, Belgrade. Russia was quick to respond. On July 30, it called for general mobilization. A few hours later, as the two empires flared up, it was Austria-Hungary's turn to do so. Immediately afterward, Germany issued an ultimatum to Russia and France telling them not to enter the war. On August 1, France and Germany decreed general mobilization and Germany declared war on Russia under the pretext that Russia had not suspended its mobilization. Until the first day of August, only Serbia and Austria had been at war. On August 1, war broke out between Russia and Germany. Two days later, on August 3, Germany declared war on France. The previous day, German troops had entered Belgium, violating its neutrality. On August 4, they crossed the Meuse in Belgium, opposite Liège. The United Kingdom accepted neither the violation of Belgian neutrality nor this invasion and immediately declared war on Germany. Belgium did the same. The next day, August 5, Montenegro also declared war on Austria-Hungary and, on August 6, also entered the European conflict by declaring war on Russia. That same day, Serbia declared war on Germany. On the tenth, France opened hostilities with Austria, and on the twelfth, the United Kingdom did the same. On August 23, the war broke across the borders of Europe with Japan's declaration of war on Germany. On November 1, the Ottoman Empire came to the aid of Austria and Germany by declaring war on Russia. Italy, for its part, did not enter the war on the side of Germany and Austria, thus giving the lie to German forecasts. Italy entered the war on May 23, 1915, alongside France, England, and Russia—in other words, with the Allies.

In the Allied camp were France, Russia, the United Kingdom, Belgium, Serbia, Montenegro, and Japan at first. Under British rule at the time were Canada, Egypt, Sudan, Kenya, British South Africa, the Union of South Africa, the Indian Empire, New Zealand, and Australia, while most of West Africa, Indochina, and Madagascar were under French administration. Italy entered the war in May 1915, Portugal in March 1916, Romania in August 1916, Greece in November 1916, the United States of America and Cuba in April 1917, Siam in July 1917, Liberia and China in August 1917, Brazil in October 1917, Panama in November 1917, Guatemala and Nicaragua in April 1918, and Costa Rica in May 1918.

On the other side in the war were Germany, Austria-Hungary, and the Ottoman Empire as well as German Southwest Africa, Cameroon, Togo, and German East Africa, all of which were under German rule. Bulgaria entered the war later.

The countries that maintained their neutrality were Spain, Denmark, Norway, Sweden, the Netherlands, Switzerland, Colombia, Venezuela, Mexico, Argentina, Uruguay, Chile, Paraguay, Afghanistan, Persia, and Ethiopia. Peru, Bolivia, and Ecuador were also neutral, but during the war they ceased all diplomatic relations with the central empires.

The soldiers in the Basque Country

This turmoil had direct repercussions in the Basque Country, especially in the Northern Basque Country, where all the men between twenty-one and forty-nine years of age were mobilized for the war. The youngest were doing their military service; the others were reservists. The French army, more precisely the 18th Army Corps, had a barracks in Baiona. Most of the soldiers from the Northern Basque Country who took part in the First World War belonged to this corps, which was created in 1873 after the new territorial military division.[20] The 18th Army Corps was part of the Aquitaine region, and its headquarters was in Bordeaux. One of its two divisions, the 36th, was located in the Baiona barracks. It was organized into two brigades, the 71st stationed in Baiona and the 72nd in Pau. Each brigade had several regiments, notably artillery and/or infantry. The infantry regiment was the one that was, during the First World War, going to be in direct contact with death and to count the most losses. The Basques were divided among several regiments, but most of them belonged to the 49th Infantry Regiment, whose barracks were in Baiona. Others belonged to the 18th Infantry Regiment, with its barracks in Pau.[21] The Basques were divided into several regiments. Each regiment was made up of 3,200 men, of whom 2,400 were divided into three battalions, and 800 others into four companies. At that time, the military presence was very strong in Baiona. In 1876, for example, soldiers represented almost half the population. That year, in addition to the 5,000 men who carried out their military service, reservists were also called to the Baiona barracks, representing 9,734 men in uniform. The city of Baiona, though, had only 18,391 inhabitants, including these soldiers.[22]

In the days following the call for mobilization, starting on July 31 and in the space of three days, twenty-five thousand soldiers passed through the city, which already contained a large military presence. Baiona was full of reservists who were forced to find space in schools, seminaries, hangars, or wherever possible. The first to go to war were the men of the 49th Infantry Regiment, especially those under twenty-three years of age. On Friday, August 7, 3,373 young men and 156 horses left Baiona through the Château Neuf, on foot, in lines, to head for the train station to the sound of drums and bugles. Wearing red and blue kepi on their heads and a thick dark blue cape, they crossed the Allées Boufflers and the Pont Saint-Esprit under a blazing sun, encouraged by thousands of anonymous citizens.[23] Some shouted from their windows while others took to the streets. The first soldiers left at 9:00 a.m., the next at noon, and the last group at 2:30 p.m. All got aboard trains requisitioned to go to the northeast of France. In Saint-Jean-Pied-de-Port there were also soldiers, those of the 18th Infantry Regiment. On August 1, 1914, they received the order to go to the barracks in Pau, from where they left for Belgium, just as had those in Baiona.

For the young men who were leaving for war, the formalities of marriage, for example, were simplified. Also, on August 5, the French government adopted an amnesty law that allowed for the integration of those who had not joined the war. In fact, thousands of young people had not done their military service and were living outside France. During the previous decades, the Basque Country had been particularly affected by draft evasion. These individuals did not necessarily leave to escape the war, though; no doubt some of them fled from military service, but many were considered evaders because they had immigrated to America before conscription. They left their country either because there was no work or food for everyone at home or because they were led to believe that they could make a fortune in America.[24] Others simply did not want to go into the army. France needed soldiers for the war, so through an amnesty law, it offered the supposed evaders the opportunity to return.[25] Some Basques were praised for having returned from America, but generally, if one consults the military files of potential evaders, it appears that most of them remained so-called evaders. It is possible that some of them did not have the means to return to the Basque Country or did not follow the news coming from Europe, or they may even have died. Nevertheless, from an official point of view, they became evaders. Unlike them, the monks who, because of the secular laws promulgated a few years earlier, had left the continental Basque Country to take refuge in the peninsular Basque Country, presented themselves to go to war.[26]

France needed men for the war, and four days after the departure of the youngest soldiers for the front, on August 11 and 12, those of the 249th

Infantry Regiment also left. On August 28 and 29, it was the turn of the men of the 142nd Territorial Infantry Regiment. Here again, people took to the streets to show their support.[27] The men of the first group were between twenty-four and thirty-four years of age. Those in the second group were between thirty-five and forty-nine years of age. Most of them were married and had families. Because young men were fitter, the men over thirty-five were supposed to stay away from the front, busy with infrastructure work. At first, 3,156 soldiers from the continental Basque Country were sent to work on protecting Paris. This is how they came to be nicknamed *les pépères* (the grandpas or quiet ones), because they had rather a quiet life. However, their future would soon be different, as these men would have to go to the front line and many of them would lose their lives.

Forty-five thousand men left the department of Basses-Pyrénées to go to war.[28] The Basques left not only from Baiona and Pau but also from barracks located in the Landes and Gironde. Some belonged to the 34th Infantry Regiment of Mont-de-Marsan (Landes), others to the 12th Infantry Regiment of Tarbes (Hautes-Pyrénées), and still others to the 57th Infantry Regiment of Rochefort and Libourne or to the 123rd of La Rochelle. In what state of mind did they leave for war? How did they receive the ringing of the bells and the call for mobilization on August 1? The press of the time spoke of a day of joy and claimed that the population was delighted that the hour of revenge against Germany had finally come. The newspapers also propagated the certainty that the war would be short.[29] The event mobilized thousands of farmers during the haymaking season. Young people had to leave their families and their fiancées.

Can we speak of joyfulness? According to the prefects' reports, everything went well during the mobilization, which was also well received in the Northern Basque Country.[30] Reports from schoolteachers describe the situation in a much more nuanced way; they highlight the surprise and sadness felt by the inhabitants of the villages, while adding that emotion and optimism were also mixed in with these feelings.[31] In the case of the Basque people, there is another factor that explains their motivation for going to war. Apart from those who had immigrated to America, the Basques had never left their villages except to go to neighboring villages. Going to war was, therefore, an adventure, the first great journey of their lives, and for many it would be the last.[32]

NOTES

1. Vallaud, *14–18: La Première Guerre mondiale*, 35.
2. Bérenger, *L' Empire austro-hongrois: 1815–1918*.
3. Tapié, *Les nationalités slaves d'Autriche-Hongrie de 1850 à 1914*.
4. Bérenger, *L'Autriche-Hongrie: 1815–1918*, 151 and 155–156.
5. Kott, *L'Allemagne du XIXe siècle*, 79.
6. Bérenger, *L'Autriche-Hongrie: 1815–1918*, 149.
7. Ambrosi, *L'apogée de l'Europe, 1871–1918*, 239.
8. Sohier, "L'enfant et la guerre à l'école primaire: En Bretagne 1871–1914," 22.
9. Bonnefous, Bonnefous, and Siegfried, *Histoire politique de la Troisième République: L'avant-guerre (1906–1914)*, 34.
10. Caron and Vernus, *L'Europe au XIXe siècle: Des nations aux nationalismes, 1815–1914*, 323–324.
11. Prior and Wilson, *La Première Guerre mondiale 1914–1918*, 34.
12. Fischer, *Les buts de guerre de l'Allemagne impériale, 1914–1918*, 65.
13. Fischer, *Les buts de guerre de l'Allemagne impériale, 1914–1918*, 71.
14. Vallaud, *14–18, la Première Guerre mondiale*, 37.
15. Fischer, *Les buts de guerre de l'Allemagne impériale, 1914–1918*, 66.
16. Fischer, *Les buts de guerre de l'Allemagne impériale, 1914–1918*, 75.
17. Fischer, *Les buts de guerre de l'Allemagne impériale, 1914–1918*, 92–93.
18. Fischer, *Les buts de guerre de l'Allemagne impériale, 1914–1918*, 95.
19. Ferro, *La Grande Guerre*, 88–89.
20. Ansoborlo, *Histoire militaire de Bayonne: 1789–1940*, 202.
21. Ansoborlo, *Histoire militaire de Bayonne: 1789–1940*, 202.
22. Ansoborlo, *Histoire militaire de Bayonne: 1789–1940*, 217.
23. Rocafort, *Avant oubli: Soldats et civils de la côte basque durant la grande guerre*, 14.
24. Fabas, "Aspects de la vie religieuse dans le diocèse de Bayonne (1905–1965)," 65.
25. Rocafort, *Avant oubli: Soldats et civils de la côte basque durant la grande guerre*, 13.
26. Hiriart-Urruti, "Eskualdun kaputchin soldadoa."
27. Ansoborlo, *Histoire militaire de Bayonne: 1789–1940*, 233.
28. Laharie, *Les Basses-Pyrénées pendant la guerre 1914–1918*, 45.
29. Ferro, *La Grande Guerre*, 57.
30. Becker, *1914: Comment les Français sont entrés dans la guerre*, 282.
31. Pourcher, "Les clichés de la Grande Guerre: Entre histoire et fiction," 145.
32. Elissondo, *Mémoires de la Soule 1914–1918: Une petite vallée du Pays Basque dans la guerre*, 42.

CHAPTER FIVE

The Position of the Southern Basque Country

Not all states decided to go to war. Some of them, such as Denmark, Sweden, Norway, Spain,[1] Holland, Switzerland, Belgium, Luxembourg, Albania, Italy, Bulgaria, Romania, and Greece, were neither in one camp nor the other. But after Germany and Austria-Hungary violated the neutrality of Belgium, Luxembourg, and Albania and occupied these territories, not all were in the same situation as they had been before. Italy was, in fact, linked to the Triple Alliance but did not enter the war. Later on it rallied to the Triple Entente. The Bulgarian and Greek armies had been weakened by the recent Balkan wars. Bulgaria nevertheless entered the war on the side of the Triple Alliance on October 5, 1915. Romania was in the camp of the Triple Alliance until the war broke out, then it chose to remain neutral, and later, on August 27, 1916, it declared war on the forces of the Triple Alliance. Despite the pressure received from all sides, from within and without, King Constantine of Greece persisted in his neutrality until, on June 29, 1917, Greece entered the war on the side of the Allies. Portugal was allied with the United Kingdom and wished to enter the war, but the United Kingdom advised against doing so because of the Portuguese army's great weakness. However, since this army controlled a large part of the Atlantic coast, it did everything possible to facilitate the Allied advance. Furthermore, it fought against the German colonies in Angola and Mozambique, though without success.

Spain was not involved in the alliances and, therefore, was not party to the troubles that led to the war. The outbreak of war between Austria and Serbia caught Spain off guard. Initially, Spain attached little importance to the war, considering it to be much like the previous conflicts in the Balkans. Spain was especially concerned about the danger of France and Russia entering the war, though. Spain's press appeared more concerned by ongoing events than Spain's leaders were. The royal court was on vacation in Donostia–San Sebastián and the king was in Santander.[2] The Spaniards were mostly preoccupied with farmwork, bullfights, and the summer heat. Politically, all eyes were on the incidents in Morocco. Central Europe seemed far away; however, at the time of the mobilization, Spaniards, Catalans, and Basques exiled in France, Belgium, England, Germany, and Switzerland were sent by train back to their native country. A total of 110,000 workers or tourists of Spanish nationality returned to the country (30,000 of whom came from the French colonies in North Africa), and the ports, as well as the municipalities near the border, had to help the poorest. This return highlighted the gravity of what was happening in Europe.

Despite their neutrality, did the Spaniards have a preference for one side? In fact, they were divided. Some were strongly in favor of neutrality because they believed that Spain had neither money nor a strong army, adding that whoever went to war did so to recover a lost land or to conquer a desirable territory, which was not the case of Spain. Likewise, those who went to war were motivated by a great national ideal, which did not exist in Spain according to the Catalan regionalist deputy Francesc Cambó.[3] Others took sides: some clearly favored the Allies, whereas others favored Germany. Among those on the side of the Allies were the opponents of the Spanish Germanophiles.[4]

King Alfonso XIII left Santander to go to Donostia–San Sebastián to visit diplomats. The Spanish monarch was a friend of France, but the pressure exerted from all sides did not make him bend, and he chose to remain neutral.[5] In 1913, the king of Spain visited France, and then, in turn, the French president made an official visit to Spain, seeing this as an opportunity to bring Spain into the entente. However, when the war broke out, Alfonso XIII argued that giving assistance to either side would not do Spain any good given that Spain lacked a powerful army, having failed to win a single victory in the conflicts in Morocco in previous years.[6] Some supporters of the neoliberal approach to the war were not prepared to accept the fact that Spain was not a member of the Triple Entente. Some proponents of neutrality believed that this position of neutrality could be beneficial to Spain if it led it to a peace conference that would end the war. Others feared that Spain would be isolated precisely because of its neutrality. The French diplomat Louis Charles de Freycenet warned in writing that because of its noncooperation, Spain would be "weakened" in the future. The king of Spain had personal (as well as diplomatic) reasons for preferring neutrality; his mother was Austrian—she was Archduchess Maria Christina of Austria—and his wife, Victoria-Eugenia of Battenberg, was the granddaughter of Queen Victoria of the United Kingdom. The head of government, Eduardo Dato, took a position in favor of neutrality, and on August 5 the Council of Ministers decided not to take part in the war.

However, in Spain many conservatives, Carlists, the Catholic Church, and the army favored Germany. They reproached France for being a secular republic. In addition, after seeing the German advance in the beginning of the conflict and the French government retreat to Bordeaux, conservatives were convinced that the Germans would quickly win the war.

The Left, in contrast, supported France and England and in particular praised their democracy.[7] These supporters of the Allies criticized neutrality, arguing that it could be detrimental to Spain because if the Germans won, neutrality could be used against them, and the same would be true if the Allies won.

Nevertheless, the majority preferred that Spain not enter the war. Whereas the populations in the interior of Spain favored Germany, Andalusia and Cantabria had trade relations and economic interests aligned with those of France and England. These two regions of Spain had in their mines raw materials such as iron, lead, pyrite, and tungsten that were indispensable to the Allies. They exported weapons, blankets, absorbent cotton, and shoes to France. In the same way, they sent fruit and dried vegetables, wine, and olive oil to European countries at war.[8]

In the Basque Country and Catalonia, the populations were more favorable to France, no doubt because they were neighboring peoples. In the Southern Basque Country, for example, between one hundred and three hundred people volunteered to join the French Foreign Legion to go to war. In Catalonia, however, not all were in favor of France because some felt that siding with the Germans would be more beneficial for the emancipation of Catalonia. Others sided with France because part of Catalonia sat in French territory, and some even joined the war on the side of France.[9] In sum, these nearby regions had more relationships with France, which influenced their position regarding the war. The Catalans, for example, helped France while taking advantage of the war situation to enrich themselves considerably.[10]

In the Basque Country, two positions, either pro Germany or pro France and England, divided Basque nationalists. Resurrección María Azkue, who was a cultural patriot and not a member of any party, was a Germanophile.[11] He was not alone—Luis Arana Goiri, president of the board of directors of the Basque Nationalist Party, was also a supporter of Germany. The brother of Sabino Arana Goiri, founder of the party, represented a more radical patriotism and militated for the independence of the Basque Country. Because of this trend, fundamental nationalism was more important than economic issues. Thus, April 24, 1916, Easter Monday, which marked the beginning of a great insurrection in Dublin, Ireland, against the British occupation had a real impact on many Basque patriots, although it was a military failure for the Irish.[12]

The moderate Basque nationalist and entrepreneur Ramón de la Sota was a supporter of the British, and the ships he built were intended for them. In recognition of this, the United Kingdom knighted him and gave him the title of Sir.[13] Like Ramón de la Sota, many members of the Basque Nationalist Party favored the Allies, as can be seen in the daily newspaper *Euzkadi*, which supported this tendency, especially through the texts of Evaristo Bustinza "Kirikiño" or Juan Bautista Bilbao "Batxi."[14] This sector—namely, the nationalist upper middle class, Biscayan capitalism, and the shipbuilding sector—included those who held economic power and thus carried great weight in the Basque Nationalist Party of the time.

Gregorio de Balparda, a liberal leftist politician from Bilbao, criticized this patriotism of the Basque Nationalist Party and denounced the fact that with the war a "plutocracy" of Basque nationalism was taking shape. By taking a political stance, he claimed that trade and economy took precedence over politics and religion. This economic stance had a strong influence on the choice that party members made in favor of neutrality. For *Euzkadi*, the Basque Country had no interest in choosing one side or the other. Ebaristo Bustintza, writing under the pen name Kirikiño, was the head of the Basque section of the newspaper and the author of numerous columns on the war. Another journalist, Juan Bautista Bilbao, known as Batxi, was a sailor who had to make many trips during the war until he was killed by a mine. He died on January 16, 1916, on the ship *Bayo*, along with twenty-seven other sailors who were on board. Fifty-nine ships from Gipuzkoa (Guipúzcoa) and Bizkaia (Vizcaya) were sunk or damaged during the war, most of them as a result of the war. A total of sixty-eight Basque passengers and sailors died at sea, and 125,000 tonnes of goods were lost.

Euzkadi put forward many arguments to justify its choice in favor of staying out of the war and, on a political level, its pro-Allied position. Among these arguments were economic ones. One of them was the possibility of sailing without interference. German propaganda claimed that ships from neutral countries, such as from the Gipuzkoa and Bizkaia coast, could not sail in international waters without expecting problems, to which *Euzkadi* replied that this was untrue. As far as maritime commerce was concerned, a victory for France and England was desired so that food and goods could reach the Basque Country more easily, especially from the east. In 1915, violent battles took place in the Dardanelles, with the opening of the Bosphorus sea passage between the Black Sea and the Mediterranean at stake. According to *Euzkadi*, if the English and French took control of the Dardanelles, wheat could reach the Basque Country. Finally, the party was convinced that if Spain entered the war, the industry of the Basque Country would come to a halt. Bidegain, Gerla Handia, muga sakona, 118. Entering the war on the side of the Germans made the newspaper fear that the Basque coast would be subject to attack from the French and the English, as these two forces were geographically closer. However, positioning oneself in favor of the Allies could also provoke reprisals from Germany.

In addition to offering these pragmatic reasons, *Euzkadi* also considered fundamental reasons for opposing the war, recalling that a war was a terrible massacre and sympathizing with the fate of the "brothers" of the Northern Basque Country who went to war. Likewise, the newspaper's editors strongly disapproved of the invasion of Belgium and Serbia by Germany and Austria-Hungary and insisted on the solidarity and understanding that they, as Basques, felt toward these smaller, weaker peoples.

Kirikiño also wrote that the bombing of the coast of the United Kingdom by the Germans was "barbaric." Driven by the nationalist position, he pronounced himself in favor of neutrality and noted that entering the war on the side of Germany could provoke a fratricidal struggle among Basques. The last thing he wanted was for the Basques of the North to be fighting those of the South. Bidegain, Gerla Handia, muga sakona, 119.

The *bertsolaritza*[15] poet Txirrita also wrote the following verses after the end of the war:

Berdun'en ezik Melilla'n ere
Egin du orrek beria:
Ango moruak bialdu ditu
Auntzak bezala mendia;
Iñoiz umillak asarretzian
Arruak bajatzen dia,
Eskarrik asko, jeneral Petaiñ
Eta Prantzi'ko jendia.
Txirrita, "Bertso berriak (Europa'ko gerra, 1914–1918)".

In Verdun as well as in Melilla
(The Kaiser) made his mischief:
He sent the Moors from there
like goats on the mountain;
When the humble rebel
The proud bend their backs
Thanks to General Pétain
And to the French people.

NOTES

1. Galiano, *España ante el conflicto europeo 1914–1915*; Morales Lezcano, "España y la Primera Guerra Mundial: La intelectualidad del 14 ante la guerra"; Espada Burgos, "España y la neutralidad en la Gran Guerra"; Morales Lezcano, Cardona, and Delaunay, *España y la Primera Guerra Mundial*.
2. Delaunay, "1914: Les Espagnols et la guerre," 120.
3. Díaz Plaja, *Francofilos y germanofilos: Los españoles en la guerra europea*, 13.
4. Díaz Plaja, *Francofilos y germanofilos: Los españoles en la guerra europea*, 27–28.
5. Cortés-Cavanillas, *Alfonso XIII y la guerra del 14*, 34–35.
6. Menéndez Pidal, *Historia de España*, vol. 38, *La España de Alfonso XIII: El estado y la política (1902–1931)*, 328–336.
7. Cortés-Cavanillas, *Alfonso XIII y la guerra del 14*, 48.
8. Delaunay, "1914: Les Espagnols et la guerre," 121.
9. Díaz Plaja, *Francofilos y germanofilos: Los españoles en la guerra europea*, 95, 97, 104, and 106.
10. Balcells, "Los voluntarios catalanes en la Gran Guerra (1914–1918)," 51.
11. Kintana, *Intelektuala nazioa eraikitzen: R. M. Azkueren pentsaera eta obra*, 184–187.
12. Caro Baroja, *Historia general del país vasco*, 163.
13. Cierva, *Hijos de la gloria y la mentira: Historia de los vascos entre España y la Antiespaña*, 433.
14. Bidegain, *Gerla Handia, muga sakona*.
15. A Basque art form that involves improvising songs in rhymed verse while singing a cappella to a specific melody.

PART TWO

The Fire

CHAPTER SIX

The Massacre of Fonteny and Gozée

Convinced that they would win the battle quickly, thousands of Basques set out from Baiona train station and from several other towns in southwestern France.[1] Those who left Baiona belonged to the 49th Infantry Regiment, at that time the 18th Army Corps, making the Basques part of the 2nd Army. On August 7, they were sent to Lorraine, in the department of Meurthe-et-Moselle. Two days later, they were in Mont-le-Vignoble. They continued their journey by train and crossed Royaumieux, Grosrouvres, and Lay-Saint-Rémy. The German offensive began on August 4. The Germans seized territory in Belgium and crossed the Meuse River, opposite the city of Liège. On August 7, the French army launched an offensive in Alsace, a region it had long wanted to recover. It occupied the city of Mulhouse without any resistance from the Germans, who were hidden in a forest. Two days later, the Germans retook the city.

The Basques in the 49th Infantry Regiment were in Moselle, guarding the castle of Toul, and in nearby Lay-Saint-Rémy, where they had not yet had any direct contact with the fighting. However, on August 16, they perceived the first threats when they heard cannons thundering in the distance. This was the German bombardment of the village of Pont-à-Mousson. It was in this same region, about fifty kilometers away, that the first Basque died of his wounds; Joseph Andrieu, a native of Bidaxune (Bidache), fell at the age of twenty-one during the fighting in Lunéville on August 14, 1914. The same day, also about fifty kilometers away, in the village of Fraize, Jean-Baptiste Dehez from Biarritz also died at the age of twenty-one. The next day, another Basque, Pierre Dibon, a native of Gixune (Guiche), died during the fighting in Fraize. He was not yet twenty-one. These men were the first Basques to die in the war. However, it was a twenty-three-year-old from Biarritz, François Latournerie, who was officially declared to be the first man from the Basque Country to die in the war.[2] He died of illness on August 11, 1914, in the village of Crépey.

These were to be just the beginning of an avalanche of death. The first cannonade occurred on August 20, during the battle of Morhange, in Moselle. Although the regiments from the Basque Country did not take part in this battle, the 144th and 344th Infantry Regiments, which had left from Bordeaux, also included Basques who took part in the fighting in the villages of Faxe, Fonteny, and Viviers. At 3:00 p.m., the Germans moved toward Fonteny, and the battle began around Faxe. The French army was lined up, its soldiers holding bayonets, but they were powerless against the firepower of the German machine guns, especially since their own shells did not explode. The Germans, who controlled the area from the surrounding forests, reduced the French force to pieces. In a single day, forty-seven Basques were killed by the bombs. Some disappeared and were later considered dead. The battle of Morhange resulted in seven thousand deaths, and ten thousand men were taken prisoner by the Germans. On the same date, German soldiers entered Brussels.

Two days later, the soldiers from the Basque Country experienced another bloody day. Sixty-nine men died in the fighting on August 22, most of them in Belgium, during the battle of Rossignol. Once again, it was not the regiments from the Basque Country that found themselves under the bombs and machine-gun fire. It was mainly the men of the 3rd Colonial Infantry Regiment from Rochefort. The French cavalry saw that the Germans had set up an important line in the middle, in the direction of the colonial infantry regiments, but the latter had not been informed of the warning issued the day before by the high command of the 4th Army, and so they went straight to a death that could have been avoided.[3]

Also that day, the 49th Infantry Regiment of Baiona was 130 kilometers farther north, on the Belgian border, near the village of Gozée. The 18th Army Corps of the Basque Country and southwestern France belonged to the 4th Army, which was taking part in the Battle of Charleroi. Its mission was to cross the Sambre River, which separated France and Belgium, to reach the Belgian city of Charleroi. The men from Baiona dug trenches between Gozée and Thuin, which was not an easy task as they exchanged fire with the Germans. However, on that day, the regiment did not suffer any casualties. The battle began the next day, August 23. German artillery attacked the soldiers around Gozée. Forty Basques were killed in Gozée itself, and if we take into account the surrounding villages, sixty-two Basques lost their lives that day, to which we must add the eight men who died the following day. On August 25, five other Basques died, some of them as a result of injuries sustained during the previous days' fighting.

The German army was imposing itself across France. French general Joseph Joffre informed the president of the Council, Raymond Poincaré, that it was impossible to resist this force, that the French did not have the capacity to go on the offensive, and that they had to hold out in order to wear down the enemy. The Germans had thirty divisions and the French only nineteen. The French launched their offensive without considering that the Germans had extremely well-prepared defenses. Thus, the French lost all the battles that took place between August 8 and 24. These battles resulted in as many deaths as at Verdun in four months and left the Germans free to invade all Belgium and a large part of France.[4] Finally, Joffre decided on a general retreat. The Battle of Charleroi ended on August 24 with a defeat of the French and the British. The day before, the British had lost the battle of Mons in Belgium.

As the days passed, the French army retreated several kilometers. Joffre ordered a withdrawal to the Seine so that the German army would not destroy the surrounding area as intended. The 49th Infantry Regiment withdrew, day after day, from Villiers, Fourmonon, the Nouvion forest, Voulpaix, Séry-lès-Mézières, and more. It continued its retreat, as did the other infantry regiments. The situation was all the more difficult as each day brought its share of victims. On August 28, during the battle of Guise, fourteen Basques perished, and the next day, twenty-four others fell in various places. African soldiers also took part in these battles alongside them. In total, during this first month of the war, 266 Basques lost their lives.

Fearing that the Germans would reach Paris, on September 2, the French government left the capital to set up its headquarters in Bordeaux. Paris was then almost in the hands of the Germans, who had taken the city of Soissons. The French prepared for the defense of Paris under the command of General Gallieni. The 142nd Territorial Infantry Regiment of Baiona also participated in the construction of the infrastructure that would allow the organization of this defense.

Things did not go as well as the Allies had hoped on the Russian front. A few days after the defeat of the French at Charleroi, from August 27 to 30, on the Eastern Front, in the town of Tannenberg (present-day Poland), Russians and the Germans were fighting. Although the Russians initially had the upper hand, the Germans eventually managed to stop their offensive, and Russia lost almost an entire army, with the death of 125,000 men. In September, though, the Russians managed to occupy the city of Przemyśl (Galicia, Poland), which was under Austrian rule; however, the Germans were to win the Battle of the Masurian Lakes in eastern Prussia.

On September 6, the French counteroffensive began with the famous Battle of the Marne. The regiments that had been retreating farther and farther each day after the rout of Charleroi were ordered to return in order to attack the Germans once again. Because the German army had spread out widely as it advanced, the Germans had difficulty keeping the whole area under their control. They had wanted to surround the French army from the south, but the French had changed their plan. The previous day, September 5, France's 4th Army had launched an offensive on the Ourcq River, breaking through the German lines; taking advantage of this breach, the 5th Army advanced considerably around the Marne. Nearby, on September 7, the 49th Infantry Regiment took part in the battle of Montmirail without suffering any losses. The following day, however, in the village of Marchais-en-Brie, soldiers came under German artillery fire. Twenty-four Basques were killed in this village and in other places. One of them was a young twenty-six-year-old priest, Dominique Charo, from Atharratze. Found wounded that day, he died on September 9. His death was the first to be reported in the Basque Country. That same day, the Germans attacked in force in several places, but they also lost many fighters and eventually retreated.

On September 13, the French army won the Battle of the Marne, and consequently Germany was unable to carry out its original plan to surround the French army, destroy it, enter Paris, and then attack Russia. Some German units lost 40 percent of their troops. The Russians on the Eastern Front also contributed to the weakening of the Germans. As a result of the German retreat, the front line was established in the vicinity of the Aisne River.

After the Battle of the Marne, the challenge centered on the territory from the department of Oise (Picardy) to the North Sea. Both sides realized that, following the Battle of the Marne, the only way to attack the enemy situated in the department of Aisne (Picardy) was to encircle it first by penetrating the northern part of the department of Oise. The fight to take over the area gave rise to several battles, notably those of Arras, Yser, and Ypres. The battle of Arras (Pas-de-Calais department) began on October 1. The fighting was violent, and the French army suffered severe hits, but in the end, on October 9, the German offensive was stopped. A few days later, on October 15, began the battle of the Yser (Nord department), the river that links France to Flanders. After twelve days of fighting, the Belgians opened the floodgates of the Nieuport dam, causing floods that stopped the Germans' advance.

The Battle of Ypres (Flanders) took place from October 23 to November 22. German strength halted the Allied advance in this city. French and English losses amounted to 100,000 men, and German losses to 130,000. Following these heavy losses, the Germans decided to remain in Ypres. Thus, the race to the sea ended, and the front was stabilized from the North Sea to Switzerland. The war of movement there, now completely over, was replaced by a war of attrition. A few weeks later, the war of movement also ended on the Eastern Front when the Germans captured the city of Łódź, near Warsaw. The war of position began.

The Basques were able to rest from fighting for a while. The first letter from the priest, writer, and stretcher-bearer Jean Saint-Pierre to the weekly magazine *Eskualduna* was not written until September 12. In the three previous days, Basque soldiers traveled 130 kilometers to clear the area where the battle of Montmirail had taken place. As the bombing grew distant, they retraced the path they had taken a few days earlier in the other direction. But when they followed their steps, they discovered a completely transformed landscape; while withdrawing, the Germans had left behind them burned and looted villages and houses. They had destroyed all in their retreat.

NOTES

1. For the following chronicles about the participation of the Basques soldiers in the war, the sources are Ansoborlo, *Histoire militaire de Bayonne: 1789–1940*; Rocafort, *Avant oubli: Soldats et civils de la côte basque durant la grande guerre*; *Historique du 49e régiment d'infanterie pendant la guerre 1914–1918*; *Historique du 172e régiment d'infanterie pendant la Grande Guerre 1914–1919*; *Historique du 123e régiment d'Infanterie: Campagne 1914–1918*; *Historique du 18e régiment d'infanterie pendant la guerre de 1914–1918*; Colonel (Le) commandant le 57e R. I. Bussy, *57e régiment d'infanterie: "Le terrible que rien n'arrête": Historique du régiment pendant la grande guerre 1914–1918*.
2. Although there were many others who were not born in the Basque Country but who seemed to be living there at the time the war broke out, the details given in the following pages concern those who were native to the Basque Country.
3. Rocafort, *Avant oubli: Soldats et civils de la côte basque durant la grande guerre*, 23.
4. Fraenkel, "Le général Joffre, cet âne qui commandait des lions," 98.

CHAPTER SEVEN

In the Heart of the Quagmire

The movement of soldiers on foot ceased with the Battle of the Marne. From September 13, 1914, most of the Basques regrouped near the Aisne River in Bourg-et-Comin, Beaurieux, and in the surrounding villages. The front that stretched from the North Sea to Switzerland was not yet completely stabilized, unlike that of the Aisne. The terrain was vast, flat, and low. One hundred meters higher up was another huge plain, the Chemin des Dames. That is where the Germans were located.

As soon as the Germans arrived, the fighting began. General Joffre sent in the 5th Army, which was in the area. September 13 saw ten Basques die there, but the regiments of the French army managed to take the village of Craonne. On September 15, thirty-three soldiers fell on the battlefield around and below the Chemin des Dames in the villages of Craonne and Craonnelle. At 5:30 a.m., a battalion of the 49th Infantry Regiment left for the top of Craonne, but the German artillery did not stop firing. After an hour, the French artillery arrived, but it was too late for them to do anything. At 4:00 p.m., the soldiers were ordered to retreat to Craonnelle. That day, twenty-three men of the 49th Infantry Regiment lost their lives, and 123 were reported missing. In addition, the village of Craonne was to remain under German control for a long period of time. On September 16, there were thirty-two more Basques of the 18th Infantry Regiment killed, most of them east of Craonne in the village of La-Ville-aux-Bois. On September 17, another sixty-four Basques were killed in this area.

September 21 was the most terrible day, marked by the death of 180 Basques, most of them belonging to the 249th Infantry Regiment. On that day, some of the battalions of this regiment lost half their men, killed by the bombs that the Germans had been throwing into their trenches since dawn. On September 26, more fighting took place in and around Hurtebise Farm. From this farm, located on the heights of the village of Oulches, the view is unobstructed both to the south and to the north. Since September 13, fighting had been going on to gain control of the farm, which had already been the scene of great battles in 1814 at the time of the Napoleonic Wars. On September 26, the Germans launched an offensive to retake the Hurtebise farm from the 49th Infantry Regiment. That day, forty-eight Basques were killed in the battle. The farm, and with it this highly strategic location, fell into German hands for a few months. On September 27, the Germans burned the farm. However, other battles were to take place there during the following months. On November 12, a shell killed two brothers from Donibane Lohizune: Pascal and Léon Gaudin.

On October 12, the 57th Infantry Regiment received the order to seize the Vauclerc mine on the high plateau of Californie, above the village of Craonnelle. The French army wanted to take control of this strategic location by dislodging the Germans who were dug in there. The men started to advance there at 5:00 a.m., but German artillery returned fire with force. At 6:30 a.m., the French launched a new attack, again without result. On October 14 at 3:00 p.m., a further attempt was made. The French reached the top of the Quatre Arbres Plateau and remained there for several hours, very close to the German trenches, protected by barbed wire. Jean Elissalde "Zerbitzari," a soldier in the 57th Infantry Regiment as well as a writer and priest from Azkaine (Ascain), took part in this battle. In his memoirs, written some twenty years later, he recounts the movements that took place that day:

> It was six in the morning when they left. Even if they hid as much as possible, the enemy could see them, alas! After covering three or four hundred meters, it was impossible to go any farther for the din of the shots and shells. Hearing the thunder that reached his ears, the general himself realized that asking us to go to the Mill at all costs was too much and, in a second message, he told us to do what we could, taking advantage of the moments when the guns fell silent. Thus, we made two or three good intrusions into the enemy terrain, but too few to go farther and get as far as we wanted. Then, after assessing the situation, the general ordered us to stop and settle in the place where we were. We did not ask for anything else.[1] (translated from Basque)

Faced with German counterattacks, they returned to their starting point on October 15. The attempt ended in failure, and casualties were high, with thirty-nine Basques, most of them belonging to the 18th Infantry Regiment, dying in the fighting between October 12 and 15. Finally, the mill at Vauclerc was destroyed. Today on its site stands a statue of Napoleon, erected in memory of the battle that took place at Craonne in 1814.

Thus, each day provided an opportunity for both sides to gain a little more ground. From the heights, the Germans controlled everything. By night, the soldiers of the French army knew better than to light a cigarette if they did not want the German soldiers posted up there to see where they were. During the day, the situation was made difficult for the French soldiers who emerged from the trenches in search of water because the Germans, who spotted them from above, sent bombs down on them. But as there was no water in the trenches, the men were forced to go down to the square in Craonnelle to obtain it, risking their lives.

As the days went on, the soldiers lived under the constant threat of death. Sometimes they were in direct contact with it when they were in the trenches, other times they were farther away, especially when they were withdrawn to Beaurieux, Fismes, Maizy, or Bourg-et-Comin. People living in these villages lived a different existence from that directly in the line of battle despite the fact that they could hear the sound of bombs in the distance. When the Basques, of whom there were hundreds in this area, gathered, it was not unusual to hear them speak Basque. Whereas the French played soccer—which was not to the taste of the Basques who found this sport strange and wild[2]—the Basques played *mus*,[3] which is a popular card game, and *pelota*.[4] Any available wall gave an excuse to play this sport, and it just so happened that the *pelota* player Chiquito de Kanbo (Cambo) was among the Basque soldiers.[5] Many people went to Mass, and the soldier-priests said the masses and prayers.[6] Sunday was a day of celebration. After Mass, the men organized *pelota* games while some played music and others danced the fandango.[7] The men would sing Basque songs for hours on end while drinking wine from a wineskin. Sometimes they would go to the local bar,[8] where the soldiers would spend their money and where, according to them, the inhabitants took advantage of their presence to sell them goods at high prices.[9] Others took advantage of their time off to hunt in the surrounding forests or fish in the rivers.[10] Finally, there were those who, in autumn, went mushroom picking.[11]

These places where the troops achieved a little respite were not very entertaining. There could be found the military leaders, the cavalry, the artillery, the military engineers, the stretcher-bearers—just about everyone of any rank or function.[12] The main French railroads reached these villages, bringing their loads of soldiers and goods. Even when the soldiers were not in combat, they often did physical exercises so that they would always be ready to go to the front on a moment's notice. During the war, they underwent military training and learned new warfare techniques.[13] Sometimes they dug new trenches or rehabilitated old ones. They also had to dig and fix the ditches that led to the trenches, install barbed wire around them, even in the middle of winter in the freezing cold.[14]

The contrast between the soldiers of these back lines and those returning from the front lines was striking.[15] After having spent a long time in the mud of the trenches, the soldiers came out filthy. On the way from the trenches to the places of rest and recreation, they presented a frequently distressing sight. In addition, crossing the forests was far from safe, as there they were not spared from bombing. As the war progressed, the forests gave way to vast spaces covered with pieces of burned wood where not a single blade of grass remained. Here and there were villages half destroyed, others totally ravaged, houses half collapsed, and yet others that were only a pile of stones.[16] Traces of the battle are still evident in the villages between the front and rear lines. The forests have grown back, but among them we can discover a succession of holes three to four meters in diameter. In this cratered terrain we can see fragments of ancient burials, the points of an iron gate buried in the earth, and a few stones that remind us that at one time a village stood there.

It is thus, in a sorry state and totally exhausted, that the soldiers returned from the trenches. While for some the time had come to take a rest, for others the time had come to return to the trenches. Everyone dreaded the moment of going into fire.

The Germans and the French, or the British, faced each other in long lines of trenches stretching from Switzerland to the North Sea. The trenches of the first and second lines, as well as those of the rear lines, were connected by narrow, deep ditches dug into the ground. Men returning from the trenches and those going to the trenches used these ditches as passages. Carrying a fifty-pound pack on their backs, they had to walk for three or four hours from the back lines to the front lines.

In addition to facing the risk of dying at any moment under machine-gun fire or bombardment, soldiers found daily life in the trenches extremely painful. When the weather was good and the temperatures mild, this was less so. But most of the time the situation was intolerable. Soldiers often had to stay in the rain in trenches that were then transformed into murky ponds.[17] They were not only soaked from head to toe but also wading in water that reached up to their knees or even their belts.[18] They live in mud, water, and dirt. Even worse than dealing with the dirt was putting up with the multitude of rats, attracted by the rain and the presence, everywhere, of the corpses of their companions.[19] The problem was not necessarily the disgusting nature of these animals; it was, rather, that they caused great damage to the infrastructure and the soldiers' food supplies, not to mention that they bit the men. So in addition to the work and fighting inherent in war, the soldiers had to spend their time killing rats. And as if the presence of these rodents were not enough, the men also had to face an invasion of lice, which they could not get rid of. Not to mention the hunger and thirst that were the daily lot of life in the trenches, the result of the lack of food and drink.[20]

In hot, dry weather soldiers had no chance to be proactive either, given the abundant dust. The heat, often unbearable, was unpleasant both when soldiers remained immobile in the trenches and when fighting. Moreover, whether winter or summer, the soldiers wore the same clothes, which became intolerably hot in midsummer and uncomfortably cold in winter when they had to face extreme cold. Although in winter the ground was drier, which pleased them, the cold was no easy thing to endure.[21] Many of the soldiers in the trenches became ill, both from the extreme cold and the scorching heat. Among those who fell sick were recently mobilized young people, many of whom died. A total of 558 Basques died of illness in the war zone, in hospitals, or after returning home.[22] Many of them were in their early twenties. As spring approached and temperatures warmed, the snow melted and it began to rain, filling the trenches with water and mud once again. For the soldiers, this was an interminable cycle.[23]

The soldiers were being forced to stay on the front lines in order to respond to attacks from their opponents, to prepare opportunities for offensives, but most importantly to monitor the surroundings. This surveillance task fell to selected men. It was dangerous work, as it required being in sight of the enemy and had to be carried out at night. The second line, another trench line, lay a kilometer back.[24] Barbed wire covered the area around the trenches and the gap between the two lines. Some soldiers were tasked with transporting packages and food from the front line to the second. Again, the task was dangerous and painful, as throughout the day the men had to carry pounds of food, clothing, and ammunition on their backs, risking death or injury from the bombs. The most dangerous area was, without a doubt, this gap between the two lines because the soldiers were not hidden from sight.[25]

Since the beginning of the war of attrition, not a day had passed without many more lives being lost. Every day, Basques lost their lives, approximately ten per day. It is impossible to speak of tranquility because of the continual presence of threat and fear. However, not until January 25, 1915, did the men face heavy fighting.[26] The Germans were entrenched in the farm of Hurtebise, but they did not control places like the Creute and the underground caves. On that day, however, the Germans went on the offensive and made way by taking over the aforementioned sites, which gave them greater control over the area.[27] For the French army, this was a symbolic failure of far-reaching proportions. Sixty-six Basques lost their lives on that fateful day.[28]

The Basques remained on the banks of the Aisne until April 1916, alternating between the trenches and the rear lines, sometimes in the midst of heavy fighting, and experiencing quieter moments from time to time. Elsewhere, too, troops were enduring a similar situation. The French and British armies were aligned facing the Germans on a front that ran from the North Sea to Switzerland. During this period, in February and March 1915, there took place violent battles in the Champagne region, from which the Basques managed to escape unharmed, but ninety thousand French soldiers died in a French offensive without result.[29]

With the Western Front stabilized, the Germans and Austro-Hungarians could put more forces on the Eastern Front. On December 2, 1914, the Austro-Hungarian army entered Belgrade, and on December 12 the Russians were defeated in Limanowa-Łapanów, ahead of Krakow. However, not everything was going as the Austro-Hungarians would have liked because on December 15 the Serbs retook Belgrade. On the twenty-third of the same month, in the Carpathians, the expectations of the Austro-Hungarians were also thwarted. They were attempting to reclaim the town of Przemyśl and to prevent the Russians from approaching Hungary, and their losses were considerable. Nevertheless, Russia was not winning. On February 7, following the German offensive in the Masuria region a few days earlier, Russia declared that all Prussia would be left to Germany. The Germans had started using poison gas against the Russians.

During the war, men used all kinds of weapons. The Basques who were at the front became most familiar with the *crapouillot*, a small trench mortar.[30] Airplanes were also appearing for the first time, with some battles being waged in the sky. In addition, the Germans began to use zeppelins, and on January 29, 1916, they bombed Paris, causing the death of twenty-six people. But one of the weapons most feared by the soldiers was poison gas, like chlorine. The Germans were the first to use these deadly gases. In April 1915, during the Second Battle of Ypres, they again used gases. Initially the Allies were caught off guard by the deadly gases; but very soon they adopted, protective measures, including the use of special masks. However, while the Germans were more advanced in their chemical industry, the French were also researching chemicals and ended up using them in turn. Ninety thousand men in total died from these gases during the First World War.

Russia, too, was fighting, but its opponent was the Ottoman Empire, meaning Turkey, particularly around Lake Van, where 200,000 Armenians were living. In revenge for the defeats inflicted by the Russians, the Turks sought "enemies within"—the Armenians—and subjected them to fierce repression. After being defeated in the Caucasus Mountains, they considered Armenians traitors. On April 24 and 25, the Turks killed thousands of Armenians, mostly in Istanbul. On May 18, the Russians won the battle of Lake Van on the border between Turkey and Persia. On May 27, Turkey adopted the Law on the Provisional Deportation of Armenians, which allowed for the mass displacement of these populations. Entire villages of Armenians were evacuated. In the period up to 1922, the Turks were responsible for the deaths of between 1.5 million and 2 million Armenians.

Although the Russians had dealt Turkey several severe blows, they were facing difficult times in their struggle against the Germans. On June 3, the Russians had to hand over the town of Przemyśl, which they had recovered a few days earlier, having lost a million men doing so. On June 20, the Russians left Galicia, fleeing the German offensive. Two days later, they had to give up the forts of Lemberg without a fight. On August 4, they abandoned the fort at Ivangorod, and the following day the Germans occupied Warsaw. On August 25, the Germans captured Brest-Litovsk. A few days later, not a single Russian remained on the left bank of the Vistula (Wisła) River.

Regarding Italy, which had just joined the war a few weeks earlier, things were not going as well as hoped. On June 23, Italy immediately recorded significant losses against the Austrians at the battle of Isonzo. On July 18, Italy lost that battle. The Bulgarians, in contrast, took Belgrade on October 6 and entered Uskub on October 22, thus cutting off to the Serbs the road from Thessaloniki.

For the French, autumn 1915 began badly. Between September 25 and October 6, they lost 140,000 men, only to advance a few meters, in the second battle in the Champagne region. Many Basques died at that time—144 men in total. For half of them, September 25 was the fatal day, with some losing their lives around the Souain mill, others in Ville-sur-Tourbe.

Early in the war, the Germans had hoped to dominate France and then Russia over a short time. Despite an initial significant advance, they failed to fulfill their objectives, and the stabilization of the war front led to a prolongation of the war. According to French propaganda as well, the war was to be very brief. The French even hoped for an immediate victory over the Germans. But in fact, despite their tireless efforts to highlight that the war was turning in favor of the Allies, the reality was quite different. It was difficult for the Allies, who were recording huge losses. Most Basques who left for Verdun on April 29, 1916, had been fighting for a year and a half, and already twenty-five hundred Basques had died in this conflict.[31]

NOTES

1. Elissalde, *LVII.a gerlan*, 23.
2. Elizalde, "Igandeak."
3. Moulier, "Josteta."
4. Saint-Pierre, "Herriak."
5. Saint-Pierre, "Herriak."
6. Elizalde, "Igandeak."
7. Saint-Pierre, "Bero."
8. Elizalde, "On dakiotela!"
9. Moulier, "Atso bat."
10. *La vie quotidienne des soldats pendant la Grande Guerre*, 159–160.
11. Saint-Pierre, "Eta hemen?"
12. Saint-Pierre, "Zer ari giren."
13. Saint-Pierre, "Toki berean."
14. Adema, "Ez ahantz."
15. Elizalde, "Oraiko gure berri."
16. Saint-Pierre, "Kuraia."
17. Elizalde, "Aroa" (1917).
18. Cazals and Offenstad, "Du Bois-le-Prêtre au 'Front intérieur': Les expériences de guerre des Papillon," 370–371.
19. Elizalde, "Arratoinak."
20. Saint-Pierre, "Lerroetatik urrun."
21. Elizalde, "Bi hitz aroaz."
22. Figure taken by the author from a recompilation of data found at www.memoiredeshommes.sga.defense.gouv.fr.
23. Elizalde, "Aroa" (1916).
24. Etchepare, "Mailka."
25. Etchepare, "Lanik nekeena."
26. See www.memoiredeshommes.sga.defense.gouv.fr.
27. *Historique du 49e régiment d'infanterie pendant la guerre 1914–1918*, 25.
28. Figure taken by the author from a recompilation of data found at www.memoiredeshommes.sga.defense.gouv.fr.
29. Vallaud, *14–18: La Première Guerre mondiale*, 145.
30. Elizalde, "Oraiko egunak!"
31. Figure taken by the author from a recompilation of data found at www.memoiredeshommes.sga.defense.gouv.fr.

CHAPTER EIGHT

The Deserters

As the men set off to war in the stifling heat of summer, they had no idea that they would also be spending the winter in the thick of the fighting. By the end of 1914, it was clear that the war was going to last longer, perhaps even much longer, than expected. Winter was drawing to a close, and there was still no end in sight. Soldiers found it increasingly difficult to be away from their families. In spring 1915, the German and French armies alike decided to grant soldiers temporary leave to return home. Starting June 30, soldiers in the French army were granted eight days leave to return home, though, of course, not all at the same time. Only 5 percent of the soldiers involved in the fighting and 10 percent of reservists were allowed to go home at the same time. The purpose of this measure was not only to keep up the soldiers' morale but also to reduce expenses and to encourage the birth rate.[1] While for city dwellers this break was synonymous with moments of freedom and exhilaration, for soldiers from rural areas it meant a return to the farm and to work in the fields, even if only for a short time.

The Basques also got their first leave, after almost a whole year at war. The first to go were those who had been at the front for more than six months, followed by fathers, married men, and older men. In the autumn, all soldiers were informed that each of them would, in turn, be able to go home. The news delighted the soldiers, who had "heavy hearts."[2] Even though they would have to spend half of this eight-day leave on the road, many wanted to take advantage of the opportunity to return to the Basque Country.

However, whether going for the first time or returning after leave, arriving at the battlefield was tough. Those going to the battlefields for the first time had their hearts in their mouths. They traveled in trucks to the rear fronts of the battlefields, where the din of the bombs was appalling. As they approached the battlefields, they could feel the earth tremors beneath their feet. As they got closer, the stench and disgusting smell of dead bodies would overcome them. And when they reached the trenches or even the path leading to them, they saw corpses everywhere. The warmth of home and the peace of the village suddenly felt far away. It was a stark contrast. Having to leave behind the love of one's family or fiancée to plunge into this hell was utterly joyless. Testimonies tell of these terrible moments. At the Baiona station, an older soldier who had been in the Basque Country on leave for a few days produced a photo of his five children and his wife. The most difficult moment for him, he said, was when his youngest child, aged two at the start of the war, did not recognize him when he returned from the front.[3] Others left home concerned after their relatives had told them how difficult it was for them to do the farmwork when the men in the house were away. In such cases, the soldiers worried even more knowing that while they were at war, their family at home were struggling.

As the war dragged on, people began to wonder more about what would happen after the end of the conflict. What would the life of each of them be like, if there was a life, at the end of the war? It didn't take much to make a soldier's heart skip a beat—all it took was for the mail to arrive late.[4] Thousands and thousands of letters went back and forth. Letters afforded the only way for those at war to get news of their loved ones and for the soldiers to tell their stories of life at the front. Some straightforward accounts managed to escape the surveillance of military censorship. One soldier, for example, complained that he had been wearing the same shirt for twenty-one days, a shirt that was soaked in sweat and was filthy and riddled with lice.[5]

In the French army, the first signs of despair appeared shortly after the war's start, in September 1914, following the defeat at Charleroi. On September 1, the minister for war granted new powers to military commanders, authorizing them to immediately shoot anyone who refused to obey orders during the fighting. State power would no longer have to examine the basis and legitimacy of decisions taken by military courts, the aim being to deter disobedient soldiers through fear.[6] The French Military Justice Act stipulated that treason "in the face of the enemy"—abandonment of post, refusal to obey, revolt, contempt of authority, and desertion—would be punishable by death. Worse still, on August 10, 1914, the right to appeal was suppressed. The military court was made up of five servicemen, and the verdict was handed down without an investigation. French military justice handed down 2,500 death sentences, of which 670 were actually carried out.

Two of these men were from the Basque Country. The first, Pierre Etxeberri, was accused of fleeing from the enemy and was shot in October 1914.[7] Born in Izpura (Ispoure), he lived in Lasa (Lasse). In 1909, he completed only three months' of military service of the three-year term specified because, when he was granted leave to spend Christmas with his family, he did not return to the army. Two months before the outbreak of war, on June 4, 1914, he had joined the troops as a volunteer. When war broke out, he went as a private. After just one month, he and the men in his company came under heavy bombardment near Avocourt in the Argonne. The bombardment took place at 1:00 p.m. on September 3. Etxeberri disappeared, and the following morning, at 5:00 a.m., on his own initiative he went a dozen kilometers farther south to join an infantry regiment at Parois. He was immediately arrested for abandoning his post. He explained that a shell had fallen on them, that he had seen many of his comrades die next to him, and that he had gone into the forest where he spent the night in hiding. On October 19, he was tried and sentenced to death. Two days later, on October 21, he was shot at Récicourt (four kilometres away) at 6:30 a.m. He was twenty-five years old at the time.

The second, Louis Mardochée Lévy, was from Baiona and was shot in January 1915.[8] He belonged to the 49th Infantry Regiment and was called up to fight around Craonne. The night of December 28–29, 1914, was to prove fatal for him. Although he had been ordered to stay in a trench at Oulches, he left for a few hours to sleep peacefully a little farther back. On January 14, 1915, he was brought before the War Council and sentenced to death for abandoning his post. The very next day, at the age of thirty, he was shot in Maizy. According to his father, he should not have gone to war because of his mental disability.

Five hundred other French soldiers were killed without trial; they were "shot as an example." On December 15, 1914, the French army shot two forty-five-year-old soldiers at the front who had been tried and sentenced to death three days earlier for self-mutilation. Another four soldiers were sentenced to death for the same reason on September 5.[9]

Most of the wounds were not self-inflicted, for soldiers were wounded in combat. According to some accounts, the wounded were pleased because their wounds meant they could leave the battlefield and could, if their wounds were serious enough, find themselves out of the war altogether.[10] Hundreds of wounded arrived in Baiona, some too seriously injured to return to the front. Others left Baiona to return to the front once they had been treated. According to several Basque journalists of the time, these wounded men were desperate to get back into action, to attack the Germans. This point of view should be seen in the context of wartime press propaganda.

As the war progressed, it became increasingly difficult to make an escape. At first, some men were allowed to stay at home for health reasons. But in 1917, many of those who had been discharged in 1914, like Jules Moulier "Oxobi," a Basque priest and writer, had to leave again for the front. The exemption measures were more restrictive, as the authorities believed that those who claimed to have health problems were cheats, traitors, or cowards who had only one concern: to save themselves. Many soldiers "went mad," but psychologists and doctors refused to recognize this, arguing that their condition did not prevent them from going to war.[11]

The other, and most common, way of escaping war was to desert. Desertion was not the same as not returning after leave: it was to flee the battlefront in the midst of a battle. The latter case was not frequent, and those who did flee were condemned to death.[12] Desertion from the battlefront was not easy, as deserters had the police on their heels and measures were taken to "sully" their families. Unable to hide at home, deserters had to flee to neutral countries, an almost impossible feat if they were acting alone.[13] They therefore needed outside support, especially from those who lived far from the border regions. The deserters first had to reach the border. Women had a strong influence on soldiers' decisions to get away from the war and were part of the networks that helped them escape.[14] In the Basque Country, deserters from France were often arrested along with the women who had helped them to escape.

Soldiers in the Basque Country, particularly those living in the mountains, had less difficulty fleeing than those from other regions, as Navarre was very close by. Overall, there were more deserters and draft dodgers in the Basque and the Catalan Pyrenees than in France. The average number of deserters across France was around 1.5 percent; in the Pyrenees regions, around 4 percent; and in the Basses-Pyrénées department, 17.6 percent.[15] There were 14,355 draft dodgers and 948 deserters in this department.

The number of deserters was high, but the number of draft dodgers should not be misinterpreted. It is true that overall, in the Basque Country and outside of it, the number of draft dodgers increased when the war began. In France, 1.2 percent of the men who were called up in 1914 became draft dodgers. By 1915, the figure had risen to 2.5 percent. From then on, the number of draft dodgers declined as a result of the severe measures put in place to arrest them and the difficulties they encountered in hiding on flat terrain. In addition, a few years earlier, an amnesty law for draft dodgers had been passed in preparation for the possible outbreak of war to give draft dodgers the opportunity to return and enlist. In spite of this, the number of draft dodgers on the coast and around border areas remained significant.[16] In the case of the Basques, it was likely that their draft dodging after 1914 was a direct consequence of the war.

In the canton of Donibane Lohizune, of 715 insubordinates, 35 percent had left long before the war and had not returned and 37 percent had been due to do military service between 1903 and 1909.[17] Most of these insubordinates had therefore left long ago, their escape facilitated by the proximity of the port of Baiona, which enabled them to embark for South or North America.

This tradition of emigration was not unrelated to cases of insubordination and desertion in wartime. Two-thirds of those Basque emigrants who had left were draft dodgers. Many Basques lived in Argentina and the United States of America, and for the new generations of soldiers, these communities could be refuges.[18] Two days before the start of the war, after noticing that many young people were heading for the "Spanish border" and the Southern Basque Country, where there was no war, the subprefect of Maule (Mauléon) warned of the risk of insubordination. He was particularly concerned that it was people from high society who were leaving.[19] According to the prefect of Maule, a third of those called up in 1914 and 1915 fled to the Southern Basque Country after mobilization. Most of the draft evaders came from rural areas. Most were farmers, shepherds, or fishermen.[20]

For the Basques, it was easy to cross the mountains, then board a ship from the Southern Basque Country to join relatives on the North American continent.[21] Better still, these relatives in America sometimes paid for the trip.[22] Yet some evaders remained in the Southern Basque Country because they had relatives there who provided them with work. They were aided by the town clerk in Luzaide (Valcarlos) in Nafarroa (Navarre), for example, who helped them obtain the documents they needed. The person in charge of emigration at Elizondo town hall (Navarre) also provided evaders with the papers they needed to leave for America. Sixteen people from Luzaide (Valcarlos) were in fact charged by French authorities for complicity in desertion.[23] Many Navarrese were Carlists and had a strong tendency to favor the Germans; it was they who offered help to deserters.[24]

What is true, above all, is that there has always been a relationship between Basques on either side of the border and that the practice of crossing to the Southern Basque Country was nothing new. It had proved its worth during the French Revolution, Louis-Napoléon Bonaparte's coup d'état in 1851, and the insurgencies of the Paris Commune. The reverse was also common, with Basques crossing to the Northern Basque Country, where speaking the same language and having family ties made relationships easy. People from Lapurdi (Labourd), Lower Navarre, or Zuberoa may have had relatives in Navarre or Gipuzkoa in the Southern Basque Country. For instance, in the past, thousands of people from Navarre lived in Zuberoa, where they worked in the espadrille factories. Some young people born in the Northern Basque Country to parents from the Southern Basque Country had French nationality, but their roots were in the South, though their attachment to France was not always certain.

For all these reasons, deserters who fled found themselves in a comfortable situation on the other side of the Pyrenees. Relatives or residents gave them work, protected them, and forwarded their letters to their families. These same relatives crossed the border to send them money or food.

A gendarmerie report dating from 1916 reveals that the number of draft dodgers and deserters was very high in the cantons of Baigorri (Saint-Étienne-de-Baïgorry) and Donibane Garazi (Saint-Jean-Pied-de-Port).[25] The latter canton had as many deserters as men who went to war (1,314 mobilized and 1,310 draft dodgers). If we add to these forty-nine more deserters, for a total of 1359, in this canton, those who did not go to war outnumbered those who did. The figures for the canton of Baigorri were even more noteworthy. There were 1,302 draft evaders and forty-five deserters, and only 594 of them went to war; in other words, for every ten men mobilized, seven did not respond to the call-up. The figures are particularly remarkable in Aldude (Aldudes) and Urepele (Urepel). In these villages, there were few deserters (six in Urepele and seven in Aldude), whereas the village of Urepele had 205 draft dodgers and that of Aldude, 263. Translated into percentages, 81 percent of those mobilized in Urepele and 87 percent in Aldude did not go to the front.

For the shepherds and smugglers who traveled through the mountains separating the Northern Basque Country from Navarre, there were no borders. The sheep moved from one side to the other, and so did the shepherds. Shepherds from Aldude and Urepele roamed the Quinto Real, which is on Navarrese territory. Shepherds from the Baigorri and Baztan Valleys, as well as those from the Arnegi (Arnéguy) area, share the same pastures. Shepherds from Navarre and Lower Navarre lived together. There were no borders for those in the Ezterenzubi (Esterençuby) region either, and the same went for Urruña (Urrugne) and Sara. As a result, it was very easy for them to evade police checks because they knew the nooks and crannies of the mountains and could hide easily. The draft dodgers did not need to live far from home, and some even worked as shepherds in Navarre, returning home in the evenings. Around thirty deserters gathered in Erratzu (Navarre), where they were joined by their fiancées. In Ibardin, some twenty meters from the Lapurdi border, a ball was organized, bringing together the deserters and their friends from Urruña, who had come to join them for the party.²⁶ The subprefect of Maule and the commissioners of Baigorri and Hendaia (Hendaye) drew up reports to denounce this situation, as they knew from intercepted mail, or having seen for themselves, the peaceful life led by these deserters.²⁷

Many of the soldiers who came to the Basque Country on eight days' leave did not return to the war. Every day, these men had seen their comrades die before their eyes, they had been wounded many times, and they knew that their turn would come. So, they took advantage of their stay in the Basque Country to cross the Pyrenees and become deserters.

The same phenomenon can be seen in Catalonia.²⁸ The choice was easier for single people and those without property. It was more complicated for others, as they had to abandon their families and run the risk of losing their farms.²⁹ This is why most deserters were aged between twenty-three and thirty-three. In their flight, they may have received help from a relative or friend in the village, but the villagers did not always keep silent, and denunciations of deserters were not uncommon.³⁰ Some people did not take kindly to soldiers fleeing the fighting while their own brothers, sons, husbands, or fathers were at war.

In 1915, noting the large number of deserters, the prefect of the Basses-Pyrénées department ordered the suspension of leave for Basques and the inspection of letters written in the Basque language. The authorities believed that these letters carried alarmist messages. In summer 1915, the prefect requested that leave be refused to soldiers from the cantons of Uztaritze (Ustaritz), Donibane Lohizune, Ezpeleta (Espelette), Baigorri, Donibane Garazi, and Atharratze, but his request was turned down.³¹ The prefect then submitted a new request to the minister of the interior. He asked that the Basques be sent to Morocco to prevent them from leaving for South America. According to him, the Basques had no patriotic feelings except for their own piece of land, which was why he wanted to send them to Morocco. The minister of the interior, Alexandre Millerand, did not accede to his request. Instead, the authorities ordered the withdrawal of passports from the deserters' families, as well as more rigorous border surveillance.³²

In addition to these measures, a list of all those who had not gone to war was posted on the wall of the town hall. In 1917, the sentences for aiding deserters were increased, and many citizens were sentenced to between one and three years in prison.³³ The aim was also to make it clear that there would be no amnesty for deserters once the war was over. Deserters would have to wait many years before they could return. If they returned during the first few years of the war, they were detained for several weeks, then tried before being released and sent to the front. The 1925 Amnesty Act reserved amnesty for those who had spent at least three months in combat or had been wounded. There was no amnesty, however, for those who had deserted in various ways. The definitive Amnesty Law of 1937 made amnesty possible after a year in prison.[34]

Be that as it may, for as long as the war lasted, the possibility remained open for deserters to return to war. Those who decided to return to combat could have their sentences lifted. The prefect and Captain Miguras intervened publicly in the Southern Basque Country with the aim of remobilizing deserters for the war, explaining that if they returned, they would not be punished.[35] Parish priests did the same, and the weekly magazine *Eskualduna* repeatedly published articles aimed at deserters or their families, encouraging them to return to the front.

The subject of desertion was extremely delicate. Letters and articles published in the press tended to play down the large number of deserters recorded in the Basque Country. The magazine *Eskualduna*, for example, insisted that most of the soldiers were exemplary. The French right-wing press also accused the Left and the Republicans of propagating negative ideas—namely that the Allies were not going to win the war.[36] This was an unacceptable prospect, especially if put forward by military personnel.[37] The Right did not want to admit the possibility of defeat. It saw only one outcome—victory—and it proclaimed the need to fight the war to the end to ensure that the blood spilled up to that point had not been in vain. There could be no peace without victory.[38] A very dim view was also taken of pacifists. In 1916, following a denunciation by the extreme right-wing review *L'Action Française*, a fierce controversy erupted around the extreme left-wing pacifist review *Le Bonnet Rouge*. Its director, Miguel Vigo-Almereyda, was arrested for receiving money from abroad. The affair also cast a shadow over the French government of the time. In the Basque Country, *Eskualduna* took a staunchly hostile stance toward the pacifist magazine.

However, it is impossible to say whether the French Left supported pacifists and rebels. In wartime, only a few groups were in favor of insubordination.[39] The Socialist International failed in uniting itself against the war. Before the outbreak of war, the leadership of the Socialist International had met to discuss how to avoid conflict. Once the war had begun, though, the socialists of each country fought for their own country. On September 5 and 8, 1915, the Swiss socialist Robert Grimm and the Russian Martov organized a meeting in

Zimmerwald (Switzerland). At the conference, the thirty-eight participants adopted a text calling for peace. One of the authors of this text was none other than Leon Trotsky. At the end of the conference, Lenin and other Russians drafted another text calling for a revolt against the war. From April 24 to April 30, 1916, a further conference was held in Kienthal (Switzerland), attended by forty-four participants. However, the initiatives of the far left had no impact on the course of the war.

NOTES

1. Cronier, "Permissions et permissionnaires," 592.
2. Saint-Pierre, "Nor baliatuko?"
3. Hiriart-Urruty, "Bortz haurren aita."
4. Audoin-Rouzeau, *A travers leurs journaux: 14–18, les combattants des tranchées*, 58.
5. Cabanes, *La victoire endeuillée: La sortie de guerre des soldats français (1918–1920)*, 28.
6. Bach, *Fusillés pour l'exemple: 1914–1915*, 234.
7. Mathieu, *14–18, les fusillés*, 357.
8. Mathieu, *14–18, les fusillés*, 541.
9. Cochet, *Survivre au front, 1914–1918: Les poilus entre contrainte et consentement*, 70.
10. Meyer, *La vie quotidienne des soldats pendant la Grande Guerre*, 188.
11. Isnenghi, *La Première Guerre Mondiale*, 55.
12. Ruquet, "Désertions et insoumissions sur la frontière des Pyrénées pendant la guerre de 14–18," 70.
13. Cochet, *Survivre au front, 1914–1918: Les poilus entre contrainte et consentement*, 216.
14. Ruquet, "Désertions et insoumissions sur la frontière des Pyrénées pendant la guerre de 14–18," 76.
15. Ruquet, "Désertions et insoumissions sur la frontière des Pyrénées pendant la guerre de 14–18," 69.
16. Boulanger, "Le refus de l'impôt du sang: Géographie de l'insoumission en France de 1914 à 1922," 5.
17. Garat, "Insoumissions et désertions en France pendant la Grande Guerre: Le cas des cantons basques," 10.
18. Ruquet, "Désertions et insoumissions sur la frontière des Pyrénées pendant la guerre de 14–18," 80.
19. Sarramone, *Les cousins basques d'Amérique*.
20. Garat, "Insoumissions et désertions en France pendant la Grande Guerre: Le cas des cantons basques," 12.
21. Ott, *War, Judgment, and Memory in the Basque Borderlands, 1914–1945*, 36.

22. Elissondo, *Mémoires de la Soule 1914–1918: Une petite vallée du Pays Basque dans la guerre*, 36.
23. Ott, *War, Judgment, and Memory in the Basque Borderlands, 1914–1945*, 40.
24. Ruquet, "Désertions et insoumissions sur la frontière des Pyrénées pendant la guerre de 14–18," 86.
25. Garat, "Insoumissions et désertions en France pendant la Grande Guerre: Le Cas des cantons basques," 31.
26. Ruquet, "Désertions et insoumissions sur la frontière des Pyrénées pendant la guerre de 1914–1918," 647.
27. Ruquet, "Insoumis et déserteurs pyrénéens de la Grande Guerre: La force des liens transfrontaliers."
28. Ruquet, "Désertions et insoumissions sur la frontière des Pyrénées pendant la guerre de 14–18," 72.
29. Elissondo, *Mémoires de la Soule 1914–1918: Une petite vallée du Pays Basque dans la guerre*, 36.
30. Elissondo, *Mémoires de la Soule 1914–1918: Une petite vallée du Pays Basque dans la guerre*, 38.
31. Garat, "Insoumissions et désertions en France pendant la Grande Guerre: Le cas des cantons basques," 17.
32. Garat, "Insoumissions et désertions en France pendant la Grande Guerre: Le cas des cantons basques," 16.
33. Garat, "Insoumissions et désertions en France pendant la Grande Guerre: Le cas des cantons basques," 15.
34. Ruquet, "Les déserteurs français de la Première Guerre Mondiale et la guerre d'Espagne," 33.
35. Ruquet, "Les déserteurs français de la Première Guerre Mondiale et la guerre d'Espagne," 33.
36. Feyel, *La presse en France des origines à 1944: Histoire politique et matérielle*, 149.
37. Cubero, *La grande guerre et l'arrière (1914–1919)*, 188.
38. Cubero, *La grande guerre et l'arrière (1914–1919)*, 203.
39. Cohen, "L'antimilitarisme des jeunesses avant 1914," 44.

CHAPTER NINE

Life in the Basque Country

Christmas Eve is a joyful night when no one is missing from home. For the soldiers in the trenches, hundreds of kilometers from their villages and families, surrounded by death, December 25, 1914, was a somber day. It was dark, too, in the Basque Country, as these verses by Jules Moulier "Oxobi" illustrate. There was no singing in church, as there had been the previous year; not a single male voice could be heard, and many priests were absent.

> Apezik ez den herrietan,
> Chilintcharik ezin entzun;
> Nigarra frango begietan,
> Eliza dorreak ilhun!
> Emazteki guti ere gaur
> On denik atheratzeko,
> Ttipi ttipiak, hoinbertze haur
> Etchetan bada zaintzeko![1]

> In villages without priests,
> Impossible to hear the slightest bell;
> Many tears in eyes,
> Sadness on the steeples!
> Few women ready
> to go out this evening,
> At home, there are so many children
> to look after!

In the homes of the Northern Basque Country, the only ones left were mainly the children, the women, and the elderly. They were responsible for all the work on the farm. The women carried out the farm chores—for example, they mowed the grass and the wheat, harvested them, and then carried them on their backs to the farm. Although this was hard work, it was worth it because the money from the farm enabled them to pay off previous debts, bring up their families, and send a little money to their husbands or brothers away at war. Even then, farms in the rural heartland Basque Country were small, on a family scale. Given that all the work had to be done with fewer hands, in many villages the different families helped each other to make the work go more smoothly.

From the front, every soldier wrote to his wife to advise her on how to carry out the various tasks.[2] Similarly, in their letters to newspapers, the men tended to discuss agriculture, in particular to describe the rural practices they had observed in the regions where they had spent time. According to the soldiers' accounts, the farmers in northern France were more technically advanced than those in the Basque Country. They used machines and had stronger horses. However, even though the French farmers had better ploughs, land, and horses, the soldiers insisted in their writings that the Basque peasants were much more valiant.[3]

Wherever these Basque farmers were in combat, they carefully observed the way of working in order to return to the Basque Country having learned something, which they were then able to apply on the farm.[4] The peasant soldier always had the work of the farm at home in mind, and this concern added to the dangers and suffering of war to accentuate his pain. Although peasants, accustomed to the hard work of the land, seemed better prepared to cope with the difficult situations they had to endure, in reality they suffered even more than urban dwellers did from being away from home, for the worry associated with farmwork never left them.[5]

Before the start of the war, the economic situation of farms was not good. During the war, with a reduced workforce, each family had to continue to feed its five or six children (or more), so everyone had to work hard to contribute to the effort. They managed to earn a little money from the farm, and every family with a member in the war received aid from the French government. For these two reasons, many women managed to pay off the debts they had accumulated before the war. Although the military requisitioned certain foodstuffs from the farms for war purposes, their work paid off.[6]

Even in wartime, this peasant society of the Northern Basque Country could continue to move forward because it remained attached to tradition and was, at heart, a conservative society. It was in these regions of small family farms that the Catholic Church was most deeply rooted and powerful. This was particularly the case in the Massif Central region in France, in the Basque Country, and in Brittany.[7] The work of peasants was difficult, their situation unenviable because they were poor, and the only way for them to get by was to work hard. If you did not work, you lost your income. The family provided the most solid and reliable support, which may explain the peasants' conservative attitudes.[8] Such was Basque society at the beginning of the twentieth century in the interior of the Northern Basque Country: family oriented, attached to the land, and hard working. These were values extolled by the parish priests and the magazine *Eskualduna*, which met with a strong positive response and support from the population.

Although it was true that the countryside served as a refuge for the Church and conservative Catholic society, some people nevertheless left inland Basque Country to live in the towns, doing so simply because their farms did not produce enough to feed everyone. The parish priests disapproved of the rural exodus, but they were not alone in seeing a danger in the decline of the rural world; the Republicans and socialists who feared the exploitation of the proletariat also saw the danger.[9] However, for Basque writers and parish priests, the rural exodus also meant the loss of Basque identity.[10] When they spoke of the dilution of this identity, they were referring not only to the fear of a decline in the Basque language but also to the disappearance of a traditional way of life. For them, faith and the Basque language were inseparable, as they constituted the pillars of the same identity.[11] Basque *pelota* was also considered to be an important, distinctive sign of a Basque Catholic. The organization of *pelota* games after Mass helped to attract people to Mass, keeping them away from the cafés once the church service was over and preventing boys and girls from dancing together.[12]

Supporters of this traditional society were highly critical of city life, particularly in wartime. *Eskualduna* published several articles and letters from soldiers who disapproved of the lifestyle and elegance of women who lived in the cities, particularly Biarritz. In 1914, with the surprise and horror of the first year of the war, community life came to a halt and no bullfights were organized. From 1915 onward, however, normal life resumed in Baiona, and the surrounding area and the atmosphere were more relaxed because the front was far away. Of course, families who had loved ones fighting in the war or loved ones who had been wounded found it difficult to relax, but others continued to go out to attend shows.

At the time, Baiona had three cinemas: La Féria; the Saint-Esprit cinema, which reopened after a period of renovation; and the Excelsior-Cinéma, which opened on October 30, 1915, but would soon face competition from two other venues. Part of the takings from some of the shows went to raise funds for the wounded or those in difficulty. This fundraising caused controversy, with many questioning whether it was legitimate to mix charity and entertainment at a time when some people were suffering. After soldiers at the Baiona military hospital asked for galas to be organized in the hospital grounds, for example, a letter published in the daily *Le Courrier de Bayonne* on March 25, 1916, expressed anger at these shows, which it said were an insult to grieving families, and condemned their lack of seriousness, as if the aim was to forget the atrocities that were taking place. Those in charge of the newspaper replied that the people, including the refugees from the war, wanted to be entertained. The Société Nautique, the Aviron Bayonnais, and the Amicale Jean-Macé also got together to organize several festivities.[13]

While it is true that many men left for war, thousands of others also came to Baiona. Some had been wounded; others had fled to Belgium. On August 25, Baiona received seventy-five lightly wounded men. Then more seriously wounded men arrived, men who had undergone operations or received first aid near the front. During the first few months, 1,025 beds were set up in the military hospital for the wounded; the Saint-Louis de Gonzague school was transformed into a 152-bed military hospital; the Delay clinic and the lycée took in 468 wounded. The Lycée Saint-Louis and the civil hospital also received wounded. After a stay in the hospital, the wounded were sent to convalescent homes in Biarritz, Kanbo, Larresoro (Larressore), and Capbreton.[14] From the start of the fighting, military medical units were organized for local people so that they could treat the wounded.[15]

Meanwhile, refugees from Belgium began arriving en masse. The first Belgians—450 in all—arrived in Baiona on October 23, 1914. Two weeks later, a new wave of refugees arrived.[16] In all, the town of Baiona welcomed some 5,000 refugees from Belgium and northeastern France. This welcome was later praised by Elisabeth, Queen of Belgium. Some local people also set up a network to help the wounded, refugees, and war orphans, welcoming them into their homes. Others were taking advantage of the situation to do business. Laundries put up signs announcing that they could provide everything needed for mourning within twelve hours. Insurance companies also offered special cover to soldiers leaving for war.[17]

Baiona was a bustling place. Fewer and fewer employees populated the factories because, as the war progressed, new generations were called up to the front. As a result, women began to work in the factories, providing themselves with an income. While some took advantage of this to earn more money, for others the situation was far from easy. Beginning in September 1914, prices soared in

Baiona. The town hall banned wholesale sales, the transportation of goods after the covered market had closed, the purchase of quantities greater than a family's consumption, or the sale of goods for more than the daily specified price. The supply of eggs, fish, fruit, and vegetables posed no problem, as these foods were produced in sufficient quantities in the region. Wheat, potatoes, and sugar arrived by boat, but not in large enough quantities. As currency was in short supply, the Baiona Chamber of Commerce distributed steel and aluminum notes and coins. The sum of 6.5 million francs was put into circulation.[18]

However, the French government demanded that the citizens deposit their silver and gold. In the Northern Basque Country, the bishop and parish priests joined in this demand and recommended that people deposit their gold with the Bank of France. The reason given was that France needed to import food, weapons, and tools, and to obtain them more cheaply, it needed more gold. People were promised not only that this gold and money would be repaid to them at 5 percent interest once the war was over but also that they were guaranteed that by selling the gold to France, they would make more profit than by selling it abroad to the Southern Basque Country. Furthermore, those who had decided to keep gold under their mattress were warned that it would be worthless in a few years' time, as the practice might no longer be legal. Another option was to raise taxes, but this measure was not viewed favorably. Most people possessed only very small quantities of gold, yet according to *Eskualduna*, a multitude of citizens went to Baiona to deposit the little gold they had.

From 1917 onward, basic foodstuffs became increasingly scarce. Bakeries were closed on Tuesdays and Wednesdays, and butcher shops closed on Thursdays and Fridays. Bread could be sold only twelve hours after baking.[19] In October 1918, a tax on mushrooms was introduced. Hotels were allowed to use hot water only on Saturdays and Sundays.

The mayor of Baiona sent a letter to the council president, Georges Clemenceau, condemning the fact that bread was being given to army horses. On March 6, a group from the 58th Artillery Regiment received six tonnes of bread for the horses. During the same period, the inhabitants of the Basses-Pyrénées went without bread for days on end, and in some villages for a fortnight. *Eskualduna* repeatedly urged its readers to eat bread sparingly, explaining that the wheat from which it was made came from America, that German submarines had several times torpedoed ships full of goods and wheat, and that many ships were stuck in port.

In the war, control of maritime space was of capital importance. The Germans also waged submarine warfare, which intensified from mid-1916 and became full-blown in 1917. In January 1916, the war indirectly affected the town of Angelu (Anglet) when a pipe exploded at the munitions factory Poudrière de Blancpignon, seriously injuring five workers. On February 12, 1917, at 5:00 p.m., the town of Baiona was the target of a German submarine attack. The Germans fired nine shells at the Forges de l'Adour, killing two workers (Jean Dupouy and Jean Peytrain), seriously injuring two others, and causing many more minor injuries.[20]

During the first ten months of 1917, the Allies lost 4.7 million tonnes of ships at sea, which had a serious effect on the transportation of goods and armaments. In 1916, the French command proposed that all ships should have an escort, but the British were not in favor of this, and it took them time to implement the decision. As well as protecting the ships, the French also proposed monitoring the coastline. In September 1917, only 17 percent of ships had protection, whereas by the end of the next year 90 percent did and less than 1 percent of them were sunk.

In February 1917, the minister for maritime affairs decided to create maritime and air bases on the French coasts.[21] Around the Basque Country, three possible sites were considered: Lake Léon, the port of Baiona, and Donibane Lohizune. The Léon site was quickly ruled out, as the lake was not a suitable location. Geographically, Donibane Lohizune, a fishing town, offered better protection for maritime forces. However, in terms of airspace, the port of Baiona was better situated. The Blanc-Pignon area could be used for aircraft takeoffs, and the Adour for landings. It was also easier to set this up in Baiona, given the existing land and the resources available. However, in the event of high seas at Baiona Harbor, a station was set up at Donibane Lohizune so that ships could go there if necessary.

The Baiona base had three hangars and, at the start, twelve bombers and three cannon aircraft. By November 1918, however, it had thirty-five aircraft. A commander, four officers (two pilots and two observers), eight pilots, and around thirty sailors were stationed at Baiona, making a total of forty-three men. The Donibane Lohizune base, at Zokoa (Socoa) to be precise, had three seaplanes. This site was linked to Baiona by a telephone line. The seaplanes flew in squadrons of three: two bombers and one gunboat. The seaplanes were equipped with two thirty-five-kilogram bombs and a machine gun. As soon as a submarine was seen on the surface of the water, a gunboat had to attack it; and when the submarine began to dive, the bombers would take over. However, it was not until the end of 1918 that gunboats were launched, as they took time to develop. As a result, until then, squadrons consisted of just two seaplanes. The first of these aircraft, although invented at the end of 1917, did not take off properly. Later the 1918 model was used.

The ships monitored the ocean. When they spotted a submarine, guns were fired to warn the boats in the vicinity so that they could attack the vessel. In eighteen months, six submarines had been spotted, but none had been sunk. Nonetheless, the safety of maritime travel was guaranteed.

Enriching the Southern Basque Country

For their part, Gipuzkoans and Biscayans also wanted safe sea journeys. For the fishermen of Gipuzkoa, Spain's neutrality was advantageous, allowing them to catch large quantities of fish even if they had old boats, having replaced their sailing boats with steamers. The advent of motorized boats led to a change in business structure. Large companies replaced the small family businesses. The owners of the shipyards created in Donostia–San Sebastián were mostly from Madrid and Biscay. They left the port of Donostia–San Sebastián to the small fishermen, and the big fishing companies moved into the port of Pasaia.[22]

The economic situation did not benefit everyone. During the war, no new businesses were set up in Donostia–San Sebastián, with European investment almost completely suspended. Between 1914 and 1920, the mining sector suffered a major decline. Tourism and construction also declined between 1914 and 1930. However, the shipbuilding sector experienced significant growth as entrepreneurs from Bilbo-Bilbao, Galicia, and Catalonia invested capital in Gipuzkoa.[23] Compañía Naviera Guipuzcoana was the company that recorded the biggest profits; it opened in 1916 with a capital of 4.5 million, and a year later its capital had risen to 19.5 million.[24]

There is no doubt that the province that grew richest as a result of the war and the shipyards was Bizkaia, and in particular Bilbo-Bilbao and the surrounding area. Moreover, it was not the only province to benefit from the First World War; the Spanish economy as a whole benefited greatly from the situation. Spanish industry and agriculture received colossal sums of money, enabling them not only to repay all the debts incurred in the nineteenth century but also to make a profit.[25] Similarly, during this period, Basque capitalists seized the opportunity to amass enormous amounts of funds.[26]

At the start of the war, the lack of political and economic security caused some concern, especially as raw materials were in short supply. The Bilbo-Bilbao Stock Exchange was in turmoil, and the Barcelona Stock Exchange was forced to close. However, the economic situation changed fairly quickly, with the textile industry expanding rapidly from 1915 onward, particularly in Barcelona. The chemical and pharmaceutical industries were also booming. Coal mining followed suit, with the number of companies and employees growing considerably and wages rising. Prices also rose sharply, and company profits doubled or even tripled.[27] Production in Eibar's arms industry was increasing, although this was not the fastest-growing sector.

Until 1915, companies in Bizkaia invested between 5 and 50 million pesetas of capital per year; by 1917, however, capital had risen to 164 million, and by 1918 to 427 million. This was particularly notable in the banking sector. Bank profits doubled in 1918 and tripled in 1919. The steel industry also experienced unprecedented growth, with production value increasing threefold between 1914 and 1916.

But the sector that benefited most from this period was the shipbuilding industry, both in shipping and in shipbuilding. As a result of the imbalance between supply and demand in international transportation and changes in regular shipping routes, in traditional port centers, and in sailing conditions, the situation of Spanish shipping completely transformed. German ships and submarines destroyed several English freighters, causing tonnes of goods to disappear and Spanish seaports to grow by 500 to 700 percent. In 1916, cash holdings were 2,729 percent higher than in 1910, and in 1919 they were 5,618 percent higher. The growth that Spain was experiencing was mainly concentrated in Bilbo, where the port of Bilbo-Bilbao alone had as many ship registrations as the whole of Spain.

The most important company was Sota y Aznar, which between 1914 and 1918 increased its annual profits from 2.5 million pesetas to 35 million pesetas. In 1920, its founder, Ramón de la Sota y Llano, was the owner and partner of several other companies, including Caminos de Hierro del Norte, Minera Sierra Menera, Banco de Bilbao, and Banco de Comercio.[28] Sota y Aznar also created the company Siderúrgica del Mediterráneo in order to control the entire iron chain: extraction, processing, sales, and transportation. Long before the war, in fact since the end of the nineteenth century, Sota had already owned assets thanks to the export of ores and the shipbuilding market. In 1900, he founded the Euskalduna shipyard and opened a factory in Teruel. During the war, Sota y Aznar's profits rose to 90 million pesetas, and its capital doubled, enabling the company to turn its attention toward the Mediterranean.[29]

This spectacular economic development also had an impact on the Bilbao Stock Exchange. Between 1915 and 1919, average share values increased by a factor of 2.3.[30] This growth resulted from the accumulation of capital and investment during this period. In addition, the development of the stock market offered great opportunities to get rich quickly. Between 1914 and 1918, this growth particularly affected shipbuilding. The value of shipyard shares increased sixfold, and the sale of these shares led to a substantial increase in capital. In 1914, for example, Compañía Naviera Vascongada was distributing a 15 percent share, which rose to 100 percent in the following years. The profits from the stock market were much greater than the capital invested in the company. In 1918, the company's liquid assets amounted to 23 million pesetas, or 2.5 times its capital, which was 50 times more than in 1914. In many other shipbuilding companies the profits distributed were enormous.

The Marítima Unión company did not distribute any shares in the prewar years. In 1915, it distributed only 6 percent, but in 1916 it increased this to 200 percent, and in 1917 to 260 percent. In 1918, Marítima de Nervión distributed 520 percent.[31] Between them, the Sota Aznar, Unión, and Vascongada groups received 240 million pesetas in cash between 1915 and 1919.

The impact of this development was also felt in Bilbo's banks. Although at the start of the war they recorded significant losses in incomes, by the end of 1915 they were making substantial profits. There was no competition from foreign companies in the Spanish market. It was at this time that branches of banks were opened in Spain's major commercial cities, and these branches then became national banks.[32] The capital of the Banco de Vizcaya increased from 8.5 million to 20 million between 1914 and 1920. At the same time, the Banco de Bilbao distributed 20 to 24 percent shares and saw its capital rise from 15 to 30 million. The Crédito de Unión Minera, furthermore, increased its capital from 20 million pesetas in 1915 to 50 million in 1919.[33] However, it was not the banking sector that made the most profits on the stock market but the shipbuilding, insurance, steel, and electricity sectors.

Nevertheless, what happened during the war was like filling a balloon with air. When the war was over, the balloon burst. In 1920, the economic situation returned to normal, and those who had been able to be the kings of Europe thanks to the war returned to their prewar situation. It was a difficult return, particularly for the shipbuilding industry. Boat sales collapsed. Shipbuilders wanted to maintain prices, but this was impossible. Consumption was also falling. The crisis spread to all sectors, and the stock market fell dramatically. Small businesses were disappearing.

In Bizkaia, the strength of nationalism was growing alongside the profits. Economic power was in the hands of the nationalist bourgeoisie who chose, as one of their battles, to oppose the tax that the Spanish budget minister, Santiago Alba, intended to introduce. He wanted to introduce a law to tax the large profits made during the war. Businessmen in Bizkaia and Catalonia, led by Catalan MP Francesc Cambó,[34] considered the measure unfair and fought against it. Against this backdrop, the Basque Nationalist Party won the 1917 elections by a large margin, obtaining an absolute majority in the Bizkaia Provincial Council.

The Basque Nationalist Party, which was very powerful at the time, believed that it was possible to obtain autonomous status. Ramón de la Sota's company, along with several other companies, generously financed the Basque Nationalist Party, after having excluded Luis Arana Goiri, the brother of the founder of the party. Sota vehemently opposed the workers' strike in 1917, fearing a contagion from the Russian Revolution. Repression put an end to the strike, and the Sotas, father and son, congratulated the army generals and the Spanish government for their firm attitude toward the strikers.[35]

Controlling the message

The warring states were keeping a close eye on what was happening in the Southern Basque Country. Their main concern was not so much the economic situation as what was being said about the war. The prefect of the Basses-Pyrénées department sent a letter to the French minister of the interior, warning him of the way in which the daily papers over there were talking about the Battle of Charleroi. He did not like the headlines emphasizing the French defeat, particularly in the August 23, 1914, issue of the conservative Bilbo-Bilbao daily *La Gaceta del Norte*. The prefect also complained about the fact that the daily *El Correo del Norte* denounced the "lies" spread by the French.[36] He stressed the importance of not allowing messages from these newspapers to enter French territory.

Until the beginning of the twentieth century, France had an influence on the Spanish press insofar as its agencies disseminated news. However, there was stiff competition from German news sources, which also wanted to have an impact on Spanish public opinion. From 1914 onward, France made every effort to weaken the influence of German news sources on the Spanish press and to disseminate its own news.[37]

Those denouncing the untruths of the French press were not so wrong. The press did not give bad news. It tried to show the good sides of events, glossing over the failures as far as possible and exaggerating the achievements. The

French government, for its part, gave the press as little information as possible so that the Germans would also know as little as possible about the condition and location of the French army. Moreover, discouraging the population was out of the question. As a result, in addition to the fact that the messaging was highly biased, censorship was also taking place.

As soon as the conflict broke out on August 3, 1914, the minister for war introduced exceptional measures, including a section on censorship, which he sent to the prefectures. The new legislation gave the French government the right to "closely monitor" the press, in particular through the prefectures and military commanders. They were forbidden to pass on certain information to the dailies and weeklies, particularly on war-related events, and the press were forbidden to publish details of the transportation of soldiers. Journalists were also ordered not to report false victories so as not to raise hopes among the readers.

The Ministry of War set up the Press Office, which had hundreds of delegates throughout France. In addition to the Press Office in Paris, regional and departmental branches were also set up to monitor not only daily newspapers but also shows, songs, and plays. In total, almost five thousand people were involved in censorship.[38] There were around three hundred local committees, each headed by a dignitary from the army and the subprefect.[39] They were a "veritable army of censors,"[40] some of whom worked full time in the printing works to check the dailies as soon as they came off the press. They supervised the preprint versions of the daily and weekly newspapers and, if they deemed it necessary, pointed out passages to be removed.

A censorship committee also existed in Baiona. On December 3, 1914, Commandant Baron, Judge Leoarat, Le Beuf, the lycée rhetoric teacher Sautet, and the engraver Mandangaran became members of the committee.[41] On March 25, 1915, Antoine Malécarie, former headmaster of the Baiona primary school, became head of the committee. In addition to these people, one member devoted himself specifically to monitoring the Basque-language magazine *Eskualduna*. The result was that *Eskualduna* was sometimes published with blank spaces, showing that fragments of articles had been cut out before printing. Censorship also affected parliamentary debates and the press reports that came out around the time of certain battles, particularly after the Battle of Charleroi and the Battle of Verdun.[42] In short, the more obvious it became that the war was going to be prolonged, the more censorship extended its grip.[43]

However, the work of the censors was not limited to controlling the newspapers; it also targeted the mail. Letters written by soldiers were closely monitored to ensure that their authors did not break the rules of censorship—for example, by mentioning their geographical location.[44] Each army had its own censorship commission, which read soldiers' and even civilians' letters. Each committee had fifteen to twenty-five members, five of them senior military officers and the rest mostly civil servants or teachers, bank employees, notaries, or priests.[45] The censors' task was not limited to place names. They had to make sure that soldiers did not criticize or spread information likely to make civilians lose hope. Knowing that they were being monitored encouraged soldiers to censor themselves.[46] Most of the daily papers in the Basque Country, as well as the magazine *Eskualduna*, accepted the arguments put forward by the censors and complied with their demands.

NOTES

1. Moulier, "Gauberri armadetan."
2. Becker, *La France en guerre 1914–1918: La grande mutation*, 41.
3. Elizalde, "Laborari etchalde handi."
4. Elizalde, "Hemengo bazterra."
5. Mariot, "Faut-il être motivé pour tuer? Sur quelques explications aux violences de guerre," 161.
6. Laharie, *Les Basses-Pyrénées pendant la guerre 1914–1918*, 76.
7. Cochet, *Survivre au front, 1914–1918: Les poilus entre contrainte et consentement*, 27.
8. Duby and Wallon, *Histoire de la France rurale*, vol. 3, *Apogée et crise de la civilisation paysanne: 1789–1914*, 501.
9. Duby and Wallon, *Histoire de la France rurale*, vol. 3, *Apogée et crise de la civilisation paysanne: 1789–1914*, 529.
10. Casenave, *De l'article de presse à l'essai littéraire: Buruchkak (1910) de Jean Etchepare*, 162–163.
11. Casenave, *De l'article de presse à l'essai littéraire: Buruchkak (1910) de Jean Etchepare*, 165.
12. Fabas, "Aspects de la vie religieuse dans le diocèse de Bayonne (1905–1965)," 68.
13. Castiella, *Un siècle à Bayonne: 1900–2000*, 56.
14. Ansoborlo, *Histoire militaire de Bayonne: 1789–1940*, 249.
15. Pontet, *Histoire de Bayonne*, 32.
16. Ansoborlo, *Histoire militaire de Bayonne: 1789–1940*, 248.
17. Castiella, *Un siècle à Bayonne: 1900–2000*, 108.
18. Pontet, *Histoire de Bayonne*, 33.
19. Castiella, *Un siècle à Bayonne: 1900–2000*, 125.
20. Castiella, *Un siècle à Bayonne: 1900–2000*, 128.

21. Lapeyre, "Une 'base aéronavale' à Bayonne: 1917–1918," 237.
22. Garate Ojanguren and Martín Rudi, *Cien años de la vida económica de San Sebastián: 1887–1987*, 86.
23. Garate Ojanguren and Martín Rudi, *Cien años de la vida económica de San Sebastián: 1887–1987*, 147.
24. Garate Ojanguren and Martín Rudi, *Cien años de la vida económica de San Sebastián: 1887–1987*, 156.
25. Vicens Vives, *Historia económica de España: 9a*, 681.
26. Roldán and García Delgado, *La formación de la sociedad capitalista en España*, 43.
27. Caro Baroja, *Historia general del país vasco*, 11:156.
28. Caro Baroja, *Historia general del país vasco*, 11:160.
29. *Historia de Euskal Herria (Orreaga)*, 49.
30. Montero, *La modernización capitalista: Ciclos económicos y desarrollo empresarial de Vizcaya entre 1891 y 1936 a través de la Bolsa de Bilbao*, 87.
31. Montero, *La modernización capitalista: Ciclos económicos y desarrollo empresarial de Vizcaya entre 1891 y 1936 a través de la Bolsa de Bilbao*, 88.
32. Montero, *La modernización capitalista: Ciclos económicos y desarrollo empresarial de Vizcaya entre 1891 y 1936 a través de la Bolsa de Bilbao*, 89.
33. Montero, *La modernización capitalista: Ciclos económicos y desarrollo empresarial de Vizcaya entre 1891 y 1936 a través de la Bolsa de Bilbao*, 90.
34. Caro Baroja, *Historia general del país vasco*, 11:161.
35. *Historia de Euskal Herria (Orreaga)*, 52.
36. Becker, *1914: Comment les Français sont entrés dans la guerre*, 529.
37. Aubert, "La presse espagnole et son public (1914–1918)," 443.
38. Almeida (d') and Delporte, *Histoire des médias en Franc: De la Grande Guerre à nos jours*, 16.
39. Forcade, "Dans l'œil de la censure: Voir ou ne pas voir la guerre," 39.
40. Rajsfus, *La censure militaire et policière 1914–1918*.
41. Departmental Archives of Pyrénées-Atlantiques: box 1 M 123.
42. Forcade, "La censure politique en France pendant la Grande Guerre," 119.
43. Livois (de), *Histoire de la presse française: 2, de 1881 à nos jours*, 401.
44. Cabanes, "Ce que dit le contrôle postal," 56.
45. Cabanes, "Ce que dit le contrôle postal," 57.
46. Rousseau, *La guerre censurée: Une histoire des combattants européens de 14–18*.

CHAPTER TEN

The Position of the Basque "Intelligentsia"

The editors of the weekly *Eskualduna* were highly disciplined in their response to orders from the French government and the army. These authors were the leading Basque writers in the Northern Basque Country at the time: the doctor Jean Etchepare, Jules Moulier "Oxobi," and Manex Hiriart-Urruty, to name only the most famous. Most of the magazine's editors were young enough to go off to war. So, on the day of mobilization, they answered the call. Those who remained at the Baiona editorial office were Manex Hiriart-Urruty, canon of Baiona; Blaise Adema; and Jules Moulier "Oxobi." Oxobi was old enough to go to war but had been discharged because of poor health. Those sent to the front included Jean Etchepare, Jean Saint-Pierre, and Jean Elissalde "Zerbitzari." Except for Etchepare, all were priests.

Jean Saint-Pierre was a young priest from Milafranga (Villefranque) mobilized as a stretcher-bearer, first with the 18th Infantry Regiment, then with the 49th. Right from the start, he began writing war chronicles. His superiors, who were full of praise for his work as a soldier, promoted him first to corporal and then, in May 1917, to sergeant. He also received two special commendations: one on May 23, 1917, and the other, the Order of the Division, on November 9 of the same year. His determination at the heart of the fighting drew admiration. A few months before the end of the war, on March 30, 1918, he was taken prisoner by the Germans after being wounded in battle. He remained in Limburg until the end of the war.

This background helps us understand why this man, who would become known as a true Basqueophile principally through his articles for the daily newspaper *Euzkadi*—written under the pseudonym Anxuberro—and who was founder of the magazine *Gure Herria* and also president of the Société d'Études Basques Eusko Ikaskuntza, also felt very French.[1] This attachment to his homeland is clearly evident in his wartime chronicles, of which here are two extracts:

People are increasingly coming out in our favor, because it's clear who's waging war in a manly way. In the big cities people are clamoring for war. In the face of such, war is better than doing nothing, in view of what could happen.[2]

But such is our eternal failing, we French, to feed on dreams that are too big, for we enthusiastically set about the task, whatever it may be, unerringly and without hesitation, surprised afterward, and crestfallen, because we stretched out our arm faster than we thought.[3] (both texts translated from Basque)

In these and other examples, Jean Saint-Pierre made it clear that he felt French. Even when writing about wartime events, he always evoked exploits and was constantly optimistic, like a loyal soldier and a good Frenchman ready to accept the difficult situation in the trenches in order to defend France.

The young writer and priest Jean Elissalde "Zerbitzari" was sent to the La Rochelle region and served in the 57th Infantry Regiment.[4] He started out in the army as a nurse and worked as a stretcher-bearer during the war. In June 1918, he was promoted to corporal. On May 21, 1917, he was rewarded for his courage and determination in going to the aid of the wounded amid the bombing. On April 13, 1918, he was mentioned for similar behavior during another battle. On August 7, he was again awarded a distinction. Finally, on November 15, 1918, he was awarded the Croix de Guerre.

His texts also reveal his attachment to France. He did not criticize the war and came across as a loyal soldier. However, his writing showed more nuances than seen in Saint-Pierre's writings, particularly because he shed light on the harshness of the situation in the trenches. He also revealed his Basqueophile leanings on several occasions. As the following extract shows, he considered himself to be as much Basque as French:

When this war started, some Basques on the other side of the Pyrenees opposed us, according to the newspapers. This news was heartbreaking for the Basque fighters. What, brother should disown his brother like that because our skies have darkened? What cruelty! And now, suddenly, last week, our beloved newspaper tells us that this was not true: that we are still united (Seven provinces make one), and that the Basques of Spain stand side by side with those of France. By supporting us so fervently, they have given us the most precious help there is. And now they want to prove their attachment to us in another way. We Basque fighters would like to thank them from the bottom of our hearts. We will never forget this, dear brothers.

Like you, we will redouble our efforts to become one with you: long live the "Zazpiak Bat" (Seven provinces that make a country)! Thank you to the men and women who are fighting for this cause in Spain. Thanking you wholeheartedly, loyal newspapers *Euzkadi* and *Napartarra* that are working hard for this same goal.[5] (translated from Basque)

Although Zerbitzari complained a great deal about the rats, the mud, and the cold, he emphasized that the Basques who endured these difficult conditions were able and willing to face any situation. This is a testimony that shows the violence of war while highlighting the heroism of the men:

> The French opened fire with machine guns, but suddenly a huge shell pulverized all of the French, except one. He had his brother with him, who was also dead. Surely, he should have lost his mind. Not at all. He overcame his grief, grabbed the machine gun and burned down every last one of the approaching enemies. That was how the French held the ground they had occupied. Thanks to another Basque soldier from Larressoro.
>
> Here are three brave soldiers, our compatriots. There are thousands like them in our armies. Under these conditions, how can you expect the French to be afraid of the Germans? Let them come with all the devils of hell, if they want, in tanks or any other machine; they won't win.[6] (translated from Basque)

The third regular journalist was Jean Etchepare, a doctor in civilian life and a soldier during the war. He, too, was rewarded by his commanders for his determination to treat the wounded under the bombardment. He was mentioned for his bravery in June 1916. He also identified with France through his writings:

> We could see all these advances and all these assaults before the border, but like one-eyed men: half-heartedly. Unfortunately, we preferred to sit back and contemplate our usual trivialities. Politics had dumbed us down, stripped us bare, broken us. From one day to the next our rulers were down and out, while we gave them more than enough time to fatten themselves up at our expense. There was no more obedience: the little people, emboldened and depraved by laziness and drink, blithely swallowed the flattery and extravagant lies of the politicians. Few marriages, even fewer births, the multitude melting away. Our beloved France was still standing thanks only to its army and a few wise men.[7] (translated from the Basque)

Jean Etchepare also glorified France and saw himself as a Frenchman among the French. However, many of Etchepare's texts were educational, as he explained in great detail how the front was organized, how the trenches were built, what the strategic issues were, and so on.⁸

Jules Moulier "Oxobi" wrote much less from the front, as he was in Baiona during the early years.⁹ In spring 1917, however, came another mobilization. This time he was not discharged but sent to the north of France. If we are to believe his testimony, he was not on the front line but on the back lines. He found himself on the medical trains. In 1917 and 1918, he wrote several chronicles, repeatedly describing the places he saw and the vicissitudes of the war. But even though he made no secret of the fact that he favored France and that he himself was involved in the war, he often spoke more of his nostalgia for the Basque Country than of his attachment to France. When war broke out, he did not show as much enthusiasm and impetuosity for the event as some others, as this verse proves:

> Eskualdunak, orhoit gaiten berme nor eta zer dugun,
> Etchetan nigarra frango zinez egiten da egun . . .
> Gureek nigar saminagorik ez dezaten ichur nehun,
> Nola herrian, halkampo, gauden gu bethi eskualdun!
>
> Basques, let's not forget what makes us Basque,
> In our homes, we cry a lot today . . .
> Let our people never shed more bitter tears,
> At home, as abroad, let us always remain Basques!¹⁰

He published these verses inspired by mobilization in November 1914. He asked the soldiers to continue to be Basques, thus clearly revealing his Basqueophile nature. However, the following year, in another verse,* he attacked deserters, underlining the shame they inflicted on their families.

Some of Jean Barbier's verses were published in *Eskualduna*. But Barbier was, above all, the author of a novel about the war, specifically the second part of the novel *Piarres* (1929). It told the story of a young peasant in the Basque Country. The first part of the novel ends with the call to arms, and the second part recounts the vicissitudes of the war. Piarres, like all young people in the Northern Basque Country, went off to war. The character imagined by Jean Barbier fits in perfectly with the model of the disciplined soldier glorified by *Eskualduna*. He was a Basque believer who loved France, who was ready to sacrifice himself for her, and who would never accept the opportunity to desert.

---

* Oxobi, "Iheskaria".

Jean Barbier was a friend of Manex Hiriart-Urruty, and like him he insisted on the traditionalist character of the Basque Country.[11]

Manex Hiriart-Urruty and Blaise Adema, who set the *Eskualduna* editorial line, were outspoken as Frenchmen and in their support for France.[12] When war broke out, Hiriart-Urruty's headline read "Biba Frantzia!" ("Long live France!"), and until his death in November 1915, every week he sent out messages in favor of the war and France, although he sometimes expressed the pain caused by the conflict in a straightforward way.

> Two moving conversations by the fire, and so many tears! How hard, how bitter! Fortunately for everyone there is still hope, if what they say is true, that the enemy is much weaker than we are, even if things are going slowly. But living so far away from each other is heartbreaking, isn't it? On top of that, we must postpone work on the railway and all the other tasks... When a man in the prime of life could be the most needed member of his family, here he is, dead without sickness! The younger the son of the house who leaves no descendants, the more the parents, brothers, and sisters, all crushed by grief, are to be pitied.[13] (translated from Basque)

From time to time he mentioned these dark aspects of the war, but more often he wrote articles maintaining that France was doing well and that it would win the war, or that the Basque soldiers were totally motivated to continue fighting, as in the following extract:

> Finally, listen to what I heard from this good soldier. This one example says it all. When I finally asked him if, once he had recovered, going off to war again after having already been there for a long time and having an arm cut off, would be harder or easier for him than the first time, he replied, gently but firmly: "It is said that many people find it difficult to go off the second time. That's not my case, nor that of many others with me. The first time, we didn't know what we were in for; now we do. Whether we live or die, we know that France, with its allies, will defeat the enemy." It's all there. Who would claim that such a soldier is not a good soldier?[14] (translated from Basque)

Eskualduna, in its editorials, day-to-day news, and letters and poems sent in by soldiers, almost always praised France, using the first-person plural to talk about the nation. For this magazine, it was very important to show that the Basques were good soldiers, that they were good Frenchmen, and that very few of them were deserters. It wholeheartedly endorsed France's objectives—namely, that the war should not end until Germany had returned to France all the territories it had confiscated. Although *Eskualduna* was a fundamentally Catholic magazine, it did not blindly follow the pope's position.

Pope Benedict XV found himself in a delicate situation. There were Catholics on both sides of the front, and therefore he refused to take a stand for either side. From the outset he sent out messages in favor of peace. In Germany and the United Kingdom, the people did not complain too much about the pope's appeals for peace because most of them were Protestants. French Catholics, in contrast, took a dim view of this appeal for peace, as they were first and foremost patriotic. The archbishop of Paris in fact criticized Benedict XV's intervention, saying that his appeals would make it even more difficult to develop Catholicism in France.

The Holy Father's appeals went unheeded, as did those of pacifist socialists; nations were at war with each other, which was the priority.[15] The pope had to maintain a difficult balance. On August 22, 1915, he explained that there were Catholics among both warring parties, which was why he could not take sides, as doing so could lead to serious quarrels within the Catholic Church.[16] In 1917 the pope wrote a letter in which he spoke of peace. The message had an unexpected reception insofar as it not only displeased the Allies but also was disregarded by the Germans and Austrians. It stated that given that the balance of power was in Germany's favor, it was necessary to enter into dialogue with that country. Neither the French government nor the Catholics accepted this text. Germany and Austria-Hungary, for their part, paid little heed to it.

Léon-Adolphe Amette, the archbishop of Paris, interpreted the pontiff's letter in his own way, saying that he was stressing the rule of law.[17] Nevertheless, in the face of all the peace proposals that were circulated, the French authorities and journalists in the Basque Country remained firm in their positions. Nobody wanted to sign peace at any price, not even *Eskualduna*, which did not favor the idea, despite the fact that when the Vatican put forward proposals that were not to France's liking, the magazine was not so critical of the pope. One of the conditions involved Germany's return of Alsace-Lorraine, and on this point the French would not tolerate the pope's proposal to enter into dialogue about this territory; for France, no dialogue was possible on this subject.[18] Similarly, many French people became angry with the pope because they felt that asking for peace in 1915 would mean France losing this "conquered" territory.[19]

The editors of *Eskualduna* often asserted that they wanted to see Germany with "a broken spine,"[20] or totally destroyed. This inflexible stance was guided by the idea that a peace offered on terms that were too mild would enable the enemy to grow stronger. Hiriart-Urruty wrote that peace had to be the fruit of a genuine victory. Only victory, in his view, would ensure against the breakout of another war.

> Think of the fact that a weakened peace, which is neither rooted nor lasting, would not be worth much, and keep this idea firmly in mind, as long as this insurmountable situation lasts. . . A hundred years' peace would not be too much, at the end of this war. To have to start again after ten or twenty years, like now, after forty-four years,[21] all the efforts made so far, the blood spilled, the misfortunes and suffering for France and all her allies would be in vain. . . If that were possible, we would have to bury the war, now and forever; or at least, for the time being.
>
> How can this be achieved? There is no other way than to break the backs of those who, with war, have spread evil.
>
> At this point, it is useless to speak of peace.[22] (translated from Basque)

Hiriart-Urruty also presents another related argument. If peace was not lasting and France did not recover all the lost territories, all the blood spilled up to now would also have been in vain. The more people die, the less likely we are to give in. Armed with this ideology, Jean Ybarnégaray, a young deputy from Donibane Garazi, was ready to give his all for France. Ybarnégaray was elected deputy in the 1914 elections, with strong support from the *xuriak*, or "whites" (reactionaries), and with widespread protection from *Eskualduna* and the sector it represented. Ybarnégaray was the symbol of the "exemplary" Basque soldier. Even though he was a member of Parliament, he was glorified above all for having been at the front from the start of the war. When he was elected, *Eskualduna*, having campaigned in his favor, was full of praise for the choice he had made.[23]

As soon as the war broke out, the "white" deputies Ybarnégaray and Léon Guichenné wanted to go to Paris, where the National Assembly was due to vote on the country's participation in the war. The two deputies were unable to get there, as the trains were full of soldiers. Finally, through the prefect, they made a telephone call to Paris to assure the French government of their support for the measures to be taken regarding the war.[24] A few weeks later, in September, Ybarnégaray announced his intention to go to the front, and he did indeed go as a private. In January 1916, he was appointed lieutenant; as Jean Saint-Pierre wrote, "It is said that a good leader makes a good soldier. This is true, just as a good shepherd always has a good flock."[25] A month later, the correspondent in Atharratze reported that Ybarnégaray had visited this village decorated with the Croix de Guerre. For his supporters, this man, who had shown himself to be valiant in battle, was also an excellent member of Parliament. *Eskualduna* highlights another of his exploits during the Battle of Verdun:

> I cannot fail to mention the qualities of some of our Basque officers. Particularly impressive was the courage of our deputy Ybarnégaray and the way he led his troops.
>
> Right from the start of the attack, taking hold of a wounded man's rifle in front of his men, he showed us what we had to do, saying, "You can miss a hare at a crossroads, but these German pigs are too heavy to miss."[26] (translated from Basque)

In the weeks and months that followed, Ybarnégaray's exploits were still talked about, as were the awards he received, the visits he made to the Basque Country, and the honors he received from General Joffre. He was always presented as a hero. The letters he wrote, and in them his tendency to applaud the Basques as good soldiers and good Frenchmen, did not go unread. In July 1917, he made a speech before all the French deputies in the Assemblée Nationale in Paris, evoking the harsh fighting on the Chemin des Dames and glorifying the exploits of Basque soldiers. He also voiced several demands: that the soldiers of the 1888–92 cohort be sent home and that all soldiers be allowed to return home more often so that they could enjoy a rest after being in the trenches. The minister of war agreed to his demands. This intervention caused quite a stir in the Basque Country and helped increase his reputation among the population. Furthermore, following the fighting on the Chemin des Dames, General Nivelle was dismissed and replaced by Philippe Pétain. Ybarnégaray's speech to the French National Assembly played a key role in this change.

After France had won the war, Ybarnégaray was one of the victorious deputies and continued to enjoy great renown. In the years that followed and right up to the end of the Second World War, he won every election and retained his position as a member of Parliament. He was the symbol of a traditionalist and conservative Basque Country that had become French, and he was the guarantor of these values.

NOTES

1. More about Jean Saint-Pierre in Charriton, *Jean Saint-Pierre "Anxuberro" (1884–1951)*.

2. Saint-Pierre, "Italiaren laguntza."
3. Saint-Pierre, "Gudu baten irabazia."
4. More information in Elissalde, *LVII.a gerlan*.
5. Elissalde, "Azken solasa."
6. Elissalde, "Nola lotsa holako soldadoak?"
7. Etchepare, "Alemanak hurbiletik IV."
8. Bidegain, "Lehen Mundu Gerra *'Eskualduna'* astekarian," 673.
9. Bidegain, "Lehen Mundu Gerra *'Eskualduna'* astekarian," 195.
10. Moulier, "Gerla."
11. Lafitte, "Oxobi hil zaiku."
12. Bidegain, "Lehen Mundu Gerra *'Eskualduna'* astekarian," 192.
13. Hiriart-Urruty, "Eguberri gerlan."
14. Hiriart-Urruty, "Soldado ona."
15. Minois, *L'Église et la guerre: De la Bible à l'ère atomique*.
16. Becker, *1914: Comment les Français sont entrés dans la guerre*, 465.
17. Mayeur, "Les catholiques français et Benoît XV en 1917," 154.
18. Latour, *La Papauté et les problèmes de la paix pendant la première guerre mondiale*, 178.
19. Fontana, *Les catholiques français pendant la Grande Guerre*, 181; Becker, *La France en guerre 1914–1918: La grande mutation*, 111.
20. Hiriart-Urruty, "Noiz finituko?"
21. This is a reference to the 1870 war between France and Prussia.
22. Hiriart-Urruty, "Berri onak."
23. Bidegain and Gostin, "1914ko hauteskundekanpaina Eskualduna astekarian."
24. Adéma, "Eskualdun deputatua."
25. Saint-Pierre, "Gure deputatu eskualduna."
26. Adéma, "Verdun."

CHAPTER ELEVEN

Off to Salonika

Ybarnégaray was not the only MP to go to war. In 1915, Joseph Garat, mayor of Baiona and a "red," or radical, deputy, also volunteered to go to war, but instead of going to the front in northeastern France, he left by ship for the Dardanelles Strait.[1] The French and British armies wanted to take control of this highly strategic territory. The Biscayans were also interested because if transportation were allowed through the strait, a new trade route could be opened up. The Dardanelles was a Turkish possession of the Ottoman Empire. However, the strait constituted an important passage linking the Aegean Sea around Greece to the Sea of Marmara, south of present-day Istanbul (then called Constantinople). The Bosphorus Strait, by contrast, linked Constantinople with the Black Sea. In other words, control of the Dardanelles Strait was imperative for proper shipping between Russia and the other Allied countries. The Germans and the Ottoman Empire were well aware of this. For them, the problem was not getting through the Dardanelles but getting out, as the British and French had set up a naval blockade and, from time to time, bombarded the fortifications surrounding the Turks.

For the Allies, things were not going as well as they would have liked. The situation in the west was deadlocked, and in the east they were losing several battles. On December 12, 1914, for example, Austria-Hungary won the Battle of Limanowa-Łapanów against the Russians. On January 23, 1915, the Austrians launched the Carpathian offensive, and although they did not achieve the expected results, they did manage to stop the Russians there. On February 7, the Germans won the Masurian Lakes offensive against the Russians and took control of the whole of East Prussia.

The Allies wanted to reverse this worrying situation, and at the end of 1914, the British announced their intention to enter Turkey and decided to attack in the Dardanelles Strait, the gateway to the city of Constantinople. This strait, which links Asia to Europe, was a strategic location for the Allies, enabling them to weaken the Turks, pressure neutral Greece and Bulgaria to support Serbia, and send goods to Russia.

On the orders of Winston Churchill, then secretary of state for the Royal Navy, the British army organized an expedition to the Dardanelles. The aim was to bombard the Turkish fortifications controlling the Dardanelles and reach Constantinople. Churchill believed not only that entry into Constantinople would surprise all the Balkan countries and rally them to the Allies but also, above all, that victory in the Dardanelles would give the British army the opportunity to penetrate Austria-Hungary and Germany from the east.[2]

However, passing through this strait, seventy kilometers long and varying in width from one to seven kilometers, was no simple matter. To further complicate matters, before the start of the war, the Germans had installed 170 cannons on both sides of the strait. The Turks fenced off the area and laid mines to prevent ships from passing through. On March 18, 1915, the British and French embarked with the intention of taking control of the strait. Once there, however, they were unable to remove the mines or even to find out where they were. As a result, of the eighteen ships that entered the strait, three were sunk and four were seriously damaged. On board one of the sunken ships, *Le Bouvet*, nine Basques were killed.

Despite their failure in the Dardanelles, the British were determined not to give in and to make another attempt to reach Constantinople. Some of the soldiers defeated in the Dardanelles regrouped in Egypt, and many others in Moudros, on the island of Lemnos, in the middle of the Aegean Sea. These soldiers were preparing for a new expedition. This time, they wanted to land on the western territory of the Dardanelles, but from the other side. This territory, named Gallipoli, eighty kilometers long and five to twenty kilometers wide, was also under Turkish domination, but in all likelihood it presented an easier access than the Dardanelles via the Aegean Sea. The attempted landing took place on April 25, and within two days the Allies lost six thousand men. Unfortunately, the Turks had kept an extremely close watch on the Aegean coast, and consequently the landing on this difficult terrain proved to be highly dangerous, and Turkish artillery made an Allied victory impossible. No Basque lay among the dead that day. However, Basques did take part in the battle, having reached the Gallipoli peninsula.

After letting the soldiers out onto the Gallipoli peninsula, the warships evacuated the area, giving way to trench warfare against the Turks. In May, fierce fighting broke out. Unlike on the Western Front, there was no respite for the soldiers, who had to remain permanently in the trenches, with very little water and in the thick of danger. At the tip of the peninsula, at Fort Seddul-Bahr at the entrance to the Dardanelles Strait, the fighting proved equally fierce. Several months before, on November 3, 1914, the British and French had launched an initial attack on this fortification. This attack had little effect, but it left the Turks with the impression that the Allies might attack the Dardanelles and so gave Turkey time to better prepare its defense. Between May and August 1915, around the fort, forty-four Basques lost their lives. The Franco-English defeat was terrible. In Gallipoli, 180,000 Allied soldiers, mostly Australians, died in the fighting. The defeat also had political consequences in London, where Churchill lost his ministry.

Among the remaining men who had taken part in the Dardanelles and Gallipoli expeditions, those making up the Armée d'Orient took refuge in Moudros. They were preparing another expedition, due to start on October 5, 1915, to help Serbia. A few days earlier, Bulgaria had called for mobilization, announcing its intention to enter the war, not on the side of the Allies but with the Triple Alliance, something the British had not expected. While the French had done what the British had wanted for the Dardanelles expedition, this time it was the French who wanted to decide how to intervene. However, Edward Grey, the United Kingdom's foreign secretary, declared that his country had no interest in getting involved in the fighting in this region, as it did not wish to fall out with Bulgaria. He decided to place all his forces on the Western Front.[3]

On October 5, Bulgaria went to war against Serbia, and the Allies felt they had to help the latter. To do this they landed in Salonika instead of going to Serbia. This was not a simple matter, as Salonika was in Greek territory, and Greece maintained its position of neutrality. While the king of Greece was not in favor of the Allies, others in Greece were. He did not give permission to land at Salonika, as he favored Germany. But the Allies ignored the ban and landed anyway. Some Basque soldiers who had left the Dardanelles earlier were already there, while others had left the port of Marseille a few days earlier and, after calling at Malta and Moudros, reached Salonika that day. The aim was to reach the Serbian valleys of Uskub and Vardar in order to aid Serbia. The Allies intended to establish their lines on the Bulgarian border to create a protected zone. However, the Bulgarians in the mountains had carefully prepared their attack, and their intention was to cut off those who had landed in Salonika, as well as the Serbs. Once again, the Allies had to turn back and remain on the defensive near Salonika. The British wanted to withdraw their troops, but the French insisted on leaving an army behind.[4]

No major battles took place, but the soldiers found themselves in a difficult situation because of the region's lack of development and unhygienic conditions. Consequently, 480,000 British were hospitalized, of whom only 18,000 were wounded, the rest being treated for illness. Basques also died in Serbia and Greece (specifically in Salonika), many of them from disease. Of the forty-eight Basques who died in Serbia, nineteen were taken by disease. Of the seventy-five Basques who died in Greece, twenty-two succumbed to disease. And of the remaining fifty-three, there were thirty-five who perished in shipwrecks, as happened on February 26, 1916, at Cape Matapan, following the German bombing of the ship *Provence II*. In Greece, though, only sixteen soldiers succumbed to war wounds. The West had largely overlooked this Armée d'Orient; its men were not in strategic battles, yet they were not allowed to return home, and no one paid them any attention.

The Bulgarians, who had made good progress, captured Belgrade on October 6, 1915. On October 19, Italy declared war on Bulgaria, but Bulgarian troops continued their advance and entered Uskub on October 22. On May 27, 1916, they crossed the Greek border and seized Fort Rupel without the Greeks putting up resistance. From August 25 to October 3, 1917, fierce fighting broke out between Serbs and Bulgarians at Kaïmaktchala, during which the Serbs lost two-thirds of their troops.

Whereas King Constantine of Greece was not in favor of entering the war, which displeased the Allies, from the outset Greek prime minister Eleftherios Venizelos wanted Greece to enter in order to help Serbia. With the support of the Allies, on September 24, 1916, he formed a provisional republican government in Salonika. The country was divided in two between the monarchical government in Athens and the one in Salonika. On December 1, the Allies landed in Piraeus and threatened Athens. But their forces were insufficient, and the Greeks pushed them back. At the same time, the Greek Royal Army was killing Venizelos's supporters. A few months later, on June 12, 1917, King Constantine abdicated after French troops entered and forced him to hand over the throne to his son Alexander. As a result, on June 29, Greece entered the war on the side of the Allies.

A few months after Greece entered the war, Romania withdrew from the conflict. The Romanians had entered the war on August 16, on the side of the Allies. Germany and Bulgaria did not spare their opponents, and the Romanians suffered repeated setbacks. On November 15, the Germans launched an offensive in the Carpathians, seizing Bucharest on December 6. Since September, the Romanians had been surrounded, and the French and Russians had been unable to bring them any help. During the conflict, 310,000 Romanians died, and their country became occupied by Germany and Austria-Hungary. After the Russian Revolution, Romania negotiated peace and signed the Focsani armistice on December 9, 1917.

NOTES

1. Archives Départementales des Pyrénées Atlantiques, Registre matricule du bureau de recrutement de Bayonne, classe 1892, matricule no. 1391, https://earchives.le64.fr/archives-en-ligne/ark:/81221/r283686z5039xk/f1?context=militaire::57287.
2. Prior and Wilson, *La Première Guerre mondiale 1914–1918*, 82–83.
3. Fassy, *Le commandement français en orient: octobre 1915–novembre 1918: Étude historique d'un commandement opérationnel français à la tête d'une force militaire alliée*, 16.
4. Prior and Wilson, *La Première Guerre mondiale 1914–1918*, 66.

CHAPTER TWELVE

Verdun and the Somme

While some soldiers were enduring hardship in the Salonika region of Greece, one of the most famous and bloody battles of the First World War had begun: Verdun, 1916. The soldiers who lived through the Battle of Verdun summed it up in one word: hell. Verdun was a garrison town close to Germany and Luxembourg, surrounded by hills covered in fortifications; in all, there were twenty-eight fortifications in the surrounding area and sixty-five thousand soldiers in Verdun itself. In the center stood a large citadel—built by Vauban in the seventeenth century and similar to those in Baiona and Saint-Jean-Pied-de-Port—in whose ancient tunnels the French army had established a major base.

France had already endured battles at Verdun against the Prussians. One previous battle had taken place in 1870, but the most famous battle and the one that remained engraved in French memory, was that of 1792 when France was at war with Austria, which was supported by Prussia. On August 19, 1792, the Prussians entered French territory and the following day reached the outskirts of Verdun. On August 31, they occupied the town, and on September 4, they headed for Paris. The French army at the time was too weakened to fight back against the Prussians and Austrians. However, on September 20 in 1792, during the Battle of Valmy, they succeeded in stopping the Prussians; and on October 14, in driving them from Verdun. All in all, Verdun became a potent symbol of victory over the Germans.

At the beginning of 1916, German army commanders wanted to strike a blow to weaken France and block the Allied offensive planned for spring 1916. They decided to fight the battle at Verdun, with the aim of breaking through the French army's line of defense, occupying a strategic city, and emerging strengthened by these military victories in the event of negotiations. For the Germans, Verdun was one of the most propitious sites for an offensive, given its relief, the trench line, the difficulty for the French in organizing a defense line, and the obstacles preventing supplies to the French army. In addition, aware of the symbolic value of Verdun, the Germans anticipated that launching an attack there would prompt the French, who did not want to lose the town, to send a large part of its army there.

That winter, the Germans began to accumulate weapons on the rear line they had established around Verdun. Previously, the Germans had made several attempts to seize these fortifications, but the French had managed to hold out around Saint-Mihiel. At the same time, the Germans consolidated their front in Alsace to divert attention. On the ground, however, no one was fooled; something was afoot at Verdun. The problem was that General Joffre had moved the fortifications' powerful artilleries to the Somme region, where he thought they would be needed for the attack being prepared there. Émile Driant, the Verdun region's deputy and lieutenant-colonel, issued a warning to the Assemblée Nationale in the days that followed, which Joffre did not like, and right up to the last moment, Joffre paid no attention to those who claimed that a major German offensive was about to take place in Verdun.

The German offensive began in the snow at 7:30 a.m. on February 21, 1916. However, it was not snowflakes that fell from the sky but a rain of shells. That day, in the space of nine hours, the Germans dropped a million shells on Verdun and the surrounding area. In just those few hours the region became disfigured, covered in a thick black fog. The dead, the wounded, the maimed were everywhere. The place no longer resembled any other on earth; it was, rather, a nightmare. On the following day, the fighting continued. It was on this day, during the Battle of Verdun, that the first two Basques lost their lives: Bertrand Erdozaintzi-Etxart, from Larzabale (Larceveau), who died on hill 304, where the fiercest fighting took place; and Michel Epherre, from Altzürükü (Aussurucq), who died in the Bois des Caures. On the same day, in the same wood, Émile Driant, the MP and lieutenant-colonel who had a few days earlier warned of the threat of this offensive, also died in battle.

The following day, February 23, the French retreated, abandoning the Wavrille forest and allowing the Germans to approach within ten kilometers of Verdun, where they began a new massacre. On February 25, a symbol was to fall: Fort Douaumont. The fort was solid, with walls 2.5 meters thick, but it was left unfortified with artillery and with only a handful of soldiers on guard. Because the outnumbered French put up no resistance, the Germans had no need to fire. Two days later, on February 27, ten Basques perished, seven of them at Douaumont. They belonged to the 418th Infantry Regiment. They had fallen under German fire and bombardment after an all-day attack. Over the next two days, another thirteen Basques were to die at this site.

Each day brought its own trail of corpses. The front was completely dismantled, and not a single French army trench remained. Soldiers had to fight concealed in the holes left by the bombs. The forests were charred. The Germans, by contrast, had trenches of solid concrete; they had also built underground shelters that communicated with the trenches. The French troops had difficulty obtaining food supplies, and above all, they had no drinking water. Soldiers reported that there were puddles full of a greenish liquid in which corpses floated, and the only way they could get a sip of water was to draw it from these puddles. Faced with this situation, Joffre asked the troops to hold out whatever the cost, and he entrusted General Pétain with command of the Battle of Verdun. Political prestige was at stake. Whoever won this battle would benefit in international public opinion.

After violent attacks on both banks of the Meuse the previous day, on April 10, the Germans occupied the Corbeaux and Cumières forests, as well as the northern slopes of Mort-Homme. But the summit of Mort-Homme remained in French hands, and the Germans lost many men in the fighting. General Pétain's prestige began to grow.

Yet the public knew virtually nothing about what was happening at Verdun. Military leaders had clearly ordered that the civilian population not be kept informed of what was happening there. They could receive only the official daily bulletin, which gave no precise information.[1] It was not permitted to give details of the location of troops around Verdun nor to broadcast information on the number of Allied dead. Even mentioning the number of Germans dead was forbidden to prevent the enemy from deducing the numbers who had died in combat.[2] Censorship groups were very active throughout the Battle of Verdun to prevent newspapers from publishing forbidden information. Censored in addition to military information was any criticism of military command, as well as descriptions that were too realistic or harsh.[3]

Despite the scarcity of information, echoes of what was happening at Verdun reached the ears of soldiers stationed elsewhere. Many Basques were still in the Aisne region, on the Chemin des Dames. They began to discuss among themselves that eventually they would have to leave for Verdun. They were terrified by what was happening there. They knew that in April movements were taking place between the regiments in their region, and knew that they, too, would be going. But they did not know where they would be sent. Many claimed it would be to Verdun, while others said no, that it was not certain, and that they may have to go to Belgium. In reality, Pétain had demanded that all the regiments of the French army should go to Verdun in turn so that no one remained too long under the appalling fire and bombardment.

Soldiers from the 49th Infantry Regiment set off for Verdun on April 21, and by the following day some were in Fleury under the Douaumont fort while others were in the Chapitre forest around the Vaux fort. The men of the 57th Infantry Regiment arrived in Verdun later, on May 5, by train, after a fortnight's stay in the Champagne region. Their experience in Verdun was far from tranquil—for example, on May 12, the troops were bombarded by thousands of shells. In addition, the French soldiers had to endure toxic gas (as did the Germans) and most of the time wore their ponderous masks.

The hardest days for the Basques were May 23, 24, and 25, when 140 of them were killed—a quarter of the total number of all Basques killed in ten months. Almost all fell at Douaumont and Fleury, half of them belonging to the 49th and 18th Infantry Regiments.[4] From May 20 onward, the Basques found themselves in the rubble of what had been the village of Fleury and around Douaumont with the French army, recovering from the onslaught. They had to endure not only the bombs and the unbreathable air but also face-to-face fighting, as well as living without food or water among corpses and dying comrades. On June 21, the men of the 49th Infantry Regiment moved away from Verdun and toward the Gruerie forest to get some rest.[5] Other regiments would also leave sometime later. After the battle, Zerbitzari gave a terrible description of the village of Fleury.

> I can't swear that they don't have dreams in their peaceful sleep. Necessarily, they must remember what they saw at Verdun: so many stretches of earth turned over, stirred up, where the eye, as far as the eye can see, cannot distinguish the slightest blade of grass; forests in shreds, where one doubts there had even been the slightest tree; hamlets and villages ransacked, where all that remains, in place of houses, there is a pile of stones . . . . But what will come back most often in our nightmares is obviously this: in a pretty white village called Fleury, near Douaumont, a young woman seated, holding a ten-month-old child in her arms, dead; and farther on, two old men, holding hands as if bidding each other farewell, also dead . . . .
>
> No, these things cannot be forgotten.[6] (translated from Basque)

Today, nothing remains where the village of Fleury once stood. Trees have been planted in tribute, and a memorial to the Battle of Verdun has been erected a few hundred meters away. No doubt far worse had been seen, but nothing was said about it. A few years later, the same Zerbitzari recalled that they were sent to Fort Thiaumont, which the Germans had seized on June 1 at the same time as Fort de Vaux, without really understanding why, but with a very clear order: rather die on the spot than retreat. They had to remain impassive in the face of the enemy and endure the unbearable smell of corpses.

The French army held out against German attacks until autumn. Holding out was already an enormous feat, as resources were dwindling. Earlier, on July 11, the Germans had launched another attack but had failed to capture Verdun. On October 24, the Allies launched an offensive to recapture the town they had lost. First they recaptured Vaux and Douaumont. Finally, on November 2, 1916, they were able to recapture what had been lost since February, putting an end to the German offensive. Officially, the Battle of Verdun ended on December 15, after sixty million shells had exploded in this small region. A total of 600,000 men, both German and French, died or disappeared in the battle. In ten months of fighting, 547 Basques also lost their lives, meaning that one in every ten Basques who died in the war did so in the Battle of Verdun. Similarly, of the 999 Basques who died during this period at Verdun and elsewhere, more than half perished at Verdun. And of those who did not die at Verdun, 206 were killed in the Battle of the Somme.[7]

Initially, Joffre did not want to give much importance to the Verdun offensive because he wanted to prepare for the battle of the Somme in northeastern France. Joffre's plan was to launch a major spring offensive, together with the British, to regain ground from the Germans and completely weaken them militarily. But the start of the Battle of Verdun upset all his plans, forcing him to postpone the Battle of the Somme and to send to Verdun many of the forces he had earmarked for the Somme.

The Battle of the Somme began in earnest on July 1. On June 24, the Allies began firing shells to destroy German-occupied ground, believing that they would thereby totally weaken the German army. Some 1.6 million shells were fired, but the German defense was particularly well prepared, with the Germans' having constructed concrete underground shelters. Convinced that the operation would be easy, the French and British attacked on July 1. But the Germans were waiting for them. Weather conditions were very bad, and the mud prevented the Allies from advancing as they would have liked. That day, the Allies and the Germans each lost twenty thousand soldiers. Two Basques were killed: Rémi Sangla, from Bardoze (Bardos); and Dominique Salaber, from Barkoxe (Barcus). The deadliest day for the Basques was July 20, when fifteen men lost their lives in the fighting. By September, the Allies had lost eighty-two thousand soldiers for an advance of nine hundred meters. The long-prepared offensive did not go according to plan, as the French were placing most of their forces in Verdun. Despite this, the Germans were forced to withdraw some troops from Verdun and send them to the Somme, enabling the Allies to recapture Verdun.

The Franco-British attack at the Somme failed from mid-July onward. From then on, they continued to fight but were aware that it would be impossible to achieve their original objective. On September 15, tanks made their first appearance at the initiative of the British. The Germans were initially taken by surprise, but it turned out that the tanks did not work as well as expected, and the Germans were quick to identify their weaknesses. The battle continued until November 18. In the end, the Allies made very little progress on the Somme, retaking between ten and forty kilometers from the Germans. The cost of the fighting, on all sides, was 1.2 million dead (650,000 German, 419,654 British, and 194,451 French). This was the deadliest battle of the First World War.

Although many more people died on the Somme than at Verdun, Verdun remains emblematic of the First World War. Why so? First, because it is the place with the highest number of dead per square meter, a result of the extreme violence of the fighting and the incredible destruction that ensued; second, because the Germans failed to turn their offensive into a victory. Although the Germans were powerful and had won many battles up to that point, the French, who were weaker, managed to halt the Verdun offensive. The city thus became a symbol of the war and was subsequently recognized by seventeen countries around the world. In fact, the city of Baiona decided to name one of its streets after Verdun.

NOTES

1. Rajsfus, *La censure militaire et policière 1914–1918*, 140.
2. Forcade, "La censure politique en France pendant la Grande Guerre," 138.
3. Navet, "Verdun et la censure," 45–56.
4. Information taken by the author from a recompilation of data found at www.memoiredeshommes.sga.defense.gouv.fr.
5. *Historique du 49e régiment d'infanterie pendant la guerre 1914–1918*, 220.
6. Elizalde, "Gure ametsak."
7. Information taken by the author from a recompilation of data found at www.memoiredeshommes.sga.defense.gouv.fr.

CHAPTER THIRTEEN

The Chemin des Dames

After their traumatic stay in Verdun, the Basques were moved from one battle to another or to places of rest. In April 1917, they returned to the area around Craonne, where they had already been stationed from September 1914 to April 1916, fighting hard against the Germans to capture the plain above the surrounding villages, the Creute quarry, the Hurtebise farm, and the Californie Plain, all of which were situated on the edge of an eighty-kilometer road, the Chemin des Dames. There the daughters of Louis XIV, King of France, used to walk along what was for them a place for strolling, hence the name Chemin des Dames. From the top the view was breathtaking and the route, surrounded by meadows and forests, presented no difficulties whatsoever. It was a peaceful, pretty, and pleasant place situated a few kilometers to the south of Laon.

In 1914, French soldiers shed much blood to reach this ridge, but without success. In November 1916, the interallied conference decided that one of the spring 1917 offensives would take place on the Chemin des Dames. The Allies were convinced that the Germans were weakened, that they had abandoned the Chemin des Dames front, and that the French could make significant progress in a single day. They believed they could launch an offensive and reach Laon, thus humiliating the Germans and putting an end to the war once and for all. The soldiers' hopes were of the same order; they, too, believed that this battle would put an end to the war and they would soon return to their homes.

General Nivelle led the offensive. The attack was to take place in February but was delayed until April. On April 16, at 6:00 a.m., the French army launched its attack against the Germans, who were not as weakened as the French had thought. The Germans took cover in solid shelters a few kilometers back or in caves along the Chemin des Dames. Conditions were challenging: the weather was extremely cold. Two-thirds of the French army's large tanks were inoperative, and its artillery resources were inadequate. And to make matters worse, the Germans had a powerful air force and had prepared their defense well. Despite everything, the French army managed to make some slight progress. They took the Germans front line and then half their second and third lines. If the aim had been to achieve an immediate and indisputable victory and reach Laon, however, the French troops were far from achieving it. In the first two days the French army suffered thirty thousand casualties. On April 16, forty-three Basques lost their lives at Craonne, Paissy, Ailles, and Cerny.

General Nivelle had promised that if the German front was not totally annihilated in forty-eight hours, he would abandon the operation.[1] In no way did the troops advance as far as they had hoped, and the operation did not produce the expected results. Yet Nivelle did not abandon the offensive. He ordered it to continue.

A rift developed between the soldiers and the military hierarchy. Nivelle's operation had raised incredible hopes among the soldiers, but they soon realized that the results would in no way live up to these hope and that they were suffering a terrible defeat and had failed in their objective.[2] In their letters written before the start of the offensive, the soldiers expressed their certainty of returning home for the summer. Their disappointment was immediate and matched the high expectations they had.[3] The day after the start of the offensive, on April 17, some distance from the Chemin des Dames but as part of the same operation in Champagne, Aubérive's soldiers decided to disobey en masse. This decision marked the beginning of the mutinies, or "trench strikes." The Aubérive soldiers were not the first to refuse to go to war. In 1916, at the height of the Battle of Verdun, several soldiers refused to go to the trenches, as a result of which sixty-two men were convicted and seven executed. In the Chemin des Dames region, four soldiers were convicted and executed in April 1916.

The mutiny of 1917 was much bigger. Between despair and anger, the fighting on the Chemin des Dames continued over the following days. On May 5, 1917, troops launched attacks in various places. The regiments to which the Basques belonged also took part. That day, fifty-seven Basques perished in the fighting at Vauclerc, Ailles, Craonne, and above all Craonnelle. The following day they had to face a German counterattack, and a further sixty-four Basques lost their lives. In one month, 253 Basques had died in this region. Since the beginning of the war, in two years and eight months, 997 Basques had been killed in the same place, and during the whole war 1,643 Basques died in the Aisne department alone. A total of 120,000 French soldiers went missing in action that month.

At the Chemin des Dames, twenty-three thousand soldiers refused to go into battle, saying they were not willing to die for nothing. From May 4 onward, more and more soldiers refused to go to the heart of the massacres. The mutiny also spread to other fronts, notably through soldiers' letters. The incitement to lay down their arms also reached the soldiers of the 49th Infantry Regiment in Baiona. A petition was circulated recalling the deaths of the battles of Craonne, Verdun, and the Somme. The men of the 49th Infantry Regiment, for their part, did not follow this call and decided to obey their military leaders.[4] The main hotbeds of disobedience developed from the beginning of May in the Reims and Soissons areas at both ends of the Chemin des Dames.[5]

Serious incidents broke out within the 18th Infantry Regiment. This regiment included many Basques who were fighting hard at Craonne between May 4 and 8. In those days alone the regiment lost 824 men. It also received rewards for bravery, six hundred in all. A quarter of the first group of survivors were allowed to return home for a week. Thereafter only, 10 percent of the two groups were granted leave, further angering the soldiers. Furthermore, a thousand new recruits were brought in to replace the casualties. Until then, local soldiers had swelled the ranks of these regiments, but as the regiments became weaker in battle, new ones arrived from all over the country to fill the gaps.

On May 27 the soldiers were sent back to Craonne, but many refused to go. First they held a rally at the Villers-sur-Fère rest area, and a few hours later they gathered again, declaring that they did not want to go into battle because they were being asked to replace others who had refused to go before them; they did not want to take the place of the mutineers. Some demonstrated loudly in the streets, firing into the air or singing "L'Internationale." Others agreed to obey. On Friday morning, it was the men of the 2nd Battalion who refused to go to the trenches. The gendarmes went looking for them, and although twenty of them agreed to obey, sixty were taken away to fight.[6] However, fourteen leaders of the protest movement were arrested: nine of them were sentenced to prison (between five-year and ten-year sentences) or public work, the other five were sentenced to death. One of them was pardoned by President Poincaré, and another managed to escape; three were shot on June 12 at Maizy.[7] None of them were Basque.

Between May and June the trench strike spread to other regions, with between sixty thousand and eighty thousand soldiers refusing to fight. The military authorities retaliated harshly, arresting many of the mutineers. Trials were held, but while it was long claimed that a multitude of soldiers had been executed, various studies have concluded that, in fact, twenty-seven soldiers who took part were shot. Since the start of the war, however, cases of disobedience or self-mutilation had led to 2,400 death sentences being handed down by the French army and 550 actual executions, most of them before November 1915.

The soldiers' anger was immense, and Nivelle was unable to continue the offensive under these conditions. Furthermore, the Chemin des Dames operation was an outright failure, even if some glorified the two- or three-kilometer advance. Around the same time, the British-led offensive in the Arras region was far more successful, as British troops were at the cutting edge in terms of equipment and artillery, which was not the case for the French.[8] On May 15, General Nivelle was relieved of command of the Chemin des Dames operation, which was then entrusted to General Pétain. Pétain gave the soldiers more rest days, after three years of relentless fighting, because it was impossible to motivate soldiers by asking them to blindly obey and then responding with severe repression in the event of disobedience. On May 23, Pétain finally decided to put an end to the Chemin des Dames operation, and General Fayolle announced that there would be no new major offensive. These changes helped calm the atmosphere.[9]

On July 11, however, the British, aided by the Canadians, launched a new offensive in the Ypres region. This was the third battle to be fought in this sector with the aim of capturing the Flemish town of Passchendaele, which had been a strategic location since the beginning of the war. The battle was interminable, as the British and Canadians made slow progress. The real attack to seize the town began on October 12 and did not end until November 6 with the capture of Passchendaele. Although the troops advanced eight kilometers, the British lost 310,000 soldiers and the Canadians almost 16,000. German losses amounted to 260,000 men. The battle was not a credit to the Allies. British general Douglas Haig took no account of the deplorable weather conditions, the difficult mud, or the risk of disease or death from asphyxiation. "March or die" was the order, as General Nivelle had also wished on the Chemin des Dames. This approach seriously damaged the Allies' prestige among their own troops.

The situation was no better in Italy during the Battle of Caporetto from October 24 to November 5. On October 23, the Austrians and Germans launched a severe offensive around the Isonzo River in the small village of Caporetto. At 2:00 a.m. on the twenty-fourth, they undertook a major attack, and by daybreak the Italian troops had been decimated. The Germans and Austrians had won the battle. Two days later, they took San Daniele, Foni, and Matajur, advancing twenty kilometers. On the twenty-seventh they occupied Cividale and on the twenty-ninth, Udine. The Italians retreated.

To assist, the French army sent soldiers to Italy, and on November 2, Allied troops began fighting in the region. On November 3, Austro-Hungarian troops crossed Tagliamento. The Italians were forced to retreat 140 kilometers, coming to a standstill northeast of Venice. Although Allied troops had not retreated in Ypres and the Chemin des Dames and had not achieved the victory they had hoped for, worse was that in Italy they suffered a terrible defeat. The year 1917 ended badly for the Allies, with angered soldiers as well as with powerful enemies in the Austrians and Germans. They then looked to the Americans for support in achieving victory, even as the news from Russia was not good.[10]

NOTES

1. Prior and Wilson, *La Première Guerre mondiale 1914–1918*, 142.
2. Cochet, *Survivre au front, 1914–1918: Les poilus entre contrainte et consentement*, 124.
3. Prior and Wilson, *La Première Guerre mondiale 1914–1918*, 143.
4. Pedroncini, *Les mutineries de l'armée française*, 95.
5. Pedroncini, *Les mutineries de l'armée française*, 72.
6. Pedroncini, *Les mutineries de l'armée française*, 113–114.
7. Rocafort, *Avant oubli: Soldats et civils de la côte basque durant la grande guerre*, 454–457.
8. Prior and Wilson, *La Première Guerre mondiale 1914–1918*, 137–138.
9. Pedroncini, *Les mutineries de l'armée française*, 75–77.
10. Ferro, *La Grande Guerre*, 154.

PART THREE

The Smoke

CHAPTER FOURTEEN

Basques and France

Published letters and word-of-mouth reveal two categories of Basques. Nearly one in five soldiers was a deserter or draft dodger, and these men's commitment to France was far from similar to that of other soldiers fighting in the war. Many of them refused to go to war because they had long since left the Northern Basque Country, some to emigrate, others because they deliberately did not want to go to the front. They had no regrets about not having gone to war, nor were they concerned about owing a debt to France. Many continued to lead a normal life, close to home, in contact with their loved ones. French officials had difficulty understanding this attitude and did not accept it in any way. The prefect of the Basses-Pyrénées, for example, reproached the Basques for having no homeland other than their own and demanded that they be closely monitored to prevent their flight.[1]

French national sentiment was still in the process of being constructed in the Basque lands, even if this was the last phase of the process. Those who had left the country in the preceding years did so at a very young age, without having spent much time at school or in the army and therefore, perhaps, before a certain French consciousness had taken root in them. Had they not left, what would they have done when war broke out? Would they have refused to go? Among those who chose to desert, we can observe that there was no great fervor for France, insofar as they refused to risk their lives for it. Nor did the mayor of Baigorri and the subprefect of Maule note any hatred of the Germans among these men. Above all, these men seized the opportunity to save their own lives and escape suffering. Theirs was not a political gesture and certainly not a collectively calculated one.

Leaving apart draft dodgers and deserters, over 80 percent of those mobilized fought at the front in the French army. Is it because they accepted the situation and out of patriotic conviction as Stéphane Audoin-Rouzeau and Annette Becker assert?[2] Or because they were forced to, as Rémy Cazals and Nicolas

Offenstadt claim?[3] To answer this question properly, we would need to study the private letters written by Basques at the front, and especially their diaries. Unfortunately, no one has yet made this collection or carried out the research.

While it is difficult to assess what the common people were really going through, what they were feeling, the messages constantly put out by an intellectual class that had its own say were well known, and there was no doubt that these intellectuals had a major impact on the population, although their stance did not reflect the opinion of all citizens. Widely circulated magazines and newspapers, such as *Le Journal de Saint-Palais*, *Eskualduna*, and *Le Journal de Bayonne*, were in complete agreement with France and the French army about the war. At the time, the editors of *Eskualduna* were some of the finest writers in the Northern Basque Country: Manex Hiriart-Urruty, Jean Saint-Pierre "Anxuberro," Jean Elissalde "Zerbitzari," Jean Etchepare, and Jules Moulier "Oxobi." Hiriart-Urruty was too old to go to war, but his fiery editorials, written in Baiona, sent a truly uplifting message. Oxobi, exempt until 1917 for health reasons, began writing chronicles from the front in 1917. From the start of the war, the other three editors recounted their experiences in chronicles published almost weekly.[4]

When they wrote about France, they naturally used the first-person plural. In their words, France almost always became "we" and the French army "our army." The official message of the weekly Basque-language Catholic magazine *Eskualduna*, distributed to thousands of homes, was therefore to constantly bring home the fact that the Basques belonged to France. The other side of the coin was the vocabulary used to characterize the Germans, who were described as beasts, wolves, savages, barbarians... The Germans were like savage eagles with their talons, and the French were like their prey. The magazine did not treat the Germans as human beings and described in no uncertain terms the pleasure of killing German soldiers or the frustration of leaving some of them alive. This pleasure or frustration was not personal but, rather, about other soldiers. If a soldier killed a lot of Germans during a battle, the magazine's editors glorified him as if he had won a game of *pelota*. In fact, they often compared the course of a battle to a game of *pelota* or *mus*. There were two opposing sides, and these Basque writers were clearly on the side of France.

The identification with France was not limited to these aspects. For as the editors of *Eskualduna* appeared to be fervent supporters of France and the French army, they did not give bad news. According to their writings, France was never in trouble; they did not acknowledge mistakes and preferred to systematically emphasize the progress of the French army and its allies. They did not mention the exploits of the Germans and always tried to convey the hope that the war would soon be over. This editorial policy was adopted as early as August 1914. At the time, everyone believed the war would be short but, after a few months, this view began to fade. In any case, despite the protracted nature of the conflict, throughout the four years of the war, *Eskualduna* was determined to give hope that the conflict would come to an end within the following six months.

However, reality showed that the war was not turning in favor of France and her allies and that Germany was truly powerful, contrary to the image of a weakened nation that was being portrayed. *Eskualduna* always left a lapse of time before acknowledging that France had lost ground, and when they did acknowledge so, it was often only after that ground had been recaptured from Germany, so as to make it look like a victory. Of course, this victory would not have occurred if the troops had not previously suffered a defeat, but the readers of *Eskualduna* were not informed of this failure.

One piece of information, however, was not withheld—that relating to the dead. Clearly mentioned was when a father or son from the Basque Country died on the battlefield. The editors were not able to give information on all the dead, of which there were many, but they wrote articles based on the deaths of certain men. Instead of referring to dying in war as an atrocity or a tragedy, they glorified the sacrifice of the soldiers who gave their lives "for the country." Of course, the country referred to was France. The fallen men were presented as heroes whose deaths were even more valuable in their eyes insofar as they had offered their lives "to the Lord," thereby securing his forgiveness and his grace. It was suggested (based on alleged testimonies from widows and mothers) that to ease the suffering of families, they write that a soldier died in the war, as relatives would rather believe that than have to live with the shame of knowing that their loved one was a deserter. They also honored the wounded, stressing in particular that these soldiers were impatient to return to combat (whether true or not). They recounted the exploits of Basque soldiers on a regular basis. Here is an article Jean Saint-Pierre sent to *Eskualduna*, in which he praised the famous *pelota* player Chiquito de Kanbo:

> We have one here who, of all the others, deserves a special mention, because he has earned great respect in the Basque country: Who doesn't know Chiquito de Kanbo, the great *pelota* player? And a fighter too!
>
> These days, soldiers have lost their comrades. A bad time to be away from comrades, with the enemy approaching. Who's going to venture out to get

help? Bullets were raining down like hail. And now our Chiquito is going at lightning speed, without fear of the whirling bullets. Long live Chiquito! Your feat is as good as that of the *pelota* player who went to Spain. And if it's God's will that you return home after the war, we'll remember it when we see you more often on the front lines. Viva la France! Long live the Basque Country!

Another Basque deserves a mention: Petri Duhalde, from Uztaritze. A family man who never even thought of running away, he went off to war, leaving his home and family behind. One evening, he found himself in the trenches with his regiment.

It's midnight.

Another regiment comes crawling up to take over where they were. Just then, poor Petri saw two Germans laying barbed wire.

What an opportunity!

Petri took sight as well as he could and was about to shoot when the captain said to him: "Duhalde, I forbid you to shoot. If you start shooting now, we will be here until tomorrow. Let's move on."

Petri, being a good soldier, left without asking for a second thought, more despondent and disappointed than if he had missed three goshawks.

The next morning he met the vicar of his village, who was also a soldier over there, and they greeted each other.

"Tell me, Petri, how many Germans have you killed?"

"Don't ask me, sir. I have enough pain. Last night, when I had two at the end of my rifle, the captain stopped me from firing! What a fool! Surely with just one shot I'd have got them both! But wait, they won't always get away with it."

Poor Petri, well done to you.

Like Chiquito and Petri, didn't the young priest Durquet, from Bastida (La Bastide Clairance), also do honor to his native land?

The Germans were firing in all directions. Our priest from Bastida stood up, in the midst of the bullets, and stretching out his arm toward his comrades gave them absolution. Then, five, six, ten times he stood up again to care for and console his wounded comrades.

What courage and what a great heart!

This priest is now a sergeant. And he wears on his uniform his beautiful Medal of Remembrance, which was presented to him in person by the highest-ranking officer of all the troops.

There are many more I should mention. But I'm running out of space. Fortunately, they are no more eager for honors than the three I have just mentioned. Besides, this is enough to show what good soldiers the Basques are, so attached to France.[5] (translated from Basque)

Stories like these were often reported during the four years of the war. As the weeks went by, the editors applauded the exploits of the soldiers, each time embellishing the sacrifice of the dead and each week glorifying France. The message went far beyond the pages of the magazine and the newspapers, as it reached people everywhere who were already feeling the pain of war. It was made clear that France was under attack and had to be defended, that the Northern Basque Country was an integral part of this France under attack, and that the Northern Basque Country had to show solidarity with its "compatriots" in the regions occupied by the Germans. With these arguments, the writers demonstrated that the Basque soldiers who went to war were first and foremost French.

The aforementioned Basque writers were keen to show that the Basques were exemplary soldiers and good Frenchmen. Recounting their exploits was part of this objective. On many occasions, they wrote that the Basques were the best of all and noted that their prestigious reputation extended as far as the National Assembly of France and the press of the United Kingdom. The Basque Country also had an unfortunate reputation for having a lot of deserters and rebels, as the prefect had denounced and as the regulations he had enacted show. However, Basque writers of the time wanted to play down the large number of deserters and insisted over and over that the Basques were good French soldiers as if to wash away the "bad reputation" associated with those who chose to desert. Not only did the writers give deserters no excuse, they did not even consider them to be men, as Jean Saint-Pierre's words attest: "Do you consider a man to be one who flees when duty calls, one who goes into hiding asking for the protection of another nation, one who when all goes well is your partner but when all goes wrong selfishly lets you down, while everyone else is in the greatest need?"[6]

Zerbitzari did not spare them either:

Today's satisfactions are also accompanied by heartbreak. So many men who don't return after their leave! What fools! They've been at war for two years, and now, when it's coming to an end, they refuse to go back. What has turned their heads? Losing priceless land, how infantile! If only they knew how much they'll soon be crying! It's incredible: they think that the pot they'll find on the other side of the mountain will be filled with gold. If only it were filled with earth.

And if the unthinkable were to happen, if the deserters were allowed to return to France, we'd spit between their eyes. Out with those who refused duty and set a bad example![7] (translated from Basque)

It is clear here that the main writers and churchmen of the time in the Northern Basque Country had a vision of society divided in two: on the one hand, the exemplary soldiers and, on the other, the undeserving deserters. The former honored France, the latter betrayed it. Zerbitzari asserted that deserters were making a mistake and pointed out that they were taking the risk of losing their possessions and of not being able to live a good life in the Southern Basque Country. If they hadn't refused to go to war, perhaps they would not have lost their homes; however, the likelihood of losing their lives was higher. Yet for those who had the opportunity to make their voices heard in public opinion, losing one's life was an honor, as we can read in the following couplets written by Jean Barbier shortly after the start of the war:

1
Alorraren erdian, arratsalde hartan,
Ogi ederra jorik, ari zen sorotan;
Kanpoari begira zagon lorietan ...
Ezkila entzuten du banbaka bet-betan!

That afternoon, in the middle of the fields,
He struck the beautiful wheat in the meadow;
And gazing, delighted, at the surroundings ...
When suddenly, he heard the bell ring twice!

2
"Gerla, Gerla, Frantziak!"... oi hitz lazgarria!
Hor utzi behar zituen etxea, herria!
Espainia hurbil da, hurbil mug'harria
"Urrun dohala gogo ahalgegarria!"

"War, war, France is at war!" Ah, what terrible words!
He had to leave his house, his village!
Spain is near, the frontier is near
"Banish this shameful thought!"

3
"Adios, ene andre, eta ene haurrak,
"Adios nik hoin maite nituen bazterrak!
"Adios, ner'eliza, hil-herri zaharrak,
"Agian nik oraino ikusi beharrak!"

"Goodbye, my wife and children,
"Goodbye, landscapes I love so much
"Goodbye, my old church, my old cemetery,
"May God grant that I may see you again!"

4
Alemanari buruz, goiz batez, harmetan,
Eskualdun soldadoak, gudu furietan,
Etsai higuingarria, orro-marrumetan,
Sista sista zeraman, xixpa errainetan.

One morning, heading toward the German, in arms,
The repulsive enemy, howling and roaring,
The Basque soldier, in the fury of battle,
Wore his rifle, with a bayonet, on his back.

5
Hor, bet-betan bala bat, ez dakit nik nundik,
Firurikan heldu da, han nunbeit urrundik.
Bere besoak aintzin, lurrean etzanik,
Eskualduna han dago, odolez husturik.

Suddenly a bullet, from who knows where, whirls in from far away.
Arms outstretched, lying on the ground,
The Basque is there, drained of his blood.

6
Ez hil eta ez bizi, begiak hestean,
Herria ikusi du bere aintzinean....
Bi egunen buruan, atzarri denean,
Herriaren izena zuen ezpainean.

Between life and death, when he closes his eyes,
he sees his village before him....
After two days, when he wakes up,
the name of his village is on his lips.

7

"Nun naiz bada ni hemen, zer zeraut gertatu?
"Ai! Oroitzen naiz orai, etsaiak kolpatu!"
Frantziarentzat banaiz hantxe odol hustu,
"Gain hartarat gateko... behar naiz moldatu."

"Where am I, what's happened to me?
"Ah, now I remember, the enemy has wounded me!
"If I bleed to death for France,
"I must find a way to reach heaven."

8

Oro hari, ondoan, amultsuki beira,
Zer nahi egiterat ekarriak dira.
Bainan hek ez aditzen Eskualdun mintzaira!
Bi begiak hetsirik, hor doa hiltzera!

They are all at his side, full of affection,
ready to do anything to help him.
But they don't understand Basque!
With his eyes closed, he is dying!

9

"Adios, edo ez, ez, berriz ikus arte!
"Jainkoa, haur, andrea, nituen hoin maite!
"Frantses-Herri maitea, libro bizi zaite!
"Nere haurrak, Frantsesek haziren zaituzte!"

"Goodbye, or rather, farewell!
"Lord, I loved my children and my wife so much!
"Dear France, live freely!
"My children, the French will raise you!"

10
Eskualdun soldadoa, hil hadi bakean!
Jainkoak harturen hau bere sahetsean:
Eskuara bazakie guziek zeruan,
Hegaldaka hoala goiti deskantsuan!

Basque soldier, die in peace!
The Lord will take you to his side:
In heaven, everyone knows the Basque language,
Fly up there in peace!

11
Eskualdun soldadoak, ohore zueri,
Ohore hor gaindika hil zirezteneri!
Hatsa eman duzue Frantses Herriari,
Zuen arima aldiz Jainko maiteari!

Basque soldiers, honor to you,
Honor to you who died on the battlefield!
You gave your breath to France,
And your soul to our dear Lord![8]

These verses sum up the messages about the war propagated in Basque by Basques for Basques: it was shameful to be a deserter but honorable to die for France, the "beloved" country. The verses attached great importance to the Basque language, particularly when it was said that Basque was spoken in heaven. Writers of this generation often evoked the Basque language and the Basques, and although they displayed their attachment to France and their desire to become one with it, they did not understate the Basque language: they were Basqueophiles.

The texts of these writers also revealed that the soldiers were homesick. This feeling was probably even more evident in their personal letters. In the quieter evenings, when the Basque soldiers gathered together, they also sang: with tears in their eyes, they sang songs like "Maitia nun zira" ("Dear, where are you?") or "Ikusten duzu goizean" ("You see in the morning") by Jean-Baptiste Elissamburu. It is hard not to feel a twinge of sadness when they were sung in the midst of exploding bombs and dead bodies, thousands of kilometers from home. The soldiers acknowledged the pain of being so far away, but this homesickness should not be seen as specific to the Basque Country because French soldiers also felt homesick when they thought of their home region. What came up most in the letters from Basque soldiers were the mountains, the sea, the village square, and other familiar places. But the most important things were the house, the hearth, their mother's soup—in other words, the warmth of home and the love of their loved ones.[9] This vision fits with the logic of the small homeland and the large homeland because the "homeland" was based on the landscapes of a region, and to love the small homeland was thus to love the large homeland.

Above all, the writers wanted to show that Basque soldiers were exemplary, that they were "men" capable of resisting and enduring. These authors were particularly keen for the laudable reputation of the Basques to spread among the officers. When a soldier was awarded the Croix de Guerre, for example, the editors of *Eskualduna* paid tribute to him. Indeed, in the local news, two types of reports predominated: the announcement of the death of a local soldier and the award of the Croix de Guerre to a soldier. In both cases, there was nothing but praise for these men—on the one hand because they gave their lives for the "homeland" and on the other because they appeared to be good, exemplary soldiers. The Basques had a reputation for bravery, and as a result, they were just as assiduous in their soldiering as they were in their work. This is why the writers insisted that the Basques were indeed capable of enduring and that they would resist to the end. When recounting a heroic deed, the journalists of *Eskualduna* took the opportunity to point out that not all were deserters and to play down their impact.

While Basque intellectuals, churchmen, and the press were trying hard to get across this kind of message, not all Basques who were in the war were so optimistic. The verse-improviser Matxin Irabola—known familiarly as Matxin Senpertarra, from Senpere (Saint-Pée-sur-Nivelle)—was of a completely different opinion. In these few verses, which were never published in the press, he gave a crude description of the war:[10]

> Gure familietan penak utzirik,
> Haur tiki zonbaitekin andriak bakarrik,
> Gizonak penatuak hor ez da dudarik,
> Orduz geroztik,
> Dabilana xutik,
> Zerbeit ikusten dik,
> Penaren partetik,
> Hilak bere konduak eginak ditik

So, we had all left the village,
Leaving our families in grief,
The women alone with several small children,
The men afflicted,
there can be no doubt,
From then on,
He who stands sees something
Through grief,
The dead have already taken their toll.

Zonbait gizon alferren kapriza gatik,
Jende miserabliak hor pekatzen ditik,
Ainitzek ez diagu hardit baten lurrik,
Bertzenaren ontutzen gabiltzak bakarrik,
Aberatsetarik,
Ainitzak segurik,
Urrun dituk sutik,
Diruaren gatik,
Gu hemen hiltzen hoien manuen gatik.

Because of the whim of a few lazy men,
The wretched must pay,
Many of us do not have an acre of land,
We are only for the benefit of others,
The rich,
Many for sure,
Are far from the fire,
Because of money,
We die here under their orders.

Izpiritu duenak errex du pentsatzen,
Gure diferentzia zonbatekoa den,
Haundiak ari dira ttikiak manatzen,
Pobrearen indarrez galonez altxatzen,
Ohorez haunditzen,
Mirailez beztitzen,
Diruaren biltzen,
Intresen doblatzen,
Gu horien manutik elgarren hiltzen.

The intelligent can easily understand
the difference that separates us,
The "big" ones order the little ones around,
They take pride on the backs of the poor,
Use honors to make themselves great,
Wrap themselves in example,
Amass money,
Double interest,
While we kill each other at their behest.

Zonbat amaren seme dolorez haziak,
Hemen uzten dituzten gaixoek biziak,
Inorantzia batez hunat etorriak,
Hekien plazak dira nigarringarriak,
Orobat erdiak,
Beltzez estaliak,
Odolez betiak,
Inozent trixtiak,
Zonbait alferren gatik hoiek guziak.

How many mothers' sons, shrouded in grief,
The poor leave their lives here,
Came here out of ignorance,
Their situation is to be mourned,
In total half,
Covered in black,
Full of blood,
Unfortunate innocents,
All for a few idlers.

Statements expressing sentiments like those in the foregoing verses by Matxin Irabola were not published in the mainstream newspapers. Yet such verses clearly show that not all the Basques were as enthusiastic and motivated to go to war as had been claimed. This aspect of the war was not necessarily what those who were writing for the newspapers of opinion wanted to highlight.

NOTES

1. Archives Départemantales de Pyrénés-Atlantiques, 1 M 95, "Lettre du préfet des Basses-Pyrénées au ministre de l'intérieur, 1er décembre 1914."
2. Audoin-Rouzeau and Annette Becker, "Violence et consentement: La 'culture de la guerre' du premier conflit mondial," 265–266.
3. Offenstadt et al., "À propos d'une notion récente: La 'culture de guerre,'" 667–674.
4. Bidegain, "Lehen Mundu Gerra '*Eskualduna*' astekarian."
5. Saint-Pierre, "Gerlarien berri."
6. Saint-Pierre, "Permisioneak."
7. Elizalde, "Diren bezalako zoroak!"
8. Barbier, "Eskualdun soldado bat gerlan."
9. Ott, *War, Judgment, and Memory in the Basque Borderlands, 1914–1945*, 35.
10. Dolosor, *Matxin Irabola: Senpereko bertsularia*, 24–26.

CHAPTER FIFTEEN

The Final Showdown

The defeat at Caporetto provoked a political crisis in Italy where the council president was forced to step down, replaced by Vittorio Emmanuele Orlando. Elsewhere, the situation was no better. In France, the anger generated by the fighting on the Chemin des Dames also had an impact on the troops in Serbia. Indeed, the men there felt that they were abandoned and were fighting in vain since they had never achieved victory. In addition, given the state of the Western Front, the French population did not look kindly on sending men to the Balkan front.[1] Some three hundred soldiers stationed in Serbia refused to go into battle. In France, there were several changes of government in 1917 until Georges Clémenceau was appointed prime minister on November 16. British enthusiasm was also waning, as many British soldiers had died in Flanders without British forces' having achieved any significant victory. In December 1916, David Lloyd George was appointed prime minister, a post he held until the end of the war.

On the other side, too, power shifted when German chancellor Bethmann-Hollweg was forced to resign in July 1917. He was replaced by Georg Michaelis, who was hardly charismatic or supported by the population. On November 1, 1917, he was dismissed, and power was militarized under Field Marshal von Hindenburg. Emperor Franz Joseph of Austria-Hungary died on November 26, 1916. Although his frail health had prevented him from really exercising his authority over the previous two years, his death brought about a change in power in Austria-Hungary.

But it was in Russia that the most striking change occurred. The war sowed the seeds of revolution on land that was already well tilled. After the February Revolution and the abdication of Nicholas II, two governments vied for power in Russia: one from the new Duma, the other from the Soviets in Petrograd. The summer unfolded against a backdrop of quarrels. Soldiers demanded peace, and those who refused war were increasingly numerous; hence, the

Germans managed to make headway. In October 1917, the Bolsheviks decided it was impossible to continue with two governments. An insurrection broke out led by Vladimir Lenin and Leon Trotsky. On November 7 (Russian October 25), the Winter Palace was stormed and Lenin seized power. This change led to Russia's signing of the Brest-Litovsk peace treaty on March 3, 1918. The United Kingdom and France, in particular, had to reorganize their troops to cope with the German troops being sent to the Western Front from the eastern one. The situation was further complicated by Romania's capitulation.

As if that were not enough, Germany inflicted another blow on France, as symbolic as it was human. On March 8 and 11, it bombed Paris, killing one hundred people. At the end of the month, on the twenty-ninth, the church of Saint-Gervais was also bombed. The death toll was eighty-eight. A year earlier, on May 26, 1917, German planes had begun bombing the United Kingdom and continued the bombing until August 24, killing 254 people, most of them women and children.

The situation darkened for the Allies, but then something else changed in 1917 when the United States entered the war, which overshadowed the defeat of Russia and Romania. Until then, the United States had not wanted to enter the war. President Wilson had opted for neutrality and was reelected in the 1916 elections having promised that the United States would continue to remain neutral. Wilson asserted that the war was causing too much harm to the countries of the world and their industries and should not be extended further. On January 22, 1917, he spoke out in favor of a "peace without victory." The Allies did not appreciate this position, but the United States was not prepared to go to war.

But war was not just fought on the lands of Europe and Asia; the sea had also been a battleground, almost from the outset. Submarine warfare officially began on February 4, 1915. On May 7, the Germans torpedoed the British ship *Lusitania*, sailing between Liverpool and New York. The sinking killed 1,198 people, including 128 Americans. The event had a huge impact on American public opinion. During the war, the sea was used to transport not only goods but also weapons and soldiers. Again, the route was a dangerous one. Sailing in the Mediterranean to the Dardanelles or Greece meant taking the risk of having one's ship torpedoed. In these naval battles, seventy-seven Basques died. Most of them (thirty-four) lost their lives off Cape Matapan in Greece, others on board *Le Bouvet* during the fighting in the Dardanelles. In addition, six men died off the coast of Portugal when the ship *Le Suffren* sank on November 25, 1916, while five others disappeared on the ship *Amiral Charnier* in Syria on

February 8, 1916. Others lost their lives in the Adriatic, Corsica, Sardinia, Marseille, and the Atlantic.

Throughout all this, Germans torpedoed Allied and neutral cargo ships. However, the situation became more complicated from 1917 onward as the United Kingdom organized convoys to protect the ships carrying goods. The Germans targeted them all, including US ships. This did not please the Americans, who continued to grant the Allies loans for shipbuilding.[2] The Germans torpedoed many American ships in early 1917, causing deaths and enormous damage. As a result, American public opinion was increasingly in favor of the country entering the war. On April 6, the US Congress decided to enter the war. On June 26, 1917, the first American soldiers arrived in Saint-Nazaire. Some stayed in Baiona, where they organized July 4 celebrations among themselves.

The Germans intended to send the soldiers they had withdrawn from the Russian front to the west in order to strike hard on the Western Front, pitting them against the French and British before the Americans sent their soldiers into action. Thus, on March 21, 1918, the Germans launched a major offensive in Picardy. This marked the beginning of a strategy of destruction in which the aim was to assault the British troops, whom they believed to be the weakest. To facilitate their passage to the English Channel, the Germans placed their forces between Arras and Saint-Quentin, destroying what was left of villages that had already suffered enormously during the war. The British were to regain the upper hand only in August. On April 5, the Germans headed for Amiens. Although they failed to occupy the town, artillery damage was severe, and the Allies were forced to retreat. Four days later, the Germans launched a new offensive in Flanders, aiming to reach the ports of Dunkirk and Calais. On April 24, the Germans seized Mount Kemmel in Flanders and launched an attack south of Ypres. However, a British counterattack did not allow them to make any significant advances.

The offensives in Flanders and the Arras region having been inconclusive, the Germans launched a new attack on May 27 on the Chemin des Dames, taking the French by surprise. The Germans began to advance toward the Marne, covering sixty-five kilometers in three days. In the space of just a few days, the French lost the little land they had gained a year earlier in the same region, at the cost of a massacre, and much more besides. As a result of this advance, the German army was then only sixty-five kilometers from Paris and considered it possible to get that far, to the extent that it worried the French deputies. The French organized their defense, cutting off the German advance at this point and stabilizing the front.[3] At the same time, in the Champagne region, the Germans occupied Soissons and Château-Thierry on May 30. A fortnight later, the Germans launched an offensive in this region and the French a counteroffensive.

These harsh spring offensives of 1918 were initially a show of force by Germany, but they failed to destroy the British army or even weaken it, just as the Germans failed to defeat the French army or conquer Paris. For the Austrians, the coming spring was no better, as they were defeated in their offensive against Italy around Piave. At the same time, American soldiers began arriving on the Western Front to reinforce the Allied troops.

That year, internal conflicts broke out in Germany and Austria-Hungary. On January 14, strikes had begun in Austria-Hungary to demand bread and peace. After two days, strikes spread to Budapest, and finally, Spartakists and communists called a strike in favor of peace. A million demonstrators gathered. The police violently repressed them, killing several of the strikers. On February 1, several incidents broke out within the Austro-Hungarian army as sailors unfurled red flags to denounce the poor quality of the food and protest the lack of home leave. Then, on February 18, Poles went on strike in opposition to the emperor of Austria-Hungary.

In Austria-Hungary, another type of protest arose alongside those of the population and soldiers—that of the oppressed nations. Between April 8 and 11, the Congress of Oppressed Nations of Eastern Europe was held in Rome with the support of the Italian government. Although the Allies were unable to agree on decisions concerning the future of Austria-Hungary, the Czechoslovakians and South Slavs demanded their independence. On May 1, 1918, they demonstrated in Prague in favor of national self-determination. On May 11, Slovak soldiers mutinied at Rimavska Sobota. Over the course of the summer, 250,000 deserters left the army. On June 2, more rebelled within the Austro-Hungarian army at Kragujevac (Serbia), and several dozen soldiers were executed.

Elsewhere, in May and July 1918, strikes against the war and the high cost of living also took place in French and British factories. However, these movements did not weaken the Allies, as had been the case in Germany and Austria-Hungary. In Germany, revolution erupted on July 13 when the Reichstag agreed to increase the war fund, adding fuel to an already explosive social climate. Sensing the risk of defeat, many soldiers refused to return to war.

From November 1917 onward the Allies had decided to organize themselves differently. Although they had communicated with each other up to that point, they had only loosely agreed on the fighting, each force acting on its own. The French criticized the English for their arrogance and for sending far fewer soldiers to war than they did. The English, for their part, accused the French of not being competent enough for war. Following Italy's setback at Caporetto, the Allies decided to review their operations at the Rapallo Conference in Italy and decided—not without difficulty—to create a single command. In spring 1918, when the Americans sent in soldiers and huge war tanks, the Allied army was considerably strengthened, and on April 14 they agreed on a single command for the American, British, and French armies. French general Ferdinand Foch took the helm.

The benefits of this cooperation became apparent the following summer. On July 18, 1918, the French and Americans launched a counteroffensive and with it achieved the second victory of the Marne. The Germans had no choice but to retreat. Less than a month later, on August 8, the French and British led the counteroffensive at Montdidier on the Somme. Two hundred thousand Germans were taken prisoner. In the Aisne, in the vicinity of the Chemin des Dames, following Charles Mangin's offensive, the Germans were forced to retreat, and from May 27 onward they evacuated all the places they had occupied. For the Germans, this was their "darkest day." The Allied attack continued over the following days, and between August 18 and September 4 the Allies launched a major offensive on the Somme. From September 26 to 28, the Allies pushed the Germans back over a vast territory stretching from Champagne to Flanders.

With the situation on the Western Front going badly for Germany, German soldiers left the Balkan front, abandoning it to the Bulgarians. By this time the Allies had reorganized the Salonika army, and on October 14 they launched an assault on the Bulgarians, condemning them to constant retreat. On September 29, Bulgaria requested an armistice and withdrew from the war. This was a heavy blow for Germany and Austria-Hungary.

On the Western Front, the Americans, the French, and the British were making more progress every day. On October 9, the Canadians entered the destroyed town of Cambrai in northeastern France. The Germans had seized it on August 26, 1914. Ypres, which had been the scene of fierce fighting since the start of the war, also fell to the Allies on October 14, 1918, with the arrival of the British. On the seventeenth, Lille was recaptured from the Germans.

In this month of October, Italy, presented as the weaker brother among the Allies, also saw the wind of change. On October 24, in a bid to recapture the Piave region, it joined the offensive against the Austrians. Meanwhile, in Austria-Hungary the pot was boiling. Also on October 24, the empire was divided into two territories after Hungary had gained the independence it had been striving for in recent months. Four days later, Austria-Hungary lost a new territory with the foundation of the Czech Republic. The following day, Croatia and Slovenia became independent states. Officially, the nations of Austria-Hungary split up on October 30. The empire disappeared on November 3 with the signing of the Villa Giusti armistice. The following day marked the birth of the Republic of Austria. On October 30, the Ottoman Empire also capitulated, signing the Moudros armistice with the British.

Germany was the last country to continue the war against the Allies, but the domestic situation was unbearable. On November 3, sailors refused to embark, and in the days that followed, even bigger strikes broke out, with protests spreading throughout Germany. On November 7, Ludwig III of Bavaria was overthrown and Kurt Eisner formed Bavaria's first socialist government. On November 9, Wilhelm II, Emperor of Germany, abdicated and the Weimar Republic was created. In the end, this country, which had shown the greatest strength throughout the war, was forced to its knees and signed the armistice on November 11, marking the end of the fighting.

The bells of the Northern Basque Country rang out joyfully on November 11, 1918, at 11:00 a.m. They signaled that the war was over. It was a day of rejoicing for the general population and the soldiers. At the battle sites, the cannons fell silent, and the bells began to ring. It was a wonderful change for everyone. The roar of cannon fire had not been a common sound in these parts, but during these four years the whistle of shells and the crash of explosions had been incessant. The soldiers had developed their hearing to guess where the bombs were coming from and where they were about to explode, which was of the utmost importance. And then, suddenly, after four years of war, the soundscape of these regions changed. This sudden silence seemed "unreal."[4]

Oxobi was in Alsace at the time, and this is how he described the moment when the bells began to ring:

> Early in the morning we waited for the bells to start ringing. They started at exactly eleven o'clock, while the sun, which until then hadn't managed to break through the clouds, slowly made its appearance.
>
> What a day! You could hear the bells ringing until noon! They filled the air. Enemy eagles hid far away in dark nests, enemy guns fled. All the doors of the houses, all the windows are magnificently decorated. At the top of the church tower, a gentle breeze flutters the French and Alsatian flags at the same time.

> In the streets, not a shout. We're stunned. When we see each other, we exchange a hearty laugh and the words "This time, it's done!"* (translated from Basque)

We can only imagine that the population at large as well as the soldiers were stunned by the incredible news. Some accounts state that village streets and squares were suddenly filled with happiness, that the demonstrations of joy by residents and soldiers alike were spectacular to behold, that flags flew from windows, that white, red, and blue flowers were worn, and that the civilians and soldiers mingled at large celebrations. But other firsthand accounts did not coincide with these representations. According to some, it was far from euphoric when the end of the war was announced. Zerbitzari, writing among those hit hard by the war, described the reaction of soldiers at the front:

> I don't know if you'll easily believe me: when the fighters heard the good news, they didn't cheer loudly. It was as if they were stunned. We were all convinced that our bones would be eaten away in the war: we were convinced of that. Then, suddenly, we were told that the war was over: How could we believe it?
>
> As night fell, after a glass of wine, I heard some Basques making the sound of the *irrintzina*. But not for long. They soon remembered all those companions who are no longer with us. The greatest joys always have their shadowy side. May our dead comrades enjoy, in heaven, the happiness they didn't have on this earth!† (translated from Basque)

It was hard for these soldiers to admit, after so many years, that the war could end like this. They did not believe it could be possible; they had expected a different outcome.[5] Similarly, how could they celebrate and feel happy after losing so many companions? On this day, the soldiers wrote fewer letters, busy as they were experiencing their joy at their first hours of peace. However, their satisfaction was incomplete because there had been so many deaths. Certainly, the version saying that in villages far from the front nothing was heard but shouts of joy and victory was widely circulated. Yet soldiers' letters told a different story.[6]

What is more, the soldiers had no information about the armistice. Soldiers in the front lines knew only one thing: the guns had fallen silent and the bells had announced the end of the war. The military leaders knew what had really

---

* Jules Moulier, "Izkilak eta banderak".
† Elizalde, "Zer dioten gerlariek".

happened, what had been decided, but they were far from the soldiers in the trenches. Negotiations between the Germans and the Allies had begun the day before in the forest of Compiègne. In fact, as early as October 7, the Germans made it known that they wished to enter talks to end the war. To do so, they had to accept a number of specific conditions: first and most important, they had to evacuate all the territories they had occupied up to that point and place the left bank of the Rhine under Allied administration. On November 6, the Germans conveyed the names of the members of their delegation, and on November 10, the meeting for the signing of the armistice began in Rethondes. The text was signed at 5:00 a.m., and a message was sent to all military leaders ordering all fighting to cease at 11:00 a.m. French time. From a legal point of view, this was a thirty-six-day ceasefire, which would be renewed at the end of this period until it became definitive in February.

Under the terms of the agreement, the Germans had to evacuate France, Belgium, Luxembourg, and Alsace-Lorraine within a fortnight. After this deadline, any German soldier captured in these territories would be taken prisoner. The Germans were also required to surrender large quantities of armaments, five thousand assembled machines, and 150,000 wagons. The agreement also ordered that the countries on the left bank of the Rhine be administered by the Allies. In addition, German soldiers were ordered to leave from across territories that had been under the control of Austria-Hungary, Romania, and Turkey before the start of the war. Certain points in the Brest-Litovsk and Bucharest armistices, which favored the Germans, were also invalidated. The cessation of fighting in East Africa was ordered, along with the evacuation of this region and the release of all prisoners in German hands. Another important point was compensation for war damage. Germany would complete its compensation payments in 2010.

Seven months later, on June 28, 1919, the peace treaty was signed in the Hall of Mirrors at the Château de Versailles. One of the aims of the treaty was to deprive Germany of its power, forcing Germany to accept the rules imposed by other nations. In addition to imposing severe economic sanctions, the signatories agreed to turn the rivers flowing through Germany into a major international canal. Another objective was to disarm Germany, which was to surrender five thousand cannons, twenty-five thousand aircraft, and all its ships to the Allies. The German army was limited to one hundred thousand men, and German military service was banned. France, however, sent its troops to both sides of the Rhine, having ordered the Germans to demilitarize the region. France's intention was to avoid a possible German attack.

In addition, as a result of this treaty, Germany lost 15 percent of the territories it had held before the war. It had to return Alsace and Lorraine to France. It returned to Belgium the cantons of Eupen and Malmedy, which were in the province of Liège but had been annexed by Prussia in 1815. Denmark, even though it had not taken part in the war, recovered part of the Schleswig-Holstein region, the Duchy of Schleswig, and the County of Holstein. These territories had been attributed to the king of Denmark in the fifteenth century but fell under the control of Prussia in 1866. Germany also lost the region of Posnania. This Polish province had become Prussian in 1793, when Russia and Prussia divided up the Polish territories. Additionally, as part of the Treaty of Versailles, a section of East Prussia became part of the new Polish state. Part of Prussia lay in the middle of Poland, separated from the other German territories by the Danzig Corridor. To the south of this corridor, Upper Silesia was a source of conflict between Poland and Germany, and over the next few years Silesia reverted to Poland. To the southwest of Silesia, the region of Moravia was ceded to Czechoslovakia. In the west, although the Saarland wished to remain part of Germany, it was placed under the administration of the League of Nations, and the ownership of its mines reverted to France, which hoped that the inhabitants of the region would decide in favor of remaining part of France. However, there were many incidents concerning this area until a plebiscite was held during the Nazi era, and 91 percent of the inhabitants of the Saarland decided on January 13, 1935, that their region should remain part of Germany. Germany's colonies in Asia and Africa also reverted to the Allies, as Germany had to cede the areas it occupied in southern Africa to the United Kingdom; Rwanda and Burundi to Belgium; Togo and Cameroon to France and the United Kingdom; and the territories in Indonesia to Australia and Japan.

Versailles

The League of Nations, the brainchild of Woodrow Wilson, was also one of the outcomes of the Treaty of Versailles. Wilson, then president of the United States, wanted to create an institution to guarantee peace in the world once the war was over. Many states took part in this institution from the outset, but those that had lost the war were initially excluded. Thus Germany did not join until 1926, only to withdraw seven years later. Yet it soon became clear that the League of Nations was incapable of guaranteeing a lasting peace.

When it was created, the League of Nations had many weaknesses. Under the Treaty of Versailles, France obtained British and American protection in the event of a German attack. However, the American Senate did not ratify the Treaty of Versailles, so the United States did not join the League of Nations. In the event of a German offensive, France could no longer be sure of American protection.

Is definitive peace just a dream, we might ask? Long before the end of the war, there was already talk of creating a body of this type, so that once peace had been achieved, the outbreak of a new war would be impossible. Among Basque writers, Jean Etchepare clearly saw what could happen in the future. He did not believe in a definitive peace.

> Some fools are already claiming that this war will be the last and that totally disgusted with war, everyone will get rid of their weapons. Please, no such dreams. People will remain armed, their lips soft, their tongues too, but their teeth sharp, each guarding his property and his rights. As before, in the future too, we will still, from time to time, devour each other. It's always up to the weakest to give way.[7] (translated from Basque)

Well before the end of the war, Etchepare had expressed his pessimism. Once the conflict was over and the Treaty of Versailles had been signed, the Germans experienced the outcome as a great humiliation. The Allies wanted to make it clear that they were the victors and that Germany was a defeated country. They wanted Germany to pay a heavy price for its acts of war. The Germans, for their part, were not prepared for a military defeat. They were convinced that they had shown considerable power and strength during the four years of conflict and that they did not lose the war because of poor political and strategic choices. Rather, they blamed Prince Maximilian of Baden to a large extent for betraying them. He had become chancellor of Germany in August 1918 and had negotiated the peace. In November, the socialist revolution broke out, and on the ninth of the month the socialist Friedrich Ebert proclaimed the Weimar Republic. Maximilian of Baden and the socialists were accused of having accepted the "peace dictated" by Versailles. The message spread by the press in the years that followed was that the army had not been weakened and that Germany had lost the war because of internal conflicts.[8] Furthermore, they had had to agree to work to pay war damages to the victorious countries. Germany, for its part, was as strong internally as it had been before the war, since it had not suffered any material damage. Its main problem was that it had lost certain territories—rich ones, at that— and that it would go into debt because of the heavy fines it had to pay, that it had to accept the military presence of the Allies in certain areas, and finally, that it had been demilitarized. In addition, although 70 percent of the population of Silesia in the 1912 referendum clearly wanted their region to remain part of Germany, Poland's refusal to accept this result only made the Germans angrier.

The war was over. Peace had been achieved. Yet this peace had in no way extinguished the embers.

NOTES

1. Fassy, *Le commandement français en orient: octobre 1915–novembre 1918: Étude historique d'un comman- dement opérationnel français à la tête d'une force militaire alliée.*
2. Prior and Wilson, *La Première Guerre mondiale 1914–1918*, 134–135.
3. Prior and Wilson, *La Première Guerre mondiale 1914–1918*, 177–178.
4. Cabanes, *La victoire endeuillée: La sortie de guerre des soldats français (1918–1920)*, 44.
5. Cabanes, *La victoire endeuillée: La sortie de guerre des soldats français (1918–1920)*, 29.
6. Cabanes, "Ce que dit le contrôle postal," 61.
7. Etchepare, "Ez urririk."
8. Fischer, *Les buts de guerre de l'Allemagne impériale, 1914–1918*, 634–635.

CHAPTER SIXTEEN

Counting the Dead

The map of the world had changed, and demographics had also undergone serious upheaval. It is difficult to establish the precise death toll, which varies from source to source and especially from state to state. Overall, the figures clearly show the scale of the slaughter: 9.4 million soldiers died (an average of 6,000 a day) and 20 million men were wounded (of whom 8 million remained disabled) during this terrible war, which lasted more than four years. However, if we count the civilian deaths, the overall figure is much higher, although it is difficult to distinguish between those who died as a result of epidemics and those who died as a result of acts of war. In addition to people, thousands, even millions of animals also died during the war, as 11 million horses, 100,000 dogs, and 200,000 pigeons were used in the war and were not spared by the bombs.[1]

Germany suffered the most casualties, with almost 2 million killed in the war. The Russians also suffered considerable losses, with 1.85 million casualties. Austria-Hungary recorded 1.5 million deaths and France 1.375 million. The United Kingdom, with 776,000 dead, and the United States of America, with 213,000 dead, were among the states least affected. In the case of the United States, it should be pointed out that US forces entered the war late and therefore spent three years fewer than the others under fire and bombardment.

Another country suffered lower numbers of military casualties than the United Kingdom, yet it deserves a special mention. Serbia lost 400,000 soldiers in the war, but there were also some 800,000 civilians lost. In all, Serbia lost a quarter of its population in the First World War. Of the men mobilized, 70 percent died. Without a doubt, both in terms of demographics and the number of men mobilized, Serbia remains the state that paid the heaviest price for the war.

Although Germany lost the greatest number of citizens in proportion, after Serbia it was Romania that suffered the greatest losses in this war, almost 10 percent of its population. France lost more than 4 percent of its population, but if we count only the soldiers killed, 3.3 percent. However, 16.7 percent of all mobilized French soldiers died in the war (between 20 and 24 percent, including colonials), making France the country with the highest number of military casualties after Serbia. Germany was also at a similar level, with 15 percent of its soldiers killed. The other countries participating in the war suffered losses of between 11 and 12 percent of their soldiers.

In demographic terms, the number of inhabitants lost in the Northern Basque Country was lower than the French average, at 2.86 percent. According to calculations, 5,324 soldiers born in the Basque Country died in the First World War, most of them (5,247) from the Northern Basque Country.[2] This figure does not include those who were not born in the Basque Country but came to live there as children or young people. In addition to these 5,324 men, more people died in the war who do not appear on the lists, as not all the dead appear on the official list of those who died for France. The lists of names on the war memorials erected in the communities of France do not necessarily include the names of those born in the community but are the names of those who lived in the locality before going off to war. In the village of Ahatsa (Ahaxe), for example, Nicolas Inhabar, Bernard Iriart, Arnaud Uhart, and Michel Uhart were not born in Ahatsa but came from the villages of Buztintze-Hiriberri (Bustince-Iriberry), Donibane Garazi, and Hozta (Hosta), respectively. Their names appear on the Ahatsa war memorial and not on that of their home village. However, Martin Grenade, born in Ahatsa, and Laurent Othart, born in Jutsi (Juxue), though listed on the Ahatsa war memorial, are not listed on the Mémoires des Hommes website. The former died in the hospital in Pau, and the latter in the hospital in Baiona. Others appear on the war memorials of several villages. These include Achile Fortis, whose name appears on the monuments of Bastida and Baiona, and Dominique Heguy, whose name appears on the monuments of Hazparne (Hasparren), Iholdi (Iholdy), and Bastida. Given such discrepancies, for this book a methodology had to be chosen to calculate the number of dead. For this purpose, the statistical data presented in the following pages have been taken from the official list from the French Ministry of Defense.[3]

To avoid repetition, names on the Ministry of Defense list have been compared with the names on the memorials to the dead.[4] This work has made it possible to correct certain errors that appeared on the Mémoires des Hommes website (some of the dead, who were born in the Basque Country, were not listed in the Pyrénées-Atlantiques department) and to identify certain names that did not appear on this website. Also to be mentioned are the cases of those who appear on the war memorials but for whom there is no information other than their first and last names. In this category are 591 names: unknown is where, when, or how they died. Some of them may have been mistaken. They may already have been included in the list of 5,324 men given. It is also possible that many of them were left off the list. Still, others may not have been born in the Basque Country. In any case, when it comes to making an estimate, we can say that between 5,324 and 5,911 of the men who died in the war were born in the Basque Country, to which we must add a further 638 men who were not born in the Basque Country but who appear on the Basque Country's war memorials. Equally numerous are the men who, though born in the Basque Country, do not appear on the Basque Country war memorials because it seems that they were not living in the Northern Basque Country when the war broke out. If we take this maximum figure into account, the percentage of war dead could represent 3.17 percent of the population of the Northern Basque Country. If this were the actual figure, the loss of men in the Northern Basque Country would be close to the French average. Two names that do not appear on the official list of the French Ministry of Defense have been added, as have the names of two men who were shot.

Of the 5,324 men identified, seventy-seven were born in the Southern Basque Country; most had French or Gascon names, but some had Basque names, such as Dorronsoro y Aguirre, Arbiza, Arrieta, Yrigoyen, and Susperregui. Of those who died, fourteen were from Donostia-San Sebastián, twelve from Bilbo-Bilbao, eighteen from Irun, four from Fontarrabia, and three each from Iruñea-Pamplona, Pasaia (Pasajes), Tolosa, Sestao, and Urdazubi (Urdax). Some of the dead were also from Zugarramurdi, Luzaide, Erratzu, Oronoz, Gartzain, Irurita, Etxalar, Almandoz, Mendigorria, Tutera (Tudela), Laudio, Zalla, Barakaldo, Arrigorriaga, Laida, Deba, Aia, Andoain, Altza, and Erranteria (Renteria).

Baiona is the town that lost the most inhabitants; 580 Bayonnais died during the war. More names appear on the town's war memorial, but many of them were born in other places. The following table (Table 16.1) shows the number of dead by locality:

Table 16.1. Basque soldiers killed, by home village

TOWN	DEATHS
TOTAL	5,324
BAIONA (BAYONNE)	580
MIARRITZE (BIARRITZ)	267
HAZPARNE (HASPARREN)	204
ANGELU (ANGLET)	145
URRUÑA (URRUGNE)	135
BOKALE (BOUCAU)	108
BIDAXUNE (BIDACHE)	103
DONIBANE LOHIZUNE (ST-JEAN DE LUZ)	101
UZTARITZE (USTARITZ)	88
SENPERE (SAINT-PÉE-SUR-NIVELLE)	68
KANBO (CAMBO)	67
ZIBURU (CIBOURE)	67
AKAMARRE (CAME)	64
MAULE-LEIXTARRE (MAULÉON-LICHARRE)	61
BESKOITZE (BRISCOUS)	58
HENDAIA (HENDAYE)	57
BASTIDA (LA BASTIDE-CLAIRENCE)	55
SOHÜTA (CHÉRAUTE)	55
AHURTI (URT)	54
DONAPALEU (SAINT-PALAIS)	54
AZKAINE (ASCAIN)	53
BARKOXE (BARCUS)	52
ARRANGOITZE (ARCANGUES)	51
BARDOZE (BARDOS)	49
BAIGORRI (SAINT-ÉTIENNE-DE-BAÏGORRY)	48
MUGERRE (MOUGUERRE)	48
AIHERRA (AYHERRE)	47
ESKIULA (ESQUIULE)	47
LARRAÑE (LARRAU)	47
ORTZAIZE (OSSÈS)	47
IRISARRI (IRISSARRY)	45
ITSASU ITXASSOU	45
MILAFRANGA (VILLEFRANQUE)	45
LEKORNE (MENDIONDE)	44
ORAGARRE (ORÈGUE)	44
SANTA GRAZI (SAINTE-ENGRÂCE)	43
ARRUETA-SARRIKOTA (ARRAUTE-CHARRITTE)	41
HELETA (HÉLETTE)	41
BIDARTE (BIDART)	40

ARBONA (ARBONNE)	39
GIXUNE (GUICHE)	39
ATHARRATZE-SORHOLÜZE (TARDETS-SORHOLUS)	37
EZPELETA (ESPELETTE)	37
MONTORI-BERRORITZE (MONTORY)	36
BITHIRIÑA (BEYRIE-SUR-JOYEUSE)	35
SARA (SARE)	35
GETARIA (GUÉTHARY)	33
BIDARRAI (BIDARRAY)	32
IHOLDI (IHOLDY)	32
DOMINTXAINE-BERROETA (DOMEZAIN-BERRAUTE)	30
AINHOA	29
ARBOTI-ZOHOTA (ARBOUET-SUSSAUTE)	28
BASUSARRI (BASSUSSARRY)	28
DONOZTIRI (SAINT-ESTEBEN)	28
MAKEA (MACAYE)	28
HIRIBURU (SAINT-PIERRE-D'IRUBE)	27
LAKARRI-ARHANE-SARRIKOTAGAINE (LACARRY-ARHAN-CHARRITTE-DE-HAUT)	27
LARZABALE-ARROZE-ZIBITZE (LARCEVEAU-ARROS-CIBITS)	27
ALTZAI-ALTZABEHETI-ZUNHARRETA (ALÇAY-ALÇABÉHÉTY-SUNHARETTE)	26
DONAIXTI-IBARRE (SAINT-JUST-IBARRE)	26
DONAMARTIRI (SAINT-MARTIN-D'ARBÉROUE)	26
MUSKILDI (MUSCULDY)	26
ARMENDARITZE (ARMENDARITS)	25
DONIBANE GARAZI (SAINT-JEAN-PIED-DE-PORT)	25
SAMATZE (SAMES)	24
BEHAUZE (BÉGUIOS)	23
BILDOZE-ONIZEPEA (VIODOS-ABENSE-DE-BAS)	23
URDIÑARBE (ORDIARP)	23
EZTERENZUBI (ESTERENÇUBY)	22
ILHARRE	22
LIGINAGA-ASTÜE (LAGUINGE)	22
PAGOLA (PAGOLLE)	22
URKETA (URCUIT)	22
AIZIRITZE-GAMUE-ZOHAZTI (AÏCIRITS-CAMOU-SUHAST)	21
LIGI-ATHEREI (LICQ-ATHEREY)	21
LANDIBARRE (LANTABAT)	20
MARTXUETA (MASPARRAUTE)	20
MITIKILE-LARRORI-MENDIBILE (MONCAYOLLE-LARRORY-MENDIBIEU)	20
ARÜE-ITHORROTZE-OLHAIBI (AROUE-ITHOROTS-OLHAÏBY)	19

(continued)

Table 16.1, cont.

TOWN	DEATHS
GOTAINE-IRABARNE (GOTEIN-LIBARRENX)	19
EZPEIZE-ÜNDÜRAINE (ESPÈS-UNDUREIN)	18
LÜKÜZE-ALTZÜMARTA (LUXE-SUMBERRAUTE)	18
MEHAINE (MÉHARIN)	18
UHARTEHIRI (UHART-MIXE)	18
AHATSA-ALTZIETA-BAZKAZANE (AHAXE-ALCIETTE-BASCASSAN)	17
AHETZE	17
LOHITZÜNE-OIHERGI (LOHITZUN-OYHERCQ)	17
MENDIBE (MENDIVE)	17
GARINDAINE (GARINDEIN)	16
LABETZE-BIZKAI (LABETS-BISCAY)	16
LARRESORO (LARRESSORE)	16
ALTZÜRÜKÜ (AUSSURUCQ)	15
AMOROTZE-ZOKOTZE (AMOROTS-SUCCOS)	15
ARNEGI-ARNÉGUY	15
BURGUE-ERREITI (BERGOUEY-VIELLENAVE)	15
GABADI (GABAT)	15
JUTSI (JUXUE)	15
LEHUNTZE (LAHONCE)	15
AMENDUZE-UNASO (AMENDEUIX-ONEIX)	14
ARROKIAGA (ROQUIAGUE)	14
BANKA (BANCA)	14
BIRIATU (BIRIATOU)	14
DONAZAHARRE (SAINT-JEAN-LE-VIEUX)	14
IZPURA (ISPOURE)	14
IZURA-AZME (OSTABAT-ASME)	14
MENDIKOTA (MENDITTE)	14
SARRIKOTAPEA (CHARRITTE-DE-BAS)	14
DONOSTIA (SAN SEBASTIAN)	14
AINHARBE (AÏNHARP)	13
ETXARRI (ETCHARRY)	13
GAMERE-ZIHIGA (CAMOU-CIHIGUE)	13
ZURAIDE (SOURAÏDE)	13
AINTZILE (AINCILLE)	12
DUZUNARITZE-SARASKETA (BUSSUNARITS-SARRASQUETTE)	12
HALTSU (HALSOU)	12
UHARTE GARAZI (UHART-CIZE)	12
ZALGIZE-DONEZTEBE (SAUGUIS-SAINT-ÉTIENNE)	12

BILBO (BILBAO)	12
ALDUDE (LES ALDUDES)	11
ALOZE-ZIBOZE-ONIZEGAINE (ALOS-SIBAS-ABENSE)	11
AZKARATE (ASCARAT)	11
HOZTA (HOSTA)	11
IRURI (TROIS-VILLES)	11
LARRIBARRE-SORHAPÜRÜ (LARRIBAR-SORHAPURU)	11
LEKUINE (BONLOC)	11
LEKUNBERRI (LECUMBERRY)	11
LUHUSO (LOUHOSSOA)	11
ÜRRUSTOI-LARREBILE (ARRAST-LARREBIEU)	11
EIHERALARRE (SAINT-MICHEL)	10
GAMARTE (GAMARTHE)	10
IZTURITZE (ISTURITS)	10
OSTANKOA (ORSANCO)	10
ARBERATZE-ZILHEKOA (ARBÉRATS-SILLÈGUE)	9
BUZTINTZE-HIRIBERRI (BUSTINCE-IRIBERRY)	9
ERANGO (ARANCOU)	9
IBARROLA (IBAROLLE)	9
JATSU GARAZI (JAXU)	9
LASA (LASSE)	9
LEXANTZÜ-ZÜNHARRE (LICHANS-SUNHAR)	9
AINHIZE-MONJOLOSE (AINHICE-MONGELOS)	8
BEHASKANE-LAPHIZKETA (BÉHASQUE-LAPISTE)	8
IDAUZE-MENDI (IDAUX-MENDY)	8
JATSU (JATXOU)	8
SUHUSKUNE (SUHESCUN)	8
UREPELE (UREPEL)	8
IRUN (IRUN)	8
BERROGAINE-LAHÜNTZE (BERROGAIN-LARUNS)	7
BUNUZE (BUNUS)	7
GARRÜZE (GARRIS)	7
IRULEGI (IROULÉGUY)	7
OZAZE-ZÜHARA (OSSAS-SUHARE)	7
ANHAUZE (ANHAUX)	6
ETXEBARRE (ETCHEBAR)	6
LAKARRA (LACARRE)	6
OZERAINE-ERRIBAREITA (OSSERAIN-RIVAREYTE)	6
HAUZE (HAUX)	5
JESTAZE (GESTAS)	5
OSPITALEPEA (HÔPITAL-SAINT-BLAISE)	5
HONDARRIBIA (FONTARRABIE)	5
BEHORLEGI (BÉHORLÉGUY)	4
URDAZUBI (URDAX)	4

(continued)

Table 16.1, *cont.*

TOWN	DEATHS
ZARO (ÇARO)	3
IRUÑEA (PAMPLONA)	3
PASAIA (PASAJES)	3
TOLOSA	3
SESTAO	3
ZUGARRAMURDI	3
ARHANTSUSI (ARHANSUS)	2
LUZAIDE (VALCARLOS)	2
ERRATZU	2
AIA	1
ALMANDOZ	1
ALTZA	1
ANDOAIN	1
ARRIGORRIAGA	1
BARAKALDO (BARACALDO)	1
DEBA (DEVA)	1
ERRENTERIA (RENTERIA)	1
ETXALAR (ECHALAR)	1
GARTZAIN	1
LAIDA	1
LAUDIO (LLODIO)	1
MENDIGORRIA	1
ORONOZ	1
TUTERA (TUDELA)	1
ZALLA	1
LEZAMA	1

(*source*: www.memoiredeshommes.sga.defense.gouv.fr and www.memorialgenweb.org)

Obviously, logic dictates that the most significant figures relate to the largest localities. In proportional terms, the population losses suffered by the town of Baiona and those recorded by the villages of Basusarri and Liginaga are not of the same order of magnitude. Baiona lost 2.08 percent of its population during the war (the population was measured according to the 1911 census); Basusarri, by contrast, lost twenty-eight inhabitants, but with a population of 386, the loss represents 7.25 percent of its population for this Lapurdi village. With twenty-two dead, Liginaga recorded almost as many losses as Basusarri, since this village of 308 inhabitants lost 7.14 percent of its population. The village of Ilharre, with a loss of 7.1 percent of its population, is in the same situation. These villages in Lapurdi, Zuberoa, and Lower Navarre recorded the heaviest losses. The following villages (in ascending order of recorded losses) also lost more than 5 percent of their inhabitants: Arrueta-Sarrikota, Lekuine, Larrañe, Arboti-Zohota, Uhartehiri, Muskildi, Aintzila, Donamartiri, Berrogaine-Lahüntze, Ibarrola, Pagola, Arrokiaga, Burgue-Erreiti, Bithiriña, Larzabale-Arroze-Zibitze, Gamarte, Sohüta, Gamere-Zihiga, Gabadi, Eskiula, Beskoitze, Lexantzü-Zünharre, Labetze-Bizkai, and Lüküze Altzümarta.

The villages that had lost between 4 and 5 percent of their population are as follows: Altzai-Altzabeheti-Zunharreta, Oragarre, Martxueta, Behauze, Donoztiri, Santa Grazi, Bidaxune, Heleta, Lakarri-Arhane-Sarrikotagaine, Donaixti-Ibarre, Arrangoitze, Getaria, Ostankoa, Bastida, Ainharbe, Iruri, Akamarre, Montori-Berroritze, Jutsi, Etxarri, Sarrikotapea, Azkaine, Ürrustoi-Larrebile, Ainhoa, Iholdi, Amorotze-Zokotze, Aiherra, Armendaritze, Buztintze-Hiriberri, Makea, Lekorne, Aiziritze-Gamue-Zohazti, Lohitzüne-Oihergi, Mitikile-Larrori-Mendibile, Urruña, Haltsu, and Irisarri.

At the other extreme are the villages that lost less than 2 percent of their population: Donibane Lohizune, Baigorri, Zaro, Sara, Banka, Lasa, Arhantsusi, Donibane Garazi, Anhauze, Donazaharre, Miarritze, Ozeraine-Erribareita, Hendaia, Maule-Lextarre, Aldude, and Urepele. Jestaze lost no inhabitants. Significantly, many of the villages on the border with Navarre had below the average number of deaths. Baigorri, Banka, Aldude, Urepele, and Sara were the villages with the highest number of deserters and rebels, which is also reflected in the number of deaths.

It is also necessary to look at victims from the point of view of their age, and in this case the figures are even more terrible. Although 5,324 Basque citizens died, this study provides data on the ages of 5,099 of them. Of the soldiers killed, 1,819 were under the age of twenty-four, representing 36 percent of all the dead. If we take a broader age range, we can say that two-thirds of the casualties were under thirty. In other words, the soldiers sent to the front line and the main targets of the bombs were young people. This situation had serious demographic repercussions, with a falling birth rate and many orphans. The following table (Table 16.2) shows the number of Basque citizens who died during the war by age group (based on the age reached during the year, not the age in completed years), though the age of two individuals is not specified.

Looking at the ages of the dead, it is clear that the Northern Basque Country, compared with France, suffered a hemorrhage. Whereas nearly 30 percent of the dead in France were under twenty-eight, in the Basque Country 47.5 percent of the victims were found in this age bracket.

Table 16.2. Basque soldiers killed, by age

	17–19 YEARS	20–29 YEARS	30–39 YEARS	40–49 YEARS	50–59 YEARS	TOTAL
0		388	231	74	2	
1		526	204	51	2	
2		455	194	34	1	
3		376	165	20	2	
4		322	193	16	0	
5		283	139	13	0	
6		231	114	14	1	
7	1	254	105	4		
8	17	213	92	4		
9	56	222	79	1		
TOTAL	74	3270	1,516	231	8	5,099

(*source*: www.memoiredeshommes.sga.defense.gouv.fr and www.memorialgenweb.org)

It is illuminating to see when most of these deaths occurred. In 1914, the first five months of the war alone claimed more lives than all the following years of conflict. In all, 1,286 Basque citizens died in 1914. In 1916, the year of the Battle of Verdun, there were 200 fewer Basque citizens killed. In August and September 1914, thousands of soldiers set off with their hearts in their mouths to face hell, and September 1914 was the most terrible month of the war for the Basques, with 617 dead. The third most difficult month was August 1914, with 265 dead, marginally fewer than in May 1916 (when 277 men died, most of them in the Battle of Verdun).

The graph on the opposite page (Figure 16.1) shows the number of Basques who died in the war year by year. The table on the opposite page (Table 16.3) shows the number of deaths month by month.

These developments reflect the movements of the war. The warfare at the beginning of open hostilities was extremely violent because the French army had to face terrible German bombardment. The French had not expected to be destroyed by shellfire, and the slaughter was unprecedented. Although the situation in the trenches was unbearable when the war of attrition began, the figures show that the intensity of the fighting had changed. Most of the Basques remained in the trenches of the Aisne department until they left for Verdun. Every month brought its share of deaths, but Verdun was something different.

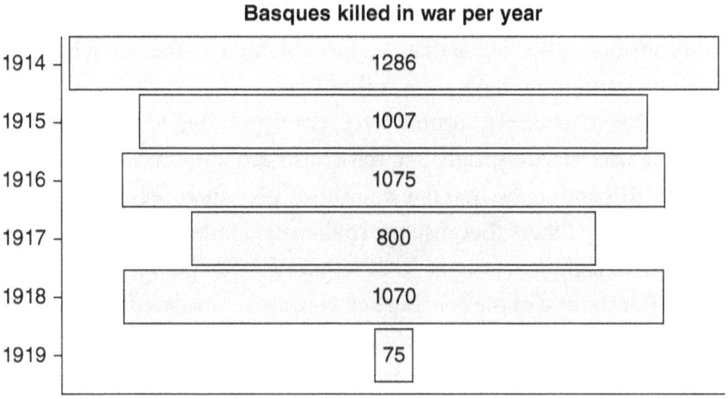

Basques killed in war per year

- 1914: 1286
- 1915: 1007
- 1916: 1075
- 1917: 800
- 1918: 1070
- 1919: 75

Figure 16.1. Basques killed in war per year
(*source*: www.memoiredeshommes.sga.defense.gouv.fr and www.memorialgenweb.org)

Table 16.3. Basque soldiers killed, by month

	1914	1915	1916	1917	1918	1919	AFTER	TOTAL
JANUARY		163	29	30	17	11		
FEBRUARY		77	95	33	22	16		
MARCH		64	59	41	53	11		
APRIL		58	81	160	71	5		
MAY		131	277	230	81	4		
JUNE		90	69	59	130	8		
JULY		78	103	44	105	4		
AUGUST	265	42	112	82	119	5		
SEPTEMBER	617	182	90	33	168	7		
OCTOBER	165	77	67	46	191	3		
NOVEMBER	108	30	42	26	79	0		
DECEMBER	131	15	51	16	32	1		
DON'T KNOW	1	0	0	0	2	0		
TOTAL	1,286	1,007	1,075	800	1,070	75	11	5,324

(*source*: www.memoiredeshommes.sga.defense.gouv.fr and www.memorialgenweb.org)

For the Basques, 1917 was a quieter year, although in April and May the death toll rose considerably, a figure that can be explained by the harsh battle of the Chemin des Dames that took place at that time.

The number of deaths in autumn 1918, corresponding to the final battles of the war, was also relatively high. Yet, the deaths did not stop with the war, as in December 1918 and in the first few months of 1919 there were still deaths, but all were caused by illness. Because the soldiers had fallen ill during the war, for statistical reasons they were considered to have died in the war. Four men died a few years after the end of the conflict but were also considered war casualties.

Many of the dead from the Northern Basque Country belonged to the 49th Infantry Regiment from Baiona. However, among those who had left the Basque Country, the dead came from numerous army units, and such was the dispersion that the proportion of dead belonging to the 49th Infantry Regiment was comparatively small at 9.39 percent, with 479 dead (out of 5,101). The second regiment with the highest number of Basque casualties—335, or 6.57 percent—was also from Baiona: the 249th Infantry Regiment. The third to leave Baiona, the 142nd Territorial Infantry Regiment, lost 208 Basque soldiers, making 4.08 percent of the dead. Another 8.57 percent of Basque citizens belonged to regiments in Pau; 5.9 percent to the 34th Infantry Regiment in Mont-de-Marsan; 4.84 percent to the 12th Infantry Regiment in Tarbes; and 3.64 percent to the 144th and 344th Infantry Regiments, based in Bordeaux. In short, at least half the Basque soldiers who fell in the war belonged to regiments in Aquitaine.

As well as the chronological distribution of the dead, their geographical distribution is significant. Given that the troops remained for many months in the Aisne, particularly between Craonne and Oulches, it is unsurprising that the largest number of Basque deaths occurred in the Aisne department. In total, 1,644 Basque soldiers lost their lives there, or 30.88 percent of all those who died—almost a third. Similarly, it is hardly surprising that the next department to receive many Basque soldiers' bodies was the Meuse, which had been devastated by the Battle of Verdun. There, 778 Basques died, or 14.62 percent of the Basque deaths. In the department of Marne, too, the Basques suffered intense fighting, and 626 of them lost their lives, or 11.66 percent.

It was in these three departments—Aisne, Meuse, and Marne—that more than half of Basque soldiers were killed during the war. In the department of the Somme, 6.27 percent of victims from the Basque Country, or 334 men, lost their lives. By contrast, 256 Basques, or 4.81 percent, died in Belgium. Those who died in the Pas-de-Calais department numbered 242, or 4.55 percent.

There were 205 in the department of Oise, or 3.85 percent. Finally, under 100 died in other places. It should be pointed out, however, that 168 soldiers died back in the Basque Country, at home or in the hospital, during the war or after it was over.

Figure 16.2 shows the number (in percentages) of men who died in each department (*département*) and country.

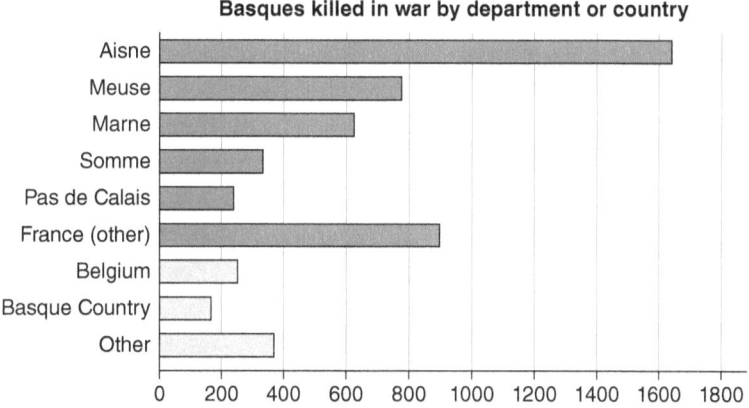

Figure 16.2. Basque soldiers killed, by French departement or country (*source*: www.memoiredeshommes.sga.defense.gouv.fr and www.memorialgenweb.org)

Figure 16.2 clearly shows that most of the Basques who were killed, 85 percent, died in France, almost all of them in the battlefields. Another 3.2 percent died in the Basque Country, almost all from disease, though a few from war wounds. Many of those who died in the Basque Country had returned wounded or sick and died in the hospital, others in their villages. In addition, 11.82 percent of the dead (630 men in all) died in other countries, most of them (248 men) in Belgium. A further 7.02 percent of losses took place outside these three areas and included seventy-five soldiers in Greece, the same number in Germany, sixty-seven in Turkey, forty-eight in Serbia, and twelve in Morocco. There were tewnty-two deaths in international waters, and the remaining deaths took place in the following countries: Bulgaria, Macedonia, Italy, Portugal, Syria, Sardinia, the Adriatic Sea, Albania, Algeria, Switzerland, Egypt, Corsica, Romania, Hungary, Ireland, Madagascar, Poland, Russia, Senegal, Tunisia, Niger, Malta, and Vietnam. It therefore appears that while most of the Basques who fought in the war did not move from northeastern France, some did find themselves in distant parts of the world.

One final point about casualties: it is clear from a study of the causes of death that most of the men were killed in the fighting, either by bullets or bombs. For each death, a form was filled in specifying the circumstances of the death. Some were described as having been "killed by the enemy"; for others, it was stated that they had died as a result of their war wounds (in most cases, in the hospital and after a considerable period). The following chart (Figure 16.3) shows the main causes of death (information was obtained on 5,101 deaths).

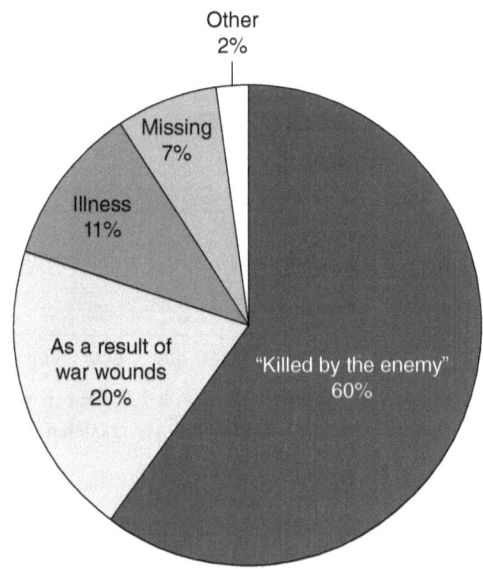

Figure 16.3. Basque soldiers killed, by cause
(*source*: www.memoiredeshommes.sga.defense.gouv.fr and www.memorialgenweb.org)

The graph in Figure 16.3 shows that more than three-quarters of the soldiers who died in the war lost their lives in battle, most of them instantly, but with almost 1 in 5 after having to endure wounds and suffering. Similarly, 1 in 10 (11.15 percent) died of disease. This clearly shows the considerable impact of the appalling conditions imposed by the war—the cold and damp, the lack of hygiene, the meager supplies, fatigue, and more. Of those who died of disease, 188 men were under the age of twenty-four, and thirty-two were under twenty, revealing that almost half the dead who were aged between seventeen and nineteen were taken by disease. This was also the case for seventy-nine of those over forty years of age, which amounted to a third of them. In short, the youngest and the oldest were the principal victims of disease; hence, the living conditions imposed by the war were especially unforgiving to the young or to those who were older.

The numbers classified as missing were also very high. Most of the missing remained buried in fields and forests ravaged by bombs. Many of the men who disappeared during heavy fighting were recorded as "killed by the enemy," but over time they were recorded to have died on the day of the bombing raid in which they disappeared. It is stated that seventy-three men were lost at sea, and twenty-nine others died as prisoners in Germany. It should also be noted that only six men died from inhaling poisonous gas. Although the gas is often mentioned, it caused barely any deaths among Basque soldiers.

Numbers for the Basque Country's wounded are not so precise. Nevertheless, given the overall proportions, it is safe to assume that more than ten thousand men were wounded. In other words, a total of over fifteen thousand men suffered the physical repercussions of war. It is not specified how many men were mobilized from the Basque Country, but in the Pyrénées-Atlantiques region the figure was around forty-five thousand. Calculated on the basis of 1911 demographics, there would have been approximately twenty thousand men mobilized from the Basque country, and it is mentioned that twenty-five thousand men passed through Baiona in the first three days of mobilization. If we make an estimate, we can deduce that 20 to 25 percent of those mobilized from the Northern Basque Country died in the war—that is, a quarter or so. If we take into account the wounded, the direct victims of the war would represent half or even more of those who went to war. These figures should be treated with caution; but in any case, the repercussions were traumatic.

NOTES

1. Baratay, *Bêtes des tranchées: Des vécus oubliés*.
2. The sources for the following data are from www.memoiredeshommes.sga.defense.gouv.fr and www.memorialgenweb.org.
3. See www.memoiredeshommes.sga.defense.gouv.fr.
4. See www.memorialgenweb.org.

CHAPTER SEVENTEEN

The Consequences

For many Basques nowadays, the First World War remains a distant subject, though for others it is more familiar; but for all, it should be known. The reason the war remains remote for many but is familiar for many others is obvious. Although it was not the only event to influence the different subsequent developments that took place in the Northern and Southern Basque Country, it was nonetheless a pivotal event, as the data clearly show. For the Southern Basque Country, it had no political repercussions. Although at the time the war constituted a major news item and had real resonance as a historical event linked to international politics, the Southern Basque Country followed the war from a distance, and subsequently, it occupied little space in its history lessons.

When war is mentioned in the Southern Basque Country, the current inhabitants of the region tend to think of only one conflict: the 1936 war that enveloped the region. This is understandable, as it was this war—not the First World War nor the Second—that shook the country to its core. The enemy was Spain, more specifically Franco and the Francoists, and the repercussions of this war continued to be felt in the decades that followed, as Franco emerged victorious; as long as he remained in power, the wounds of the 1936 war remained raw. The 1936 war, as did the wars that preceded it, reflects the Basque Country's relationship with Spain, given that in this war most Basques fought against the Spanish.

By contrast, when war is mentioned in the Northern Basque Country, even a century later, it is the First World War—the "War of '14" or the "Great War"—that most people bring to mind. It could also bring to mind the Second World War, which is a different matter. Or it could conjure thoughts of the Algerian War, which is yet another case in point. All three conflicts have one thing in common, though: the Basques went to war with France, for France, and above all, as Frenchmen. The relationship between the inhabitants of the Northern

Basque Country and France is nothing like that existing between the inhabitants of the Southern Basque Country and Spain. One of the keys to understanding the Northern Basque Country is to know and understand the First World War.

It did not all start in 1914, nor did it all end in 1918, of course, yet the First World War was the main chapter in the Frenchification of the Basque people in the Northern Basque Country, a major step in the process of French nation-building. Although the essential seeds of the Jacobin French nation had been sown during the French Revolution, they were slow to develop. The most important stage in the construction of French unity had begun in 1871, particularly through the schools and the army. More than half the population at that time did not know French, but schooling became compulsory, and by the beginning of the twentieth century almost everyone knew French, at least to some extent. At school and in the army, people were taught to love France; they were taught that sooner or later they would have to defend her, and they were constantly encouraged to think about reclaiming Alsace and Lorraine and taking revenge on Germany. This was the age of nationalism, and not only in France. The awakening of a national consciousness went hand in hand with economic development and urbanization. Whereas in the Southern Basque Country, especially in Biscay, Basque nationalism was on the rise, in the Northern Basque Country this was not so. The North had not really experienced urbanization or economic development, so Basque national consciousness did not yet exist there. Those Northern Basques who had experienced urbanization and economic development were affected by the development of French national consciousness. Except for a handful of elected officials, Basque leaders and churchmen glorified France and considered the Northern Basque Country a part of it. Across the Left/Right, anticlerical/clerical, and Republican/monarchist divides, all had a common enemy, and it was named with one voice: Germany.

While attachment to the French nation may not have been as deeply rooted in 1914, it was well on the way to becoming so, as the ground had been well tilled in the preceding decades. In the end, pacifists carried little weight, apart from a few incidents in Baiona, and there was no one to "refuse to go to war for a homeland that is not mine." There were those who fled the war, not out of Basque patriotism but to escape the fighting. Certainly, the day of mobilization was not as joyous as some have written. It may even have been a day of sadness, but the men had no idea of the barbarity they would have to endure. They were perfectly aware of who the enemy was, and they had accepted that they would do more than bring Germany to its knees, they would bring it to the ground. They would experience in practice what they had learned in theory over decades: they would not be bringing Germany only to its knees.

Although 5,322 Basques were awarded the "Mort pour la France" (Died for France) medal, this has yet to be granted to the two men who were sentenced to death and shot. At the beginning of 2014, they had yet to be pardoned. In all, 5,324 men died, and no doubt some others not on official lists as well. But one cannot say that the number of households or families affected by these deaths was as great as the number of deaths because many households lost more than one member—not just one son or even father and son. The number of families who had the pain of losing only one of their own was smaller than the number who died. Nonetheless, the war left thousands of widows and orphans, and thousands of parents also had to live with the grief of losing a son. Thousands more Basques returned wounded and many were disabled. Two generations of males were severely reduced in number, with consequences on the demographics of the villages.[1]

However, authorities, churchmen, and journalists continued to preach the prewar message: the dead son, brother, or father had fallen for France, "pour la patrie." (They implied that those who had lost an arm or a leg, or even those who had returned disfigured, could also be proud of themselves.) Moreover, theirs was a heroic death and a sacrifice that honored them. It would have been hard for the authorities, churchmen, and journalists to admit that the deaths were for nothing, that they were unjust. To believe that their loved ones had died victorious, in the name of justice and "civilization," fighting against "barbarians," gave people more comfort. The work previously undertaken by the school and the army was crowned by the loss of blood. At school, Basques, as well as others, had been linked to France in theory, but with the war they felt the link to France in their flesh, through their blood. Because of that, the war's impact on Basque culture was important. Demobilized Basque soldiers had been culturally assimilated into French society.[2] Moreover, thousands of widows and orphans, thousands of the wounded and invalids, experienced their grief as the link that bound them to France, and France welcomed them into her bosom, as many war memorials show.

The political consequences of the First World War in the Northern Basque Country did not end on November 11, 1918, because the process of nation-building continued. Just as the prewar population had been prepared for war politically, psychologically, and physically, so the postwar population was subjected to political use of the conflict. To this end, pensions were distributed to widows, orphans, and invalids. Commemoration was also given great importance, with the first commemoration taking place when the soldiers returned home. For example, when the soldiers of the 49th Infantry Regiment returned to Baiona on July 27, 1919, after the war had officially ended on June 24 with Germany's admission of defeat, they were welcomed with honors in the streets of Baiona. A parade moved through the streets, bunches of flowers were offered to the dead, war crosses were borne. In every street, as soldiers passed they could see placards paying them tribute with inscriptions such as "Merci aux sauveurs de la Patrie" (Thank you to the saviors of the Motherland), and around them flew thousands of French flags. At the ceremony held at the town hall, Lieutenant-Colonel Louis Gaussot exclaimed, in French, "Vive Baiona! Vive le Pays Basque!" (Long live France! Long live the Republic!). This was followed by "La Marseillaise" and the Basque song "Gernikako Arbola" ("The Tree of Guernica").[3]

When the Basque Country was evoked at this ceremony, it was to link it to France, in line with the concept of "petite patrie et grande patrie," or small homeland and large homeland, developed at the end of the nineteenth century. War memorials fulfilled the same function. From 1919 onward, these monuments were built in every village. Each village took the initiative and, depending on its budget and the number of dead in the community, erected a monument of relevant size. Some monuments were sober, bearing only the inscription "Morts pour la France" or "Morts pour la patrie," while others took on political, religious, or even symbolic significance with the addition of sculptures. The messages conveyed by these monuments—such as those in Donibane Lohizune, Hendaia, Baiona, Biarritz, Getaria, Urruña, Ziburu, or Maule—provide much basis for future analysis. Some monuments are more ornate than others, but the message always revolves around sacrifice or martyrdom and symbolizes life offered to the motherland. The one in Maule is particularly significant, as it depicts a child being shown the list of the dead, thus representing the passing on of a legacy.

Another monument, the one erected on the Chemin des Dames in the community of Craonnelle, pays tribute to all that the Basques did for France. This large obelisk commemorates the role played by the Basques, the Béarnais, and the Landais in those lands in support of France. It was built on a summit from which the villages of Craonnelle and Oulches can be seen. When visitors to this region consider the war, they can see the decisive role played by the Basques, made obvious by the Basque names on many of the graves in the Craonnelle military cemetery. Known as the Monument des Basques, the obelisk is now one of the region's main monuments and places of remembrance. It was inaugurated in 1928, and since then it has been a symbol of the bond between the Basques and France. The idea for the monument came from several veterans from the Basque Country, the area of Béarn, and of the Landes; and a fundraising campaign was organized in order to erect it. The communities of the Northern Basque Country also contributed to the financing of this work.

The purpose of war memorials, in addition to paying tribute to the dead, was to organize commemorative ceremonies around them, to recall and glorify the blood shed for France by each village. As Hubert Pérès explains, the installation of the monument to the dead in the village square was strongly motivated by the fact that the dead had given their lives for a nation or a homeland; but at the same time, the dead were the children of the village.[4] The nation was an abstract concept, whereas the village was a more tangible one. It would have been different if the names of all the dead had been inscribed on a stone in Paris, where without an emotional connection the inhabitants would have experienced the memorial as something distant. Placing war memorials in the village square was meant to bring the village and the nation together. For the monument physically proved that the village belonged to the French nation. The presence of France is, thus, felt daily in all the village squares through the words "Morts pour la France" (Dead for France) inscribed on the monuments, through the French flags displayed, and through the annual November 11 ceremonies. Just as the end of the First World War is celebrated on November 11, a similar ceremony is held in the Basque Country on May 8 to mark the end of the Second World War. As a rule, tributes to veterans are held twice a year, and their main function is to ensure that every village in the Basque Country, like every village in France, feels that it belongs to France.

This war was not the final event to unite the Northern Basque Country with France, but it was the most important. Not until the second half of the twentieth century did a different national vision emerge. From the point of view of today's Basque nationalists, the Basques gave their lives for a country that was not theirs. However, for a large majority of the population, and until recently, this was not the case. The families of the dead did not protest because their sons, fathers, and brothers died for a country that was not theirs.

The same phenomenon can be seen in Brittany and Corsica. Numerical disagreements have always taken place over the number of dead sacrificed for France from these two territories. Around 12,000 Corsicans lost their lives in this conflict. The Corsican death toll was slightly higher than the French average, at 3.3 percent. Also, 130,000 Bretons died in the war, representing between 3.6 and 4.5 percent of the population of that region. As in the case of the Northern Basque Country, Bretons and Corsicans were linked to France by loss of blood. Figures for the Northern Basque Country are lower than French averages, but when we look at age groups, they are truly significant. Nearly half of the Basques who died in the war were under twenty-eight. The French average for this age group was less than 30 percent. It is impossible to justify with numbers alone whether there was an intention to sacrifice Basque youth, but the idea may be worth investigating.

In short, the Northern Basque Country became much more French as a result of the bloodshed of the 1914 war and the monuments and tributes that followed. The veterans themselves, and the celebrations organized around them, played an important role in this Frenchification, and even more so at the end of the Second World War, although in the latter case there were fewer Basques among the victims (as France was to immediately lose the war against Germany).

Among the 1914 veterans, there were manifold profiles; some were linked to the communist movement, while others had slipped toward the extreme Right. The former was against war. However, most of the profiles were of pacifists, and they did not want another war. Under the influence of the pacifist movement, France did not venture to take military action against Nazism. Given Marshal Pétain's status among them, veterans readily accepted the agreement signed with Hitler in 1940. Those close to the Catholic Church in the Northern Basque Country, as well as Jean Ybarnégaray, the MP at the time, remained loyal to Pétain.

Only twenty-one years separated the end of the First World War from the start of the Second. Germany regained its power. In 1918, while the French tasted the joy of victory, the end of hostilities had left a very different taste in Germany, where the population experienced the Treaty of Versailles as a humiliation. Germany, as such, had not really suffered any material damage, since the war had mainly been fought in neighboring countries. The Germans had not believed that a military defeat was possible, and they now felt the limits imposed on their army, as well as the harshness of the economic sanctions, as an injustice. Hitler himself was a war veteran, and this sense of humiliation was not unconnected with his later intentions. The signatories to the Treaty of Versailles had been keen to show Germany as the defeated country and to sanction it. However, by failing to sufficiently empower the League of Nations—whose objective was to ensure peace—the nations of the world were unable to implement and guarantee the measures needed to make peace a lasting reality. This dark chapter in history shows that an ill-conceived peace based on humiliation can never be a good long-term solution.

NOTES

1. Jacob, *Hills of Conflict: Basque Nationalism in France*, 55.
2. Jacob, *Hills of Conflict: Basque Nationalism in France*, 55.
3. *Historique du 49e régiment d'infanterie pendant la guerre 1914–1918.*
4. Pérès, "Identité communale, République et communalisation: À propos des monuments aux morts des villages," 667.

BIBLIOGRAPHY

Adéma, Blaise. "Eskualdun deputatua." *Eskualduna*, 20 July 1917.
———. "Ez ahantz." *Eskualduna*, 8 December 1916.
———. "Verdun." *Eskualduna*, 10 November 1916.
Adema, Gratien. "Maria bekhaturik gabe kontzebitua." *Eskualduna*, 7 August 1908.
Almeida (d'), Fabrice, and Christian Delporte. *Histoire des médias en France: De la Grande Guerre à nos jours*. Paris: Flammarion, 2003.
Altzibar, Xabier. "Zazpiak bat gaia XIX. Mendean" [The zazpiak bat topic in the nineteenth century]. In *Antoine d'Abbadie (1897–1997), Congrès international Eusko Ikas- kuntza, Ez ohizko kongresua. Eskualtzaindia. XIV biltzarra*, 663–688. Donostia–San Sebastián: Eusko Ikaskuntza, 1998.
Ambrosi, Christian. *L'apogée de l'Europe, 1871–1918*. [1987]. Paris: Armand Colin, 1996.
Ansoborlo, Jean. *Histoire militaire de Bayonne: 1789–1940*. Bayonne: Société des Siences Lettres et Arts de Bayonne, 1995.
Archives Départemantales de Pyrénées-Atlantiques, 1 M 95, "Lettre du préfet des Basses-Pyrénées au ministre de l'Intérieur, 1er décembre 1914."
Aubert, Paul. "La presse espagnole et son public (1914–1918)." PhD diss., Université de Pau et des Pays de l'Adour, 1983.
Audoin-Rouzeau, Stéphane. *A travers leurs journaux: 14–18, les combattants des tranchées*. Paris: Armand Colin, 1986.
Audoin-Rouzeau, Stéphane and Annette Becker. "Violence et consentement: La "culture de guerre" du premier conflit mondial." In *Pour une histoire culturelle*. Edited by Jean-Pierre Roux and Jean-François Sirinelli, 251–271. Paris: Seuil, 1997.
Bach, André. *Fusillés pour l'exemple: 1914–1915*. Paris: Tallandier, 2003.
Balcells, Albert. "Los voluntarios catalanes en la Gran Guerra (1914–1918)." *Historia 16*, no. 121 (1986): 51–62.
Baratay, Eric. *Bêtes des tranchées: Des vécus oubliés*. Paris: CNRS, 2013.
Barbier, Jean. "Eskualdun soldado bat gerlan." *Eskualduna*, 27 November 1914.
Bascans, Aline, and Xipri Arbelbide. "Uztaritzeko seroren eskolen hestea." In *Elizak eta Estatua bereizteko legea: ondorioak Euskal Herrian (1905–1906)*, 31–37. Donostia–San Sebastián: Eusko Ikaskuntza, 2008.
Becker, Jean-Jacques. *1914: Comment les Français sont entrés dans la guerre*. Paris: Presses de la Fondation Nationale des Sciences Politiques, 1977.

———. *La France en guerre 1914–1918: La grande mutation*. Brussels: Editions Complexe, 1988.

———. "La population française face à l'entrée en guerre." In *Les Sociétés européennes et la guerre, 1914–1918: Actes du colloque d'Amiens-Nanterre, 8–11 décembre 1988*. Edited by Jean-Jacques Becker and Stéphane Audoin-Rouzeau, 35–38. Nanterre: Publication de l'université de Nanterre, 1990.

Becker, Jean-Jacques, and Stéphane Audoin-Rouzeau. *La France, la nation, la guerre: 1850–1920*. Paris: Sedes, 1995.

Bérenger, Jean. *L'Autriche-Hongrie: 1815–1918*. [1994]. Paris: Armand Colin, 1998.

———. *L'Empire austro-hongrois: 1815–1918*. Paris: Armand Colin, 2011.

Bidegain, Eneko. *Gerla Handia, muga sakona*. Donostia–San Sebastián: Utriusque Vasconiae, 2009.

———. "Lehen Mundu Gerra '*Eskualduna*' astekarian." PhD diss. Bordeaux 3; EHU, 2012.

Bidegain, Eneko, and Gostin, Andres. "1914ko hauteskundekanpaina Eskualduna astekarian." *Uztaro*, no. 90 (2014): 25–40.

Bonnefous, Georges, Édouard Bonnefous, and André Siegfried. *Histoire politique de la Troisième République. L'avant-guerre (1906–1914)*. [1956]. Paris: Presses universitaires de France, 1965.

Boulanger, Philippe. "Le refus de l'impôt du sang: Géographie de l'insoumission en France de 1914 à 1922." *Guerres mondiales et conflits contemporains*, no.188 (1997): 3–25.

Brunel, Christian. "L'Académie bretonne au grand séminaire de Quimper." In *Les parlers de la foi, religion et langues régionales*. Edited by Michel Lagree-k argitaratua, 31–46. Rennes: Presses Universitaires de Rennes, 1995.

Cabanel, Patrick. *1905, la séparation des Églises et de l'État*. La Crèche: Geste, 2005.

———. *La question nationale au XIXe siècle*. Paris: La Découverte, 1997.

———. "Sentiments nationaux et terre "irredente." In *Encyclopédie de la Grande Guerre 1914–1918. Histoire et culture*. Edited by Stéphane Audoin-Rouzeau and Jean-Jacques Becker, 35–47. Paris: Bayard, 2004.

Cabanes, Bruno. "Ce que dit le contrôle postal." In *Vrai et faux dans la Grande guerre*. Edited by Christophe Prochasson and Anne Rasmussen, 55–76. Paris: La Découverte, 2004.

———. *La victoire endeuillée: La sortie de guerre des soldats français (1918–1920)*. Paris: Seuil, 2004.

Camino, Iñaki. "Hitzaurrea." In *Gontzetarik jalgiaraziak*. Edited by Jean Hiriart-Urruty. Donostia–San Sebastián: Euskal Editoreen Elkartea, 1994.

Caro Baroja, Julio. *Historia general del país vasco*. Vol. 11. Bilbo-Bilbao and Donostia–San Sebastián: La Gran enciclopedia vasca; L. Haranburu, 1981.

Caron, Jean-Claude, and Michel Vernus. *L'Europe au XIXe siècle: Des nations aux nationalismes, 1815–1914*. Paris: A. Colin, 1996.

Casenave, Jon. *De l'article de presse à l'essai littéraire: Buruchkak (1910) de Jean Etchepare*. Madrid: Universidad Nacional de Educación a Distancia, 2002.

Castiella, Manuel. *Un siècle à Bayonne: 1900–2000*. Anglet: Atlantica, 2003.

Cazals, Rémy, and Nicolas Offenstad. "Du Bois-le-Prêtre au 'Front intérieur': Les expériences de guerre des Papillon." In *Si je reviens, comme je l'espère: Lettres du front et de l'arrière*. Paris: Grasset, 2003.

Cazals, Rémy, and Frédéric Rousseau. *14–18, le cri d'une génération*. Toulouse: Privat, 2001.

Charle, Christophe. "Région et conscience régionale: Questions à propos d'un colloque." *Actes de la recherche en sciences sociales* 35 (1980): 37–43.

Charriton, Pierre. *Pierre Broussain, sa contribution aux études basques (1895–1920)*. Bordeaux: CNRS, 1985.

———. *Jean Saint-Pierre "Anxuberro" (1884–1951)*. Vitoria-Gasteiz: Eusko Jaurlaritza, 2003.

Cholvy, Gérard. "Régionalisme et clergé catholique au XIXe siècle." In *Régions et régionalisme en France du XVIIIe siècle à nos jours*. Edited by Christian Gras and Georges Livet, 187–201. Paris: Presses universitaires de France, 1977.

Cierva, Ricardo (de la). *Hijos de la gloria y la mentira: Historia de los vascos entre España y la Antiespaña*. Madrid: Editorial Fénix, 2004.

Cochet, François. *Survivre au front, 1914–1918: Les poilus entre contrainte et consentement*. Saint-Cloud: 14-18 Editions, 2005.

Cohen, Yolande. "L'antimilitarisme des jeunesses avant 1914." *Matériaux pour l'histoire de notre temps*, no.16 (1989): 42–48.

Colonel (Le) commandant le 57e R.I. Bussy. *57e régiment d'infanterie: "Le terrible que rien n'arrête": Historique du régiment pendant la grande guerre 1914–1918*. Rochefort: Imprimerie Norbertine, 1921.

Cortés-Cavanillas, Julián. *Alfonso XIII y la guerra del 14*. Madrid: Alce, 1976.

Cronier, Emmanuelle. "Permissions et permissionnaires." In *Encyclopédie de la Grande Guerre 1914–1918: Histoire et culture*. Edited by Stéphane Audoin-Rouzeau and Jean-Jacques Becker, 591–600. Paris: Bayard, 2004.

Cru, Jean-Norton. *Du témoignage*. Paris: Gallimard, 1930.

Cubero, José-Ramón. *La Grande Guerre et l'arrière (1914–1919)*. Pau: Cairn, 2007.

Darrigrand, Pierre. "La guerre de 1870–1871 à Bayonne et dans les environs." *Revue d'histoire de Bayonne, du Pays-Basque et du bas-Adour*, no. 154 (1999): 255–302.

Delaunay, Jean-Marc. "1914: Les Espagnols et la guerre." In *Les Sociétés européennes et la guerre, 1914–1918: Actes du colloque d'Amiens-Nanterre, 8–11 décembre 1988*. Edited by Jean-Jacques Becker and Stéphane Audoin-Rouzeau, 117–132. Nanterre: Publication de l'Université de Nanterre, 1990.

———. "La grande guerre ou la clé du retour." *Mélanges de la Casa de Velazquez*, no. 19 (1983): 347–368.

Díaz Plaja, Fernando. *Francofilos y germanofilos: Los españoles en la guerra europea*. [1973]. Madrid: Alianza, 1981.

Dolosor, Franck. *Matxin Irabola: Senpereko bertsularia*. Baiona-Bayonne: Elkar, 2010.

Doucet, Marc. "Estadoaren eta Elizaren arteko borrokak 1900 inguruan: Fraide batzuen ihardespena Belokeko fraidetxean." In *Elizak eta Estatua bereizteko legea: Ondorioak Euskal Herrian (1905–1906)*, 39–47. Donostia–San Sebastián: Eusko Ikaskuntza, 2008.

Duby, Georges, and Armand Wallon. *Histoire de la France rurale*. Vol. 3, *Apogée et crise de la civilisation paysanne: 1789–1914*. Paris: Le Seuil, 1976.

Elias, Norbert. *La civilisation des moeurs* [Über den Prozess der Zivilisation]. Translated by Pierre Kamnitzer [1973]. Paris: Presses Pocket, 2002.

Elissalde, Jean. *LVII.a gerlan*. Edited by Patri Urkizu. Zarautz: Alberdania, 1995.

Elissondo, Robert, ed. *Mémoires de la Soule 1914–1918: Une petite vallée du Pays Basque dans la guerre*. Maule: Ikerzaleak, 2006.

Elizalde, Jean. "Aroa." *Eskualduna*, 14 July 1916.

———. "Aroa." *Eskualduna*, 2 November 1917.

———. "Arratoinak." *Eskualduna*, 4 August 1916.

———. "Azken solasa." *Eskualduna*, 12 January 1917.

———. "Bi hitz aroaz." *Eskualduna*, 7 July 1918.

———. "Diren bezalako zoroak!" *Eskualduna*, 2 July 1916.

——— "Gure ametsak." *Eskualduna*, 9 June 1916.

——— "Hemengo bazterra." *Eskualduna*, 27 July 1917.

——— "Igandeak." *Eskualduna*, 3 November 1916.

——— "Laborari etchalde handi." *Eskualduna*, 11 August 1916.

———. "Nola lotsa holako soldadoak?" *Eskualduna*, 18 January 1918.

———. "On dakiotela!" *Eskualduna*, 21 January 1916.

———. "Oraiko egunak!" *Eskualduna*, 21 July 1916.

———. "Oraiko gure berri." *Eskualduna*, 12 October 1917.

———. "Zer dioten gerlariek", *Eskualduna*, 22 November 1918

Elosegi, Xabier. "Jean-Baptiste Elizanbururen bizitza." *Euskera* 37 (1992): 83–107.

Espadas Burgos, Manuel. "España y la neutralidad en la Gran Guerra." *Historia 16*, no. 5 (1983).

Etchepare, Jean. "Alemanak hurbiletik IV." *Eskualduna*, 13 November 1914.

———. "Ez urririk." *Eskualduna*, 22 June 1917.

———. "Lanik nekeena." *Eskualduna*, 21 January 1916.

———. "Mailka." *Eskualduna*, 21 January 1916.

Fabas, Philippe. "Aspects de la vie religieuse dans le diocèse de Bayonne (1905–1965)." PhD diss., Michel de Montaigne, Bordeaux III, 1999.

Fassy, Gérard. *Le commandement français en orient: octobre 1915–novembre 1918: Étude historique d'un commandement opérationnel français à la tête d'une force militaire alliée*. Paris: Economica, 2003.

Ferro, Marc. *La Grande Guerre*. [1969]. Paris: Gallimard, 1990.
Feyel, Gilles. *La presse en France des origines à 1944: Histoire politique et matérielle*. Paris: Ellipses, 1999.
Fischer, Fritz. *Les buts de guerre de l'Allemagne impériale, 1914–1918* [Griff nach der Weltmacht]. Translated by Geneviève Migeon and Henri Thiès. Paris: Ed. de Trévise, 1970.
Fontana, Jacques. *Les catholiques français pendant la Grande Guerre*. Paris: Cerf, 1990.
Forcade, Olivier. "Dans l'oeil de la censure: Voir ou ne pas voir la guerre." In *Vrai et faux dans la Grande Guerre*. Edited by Christophe Prochasson and Anne Rasmussen, 35–54. Paris: La Découverte, 2004.
———. "La censure politique en France pendant la Grande Guerre." PhD diss., Université Paris-X Nanterre, 1999.
Fraenkel, Roger. "Le général Joffre, cet âne qui commandait des lions." In *Atlas, Histoire critique du XXe siècle*, 98. Paris: Le Monde Diplomatique, 2010.
Galiano, Alvaro Alcalá. *España ante el conflicto europeo 1914–1915*. Est. tip. "Sucesores de Rivadeneyra," 1916.
Garat, Jacques. "Insoumissions et désertions en France pendant la Grande Guerre: Le cas des cantons basques." Master's thesis, EHESS, 1983.
Garate Ojanguren, Montserrat, and Javier Martín Rudi. *Cien años de la vida económica de San Sebastián: 1887–1987*. Donostia–San Sebastián: Fundación Social y Cultural KUTXA, 1995.
Gerbod, Paul. "L'éthique héroïque en France (1870–1914)." *Revue Historique* 544 (1982): 409–429.
Girardet, Raoul. *Le nationalisme français. Anthologie 1871–1914*. Paris: Seuil, 1983.
Goñi, Beñat. "Interdiction du catéchisme en basque." In *Elizak eta Estatua bereizteko legea: Ondorioak Euskal Herrian (1905–1906)*. Edited by Xipri Arbelbide, 49–55. Donostia–San Sebastián: Eusko Ikaskuntza, 2008.
Goyhenetche, Manex. *Histoire générale du Pays Basque: Le XIXe siecle 1804–1914*. Donostia–San Sebastián, Baiona: Elkarlanean, 2005.
———. "Les origines sociales de l'association Eskualzaleen Biltzarra." *Bulletin du Musée Basque* (1993): 1–68.
Guiomar, Jean-Yves. "Régionalisme, fédéralisme et minorité nationales en France entre 1919 et 1939." *Le mouvement social* 70 (1970): 89–108.
Hiriart-Urruti, Manex. "Berri onak." *Eskualduna*, 19 March 1915.
———. "Bortz haurren aita." *Eskualduna*, 26 July 1915.
———. "Eguberri gerlan." *Eskualduna*, 25 December 1914.
———. "Eskualdun kaputchin soldadoa." *Eskualduna*, 11 December 1914.
———. "Noiz finituko?" *Eskualduna*, 2 April 1915.
———. "Soldado ona." *Eskualduna*, 9 July 1915.
Historia de Euskal Herria (Orreaga). Tafalla: Txalaparta, 1995.

Historique du 18e régiment d'infanterie pendant la guerre de 1914–1918. Nancy: Imprimerie Berger-Levrault, 1920.
Historique du 49e régiment d'infanterie pendant la guerre 1914–1918. Nancy: Berger-Levrault, 1919.
Historique du 123e régiment d'Infanterie: Campagne 1914–1918. Paris-Nancy: Librairie Chapelot, 1919.
Historique du 172e régiment d'infanterie pendant la Grande Guerre 1914–1919. Paris: Imprimerie P. Orsoni, 1919.
Isnenghi, Mario. *La Première Guerre Mondiale* [La prima guerra mondiale]. Translated by Fabrice d'Almeida. Firenze: Casterman, 1993.
Itçaina, Xabier. *Les virtuoses de l'identité. Religion et politique en Pays Basque.* Rennes: Presses Universitaires de Rennes, 2007.
Jacob, James. *Hills of Conflict: Basque Nationalism in France.* Reno: University of Nevada Press, 1994.
Jeissmann, Michael. *La patrie de l'ennemi, la notion de l'ennemi national et la représentation de la nation en Allemagne et en France de 1792 à 1918.* Paris: CNRS Editions, 1997.
Joly, Bertrand. "Le souvenir de 1870 et la place de la Revanche." In *Encyclopédie de la Grande Guerre 1914–1918: Histoire et culture.* Edited by Stéphane Audoin-Rouzeau and Jean-Jacques Becker, 109–124. Paris: Bayard, 2004.
Jourdan, Jean-Paul. "Noms des morts à la guerre ou des suites au Pays Basque et à Bayonne." *Bulletin de la Société des Sciences, Lettres et Arts de Bayonne* (2012).
Kintana, Jurgi. *Intelektuala nazioa eraikitzen: R. M. Azkueren pentsaera eta obra.* Euskaltzaindia, 2008.
Kott, Sandrine. *L'Allemagne du XIXe siècle.* Paris: Hachette, 1999.
Krumeich, Gerd. "L'entrée en guerre en Allemagne." In *Les Sociétés européennes et la guerre, 1914–1918: Actes du colloque d'Amiens-Nanterre, 8–11 décembre 1988.* Edited by Jean-Jacques Becker and Stéphane Audoin-Rouzeau, 65–74. Nanterre: Publication de l'université de Nanterre, 1990.
Kurtz, Harold. *Le Deuxième Reich: l'Allemagne de Guillaume II* [The Second Reich: Kaiser Wilhelm II and his Germany]. Translated by F. Didier-Lauber. Ed. Rencontre, 1971.
Labaien, Antonio Maria. *Elizanburu bere bizitza ta lanak: Su vida y obras.* Donostia: Auñamendi, 1978.
Lachaga, José Maria. *Eglise particulière et minorités ethniques, jalons pour l'évangélisation des peuples minoritaires.* Paris: Le Centurion, 1978.
Lafitte, Piarres. "Oxobi hil zaiku." *Herria*, 13 February 1958.
Laharie, Claude. *Les Basses-Pyrénées pendant la guerre 1914–1918.* Pau: Archives départementales des Pyrénées-Atlantiques, 1982.
Langlois, Claude. "Catholiques et laïcs." In *Les lieux de mémoire.* Vol. 2, *La Nation, les Frances.* Edited by Pierre Nora, 2327–2357. Paris: Gallimard, 1997.

Lapeyre, Gaston. "Une 'base aéronavale' à Bayonne: 1917–1918." In *Passé, présent et avenir du Port de Bayonne. Congrès des 16–17 avril 1999*, 235–244. Baiona: Société des Sciences Lettres et Arts de Bayonne, 2000.

Latour, Francis. *La Papauté et les problèmes de la paix pendant la première guerre mondiale*. Paris: L'Harmattan, 1996.

Livois (de), René. *Histoire de la presse française: 2, de 1881 à nos jours*. Lausanne: Spes, 1965.

Mariot, Nicolas. "Faut-il être motivé pour tuer? Sur quelques explications aux violences de guerre." *Génèses*, no. 53 (2003): 154–177.

Martinien, Aristide. *La Guerre de 1870–1871—La Mobilistation de l'Armee—Mouvements des dépots*. Paris: L. Fournier, 1912.

Mathieu, Frédéric. *14–18, les fusillés*. Malakoff, France: Éd. Sébirot, 2013.

Mayeur, Jean-Marie. "Les catholiques français et Benoît XV en 1917." In *Chrétiens dans la Première Guerre mondiale*. Edited by Nadine-Josette Chaline, 153–165. Paris: Cerf, 1993.

Menéndez Pidal, Ramón. *Historia de España*. Vol. 38, *La España de Alfonso XIII: El estado y la política (1902–1931)*. Madrid: Espasa Calpe, 1995.

Meyer, Jacques. *La vie quotidienne des soldats pendant la Grande Guerre*. Paris: Hachette, 1966.

Micheu-Puyou, Jean. *Histoire électorale du département des Basses-Pyrénées sous la IIIe et la IVe République*. Paris: Librairie générale de droit et de jurisprudence, 1965.

Minois, Georges. *L'Église et la guerre: De la Bible à l'ère atomique*. Paris: Fayard, 1994.

Miquel, Pierre. *La grande guerre au jour le jour*. Paris: Fayard, 1988.

Montero, Manuel. *La modernización capitalista: Ciclos económicos y desarrollo empresarial de Vizcaya entre 1891 y 1936 a través de la Bolsa de Bilbao*. Historia contemporánea 30. Bilbo: Euskal Herriko Unibertsitatea, 2005.

Morales Lezcano, Victor. "España y la Primera Guerra Mundial: La intelectualidad del 14 ante la guerra." *Historia 16*, no .63 (1981): 44–52.

Morales Lezcano, Víctor, Gabriel Cardona, and Jean-Marc Delaunay. *España y la Primera Guerra Mundial*. Grupo 16, 1985.

Moulin, Annie. *Les paysans dans la société française: De la Révolution à nos jours*. Paris: Seuil, 1988.

Moulier, Jules "Oxobi." "Atso bat." *Eskualduna*, 1 March 1918.

———. "Gauberri armadetan." *Eskualduna*, 25 December 1914.

———. "Iheskaria", *Eskualduna*, 16 April 1915.

———. "Gerla." *Eskualduna*, 11 November 1914.

———. "Izkilak eta banderak", *Eskualduna*, 22 November 1918.

———. "Josteta." *Eskualduna*, 15 March 1918.

Navet, Françoise. "Verdun et la censure." *Guerres mondiales et conflits contemporains*, no. 182 (1996): 45–56.

Notes sur l'éducation morale du soldat: 13e corps d'armée. 25e division. 49e brigade. 38e régiment d'infanterie. Lyon: Imp S Pelletier, 1879.

Offenstad, Nicolas, Philippe Olivera, Emmanuelle Picard, and Frédéric Rousseau. "À propos d'une notion récente: La "culture de guerre." In *Guerres, paix et sociétés, 1911–1946*. Edited by Frédéric Rousseau, 667–674. Neuilly: Atlande, 2004.
"Orok bat." *Eskualduna*, 7 August 1914.
Orpustan, Jean-Baptiste. "Rôle et pouvoirs de l'Eglise." In *La nouvelle société basque*, 108–158. Paris: L'Harmattan, 1980.
Ott, Sandra. *War, Judgment, and Memory in the Basque Borderlands, 1914–1945*. The Basque Series. Reno: University of Nevada Press, 2008.
Ozouf, Mona. *L'Ecole, l'Eglise et la République (1871–1914)*. [1963]. Paris: Cana, 1982.
Pedroncini, Guy. *Les mutineries de l'armée française*. Paris: Presses universitaires de France, 1967.
Pérès, Hubert. "Identité communale, République et communalisation: A propos des monuments aux morts des villages." *Revue de Science politique* 39, no. 5 (1989): 665–682.
Pontet, Josette. *Histoire de Bayonne*. Toulouse: Privat, 1991.
Pourcher, Yves. "Les clichés de la Grande Guerre: Entre histoire et fiction." *Terrain*, no. 34 (2000): 143–158.
Prévotat, Jacques. *L'Action française*. Paris: Presses universitaires de France, 2004.
Prior, Robin, and Trevor Wilson. *La Première Guerre mondiale 1914–1918*. [The First World War]. Translated by Alex Girod. Paris: Editions Autrement, 2001.
Prost, Antoine, and Jay Winter. *Penser la Grande Guerre: Un essai d'historiographie*. Paris: Seuil, 2004.
Rajsfus, Maurice. *La censure militaire et policière 1914–1918*. Paris: Le Cherche Midi, 1999.
Rocafort, Joël. *Avant oubli: Soldats et civils de la côte basque durant la grande guerre*. Biarritz: Atlantica, 1997.
Roldán, Santiago, and José Luis García Delgado. *La formación de la sociedad capitalista en España*. Madrid, 1973.
Roth, François. *La guerre de 1870*. [1990]. Paris: Fayard, 1993.
Rousseau, Frédéric. *La guerre censurée: Une histoire des combattants européens de 14–18*. Paris: Seuil, 1999.
Ruquet, Miquèl. "Les déserteurs français de la Première Guerre Mondiale et la guerre d'Espagne." *Le Midi Rouge, Bulletin de l'Association Maitron Languedoc-Roussillon*, Perpinya, 2007, 32–36.
———. "Désertions et insoumissions sur la frontière des Pyrénées pendant la guerre de 1914–1918." PhD diss., Université de Perpignan Via Domita, 2009.
———. "Désertions et insoumissions sur la frontière des Pyrénées pendant la guerre de 14–18." In *Mémoire et trauma de la Grande Guerre: Bretagne, Catalogne, Corse, Euskadi, Occitanie*. Edited by Gwendal Denis, 65–93. Rennes: Rennes 2 Université Haute Bretagne, 2010.

———. "Insoumis et déserteurs pyrénéens de la Grande Guerre: La force des liens transfrontaliers." n.d.
Saint-Pierre, Jean. "Bero." *Eskualduna*, 11 August 1916.
———. "Eta hemen?" *Eskualduna*, 22 September 1916.
———. "Gerlarien berri." *Eskualduna*, 4 December 1914.
———. "Gudu baten irabazia." *Eskualduna*, 11 May 1917.
———. "Gure deputatu eskualduna." *Eskualduna*, 14 January 1914.
———. "Herriak." *Eskualduna*, 25 June 1915.
———. "Italiaren laguntza." *Eskualduna*, 7 May 1915.
———. "Kuraia." *Eskualduna*, 75 March 1915.
———. "Lerroetatik urrun." *Eskualduna*, 10 June 1916.
———. "Nor baliatuko?" *Eskualduna*, 16 July 1915.
———. "Permisioneak." *Eskualduna*, 23 July 1915.
———. "Toki berean." *Eskualduna*, 27 October 1916.
———. "Zer ari giren." *Eskualduna*, 19 May 1916.
Saly, Pierre, Alice Gérard, Céline Gervais, and Marie-Pierre Rey. *Nations et nationalismes en Europe: 1848–1914*. Paris: Armand Colin, 1996.
Sarramone, Alberto. *Les cousins basques d'Amérique*. Biarritz: J&D Editions, 1997.
Sohier, Anne. "L'enfant et la guerre à l'école primaire: En Bretagne, 1871–1914." In *Mémoire et trauma de la Grande Guerre: Bretagne, Catalogne, Corse, Euskadi, Occitanie*. Edited by Gwendal Denis, 11–30. Rennes: Rennes 2 Université Haute Bretagne, 2010.
Soutou, Georges-Henri, and Jean-Baptiste Duroselle. *L'or et le sang: Les buts de guerre économiques de la Première Guerre mondiale*. Paris: Fayard, 1989.
Tapié, Victor-Lucien. *Les nationalités slaves d'Autriche-Hongrie de 1850 à 1914*. Les Cours de Sorbonne. Paris: Centre de Documentation Universitaire, 1962.
Thiesse, Anne-Marie. *Ils apprenaient la France: L'exaltation des régions dans le discours patriotique*. Paris: Éditions de la Maison des sciences de l'homme, 1997.
———. *La création des identités nationales: Europe, XVIIIe–XXe siècle*. [1999]. Paris: Seuil, 2001.
Txirrita, "Bertso berriak (Europa'ko gerra, 1914–1918)." In *Ustu ezin zan ganbara (Txirritaren zenbait bertso eta gertaera)*. Edited by Antonio Zavala, 19–22. Tolosa: Auspoa liburutegia, 1976.
Urkiza, Julen. *Elizaren Historia Euskal Herrian: Ikerlan materialak*. Vol. 1 of *Vasconia sacra*. Markina: El Carmen, 1995.
Vallaud, Pierre. *14–18: La Première Guerre mondiale*. Paris: Acropole, 2008.
Vicens Vives, Jaime. *Historia económica de España: 9a*. Barcelona: Ed. Barcelona, 1972.
Vigier, Philippe. "Régions et régionalisme en France au XIXe siècle." In *Régions et régionalisme en France du XVIIIe siècle à nos jours*, 161–176. Paris: Presses universitaires de France, 1977.

Walter, Henriette, and Michel Lagree. *Les parlers de la foi, religion et langues régionales*. Rennes: Presses Universitaires de Rennes, 1995.

Wawro, Geoffrey. *The Franco-Prussian War: The German Conquest of France in 1870–1871*. Cambridge: Cambridge University Press, 2003.

Weber, Eugen. *L'Action française* [Action Française, royalism and reaction in twentieth-century France]. Translated by Michel Chrestien. Paris: Stock, 1964.

———. *La fin des terroirs, la modernisation de la France rurale, 1870–1914* [Peasants into Frenchmen: The modernization of rural France, 1870–1914]. Translated by Antoine Berman and Bernard Génies. Paris: Fayard, 1984.

INDEX

2nd Army, 51
2nd Battalion, 109
3rd Colonial Infantry Regiment, 52
4th Army, 52, 54
5th Army, 54, 56
12th Infantry Regiment, 40, 150
18th Army Corps, 38, 51–52
18th Infantry Regiment, 38–39, 56–57, 87, 104, 109
34th Infantry Regiment, 40, 150
49th Infantry Regiment, 27, 38–39, 51–54, 56–57, 66, 104, 109, 150, 157
57th Infantry Regiment, 40, 57, 88, 104
58th Artillery Regiment, 78
142nd Territorial Infantry Regiment, 40, 53, 150
144th Infantry Regiment, 52, 150
249th Infantry Regiment, 39–40, 56, 150
344th Infantry Regiment, 52, 150
418th Infantry Regiment, 102

Action Française, 10, 12n18, 19, 28, 71
Adema, Blaise, 87, 91, 95n24, 95n26
"Agur Euskal Herriari", 8
Ahatsa, 140, 144
Ahaxe, 144, 140. *See also* Ahatsa
Aia, 141, 146
Aiherra, 147
Ailles, 108
Ainharbe, 144, 147
Ainhoa, 143, 147
Aintzila, 147
aircraft, 79–80, 135

Aisne, 54, 103, 108, 132, 148, 150–151
Aisne River, 54, 56, 61
Aiziritze-Gamue-Zohazti, 143, 147
Akamarre, 142, 147
Alba, Santiago, 83
Aldude, 69, 145, 147
Aldudes, 69, 145. *See also* Aldude
Allées Boufflers, 39
the Allies, 37, 42–46, 53, 61–62, 71, 79, 92, 96–99, 105–106, 107, 110–111, 129–133, 135–138
Allied troops, 111, 131
Almandoz, 141, 146
Alsace, 5–6, 9–11, 19–20, 51, 102, 133, 136, 155
Alsace-Lorraine, 6, 9, 92, 135
Altza, 141, 146
Altzai-Altzabeheti-Zunharreta, 143, 147
Altzürükü, 102, 144
Amette, Léon-Adolphe, 92
Amicale Jean-Macé, 77
Amiens, 130
Amiral Charnier, 129
Amnesty Act, 71
Amnesty Law, 71
Amorotze-Zokotze, 144, 147
Andalusia, 44
Andoain, 141, 146
Andrieu, Joseph, 51
Angelu, 79, 142
Anglet, 79, 142. *See also* Angelu
Anhauze, 145, 147
anti-militarism, 27
anti-militarist, 27–28

172 | Index

anti-nationalist, 28
anti-Semitic, 14
Anxuberro, 87, 94n1, 116. *See also* Saint-Pierre, Jean
Aquitaine, 38, 150
Arboti-Zohota, 143, 147
Archduchess Maria Christina, 43
Archduke Franz Ferdinand, 31. *See also* Ferdinand, Franz
Argonne, 66
Arhantsusi, 146, 147
Armée d'Orient, 98–99
Armendaritze, 143, 147
armistice, 6, 9, 132–135
Arnegi, 69, 144
Arnéguy, 69, 144. *See also* Arnegi
Arrangoitze, 147
Arras, 54, 110, 130
Arrigorriaga, 141, 147
Arrueta-Sarrikota, 142, 147
Ascain, 57, 142. *See also* Azkaine
Assemblée Nationale, 94, 102. *See also* National Assembly
Atharratze, 29, 54, 70, 93
Athens, 99
Aubérive (soldiers), 108
Audoin-Rouzeau, Stéphane, 11n1, 12n21, 21n11, 72n4, 115, 127n2
Aussurucq, 102, 144. *See also* Altzürükü
AustroHungarian Empire, 34
Aviron Bayonnais, 77
Avocourt, 66
Azkaine, 24, 57, 142, 147

Bad Duchy, 13
Baigorri, 69–70, 115, 142, 147
Baiona, 6, 25, 27, 38–40, 51–53, 65–66, 68, 76–79, 84, 87, 90, 96, 101, 106, 109, 116, 130, 140–142, 146, 150, 153, 155, 157
Balkan front, 128, 132

the Balkan problem, 36
Balparda, Gregorio de, 45
Banco de Bilbao, 81–82
Banco de Vizcaya, 82
Banco de Comercio, 81
Bank of France, 78
Banka, 144, 147
Barakaldo, 141
Barbier, Jean 90–91, 120, 127n8
Barcelona, 81
Barcelona Stock Exchange, 80
Barcus, 105, 142. *See also* Barkoxe
Bardos, 105, 142. *See also* Bardoze
Bardoze, 105, 142
Barkoxe, 105, 142
Basque Catholic Church, 20
Basque language, 15–16, 18–20, 70, 76, 123. *See also* Euskara
Basque nationalism, 45, 155, 160n1-2
Basque Nationalist Party, 20, 44–45, 83
Basse-Navarre, 25. *See also* Lower Navarre
Basses-Pyrénées, 27, 30n11, 40, 41n28, 67, 70, 78, 83, 85n6, 115, 127n1
Bastida, 118, 140, 142, 147
La Bastide Clairance, 118, 142, *See also* Bastida
Basusarri, 143, 146
battle of Arras, 54
Battle of Caporetto, 110
Battle of Charleroi, 52–53, 83–84
battle of Guise, 53
battle of Isonzo, 62
Battle of Limanowa-Łapanów, 96
Battle of the Marne, 54, 56
Battle of the Masurian Lakes, 53
battle of Mons, 53
battle of Montmirail, 54–55
battle of Morhange, 52
battle of Rossignol, 52
battle of Sedan, 6

Index | 173

Battle of the Somme, 105
battle of Woerth, 6
Battle of Valmy, 101
Battle of Verdun, 84, 94, 101–105, 108, 148, 150
Battle of Ypres, 54, 61
battle of the Yser, 54
Batxi, 45. *See also* Bilbao, Juan Bautista
Bayo, 45
Bayonne, 6, 11n5, 12n6, 23n50, 41n20–24, 41n27, 55n1, 85n12–18, 86n19–21, 100n1, 142. *See also* Baiona
Baztan, 69
Béarn, 158
Béarnais, 157
Beaurieux, 56, 58
Becker, Annette, 11n1, 12n21, 21n11, 30n12–14, 30n18–19, 30n23, 41n30, 85n2, 86n36, 95n16, 95n19, 115, 127n2
Behauze, 143, 147
Belgrade, 37, 61–62, 99
Belloc, 26
Berrogaine-Lahüntze, 145, 147
bertsolaritza, 46
Beskoitze, 142, 147
Biarritz, 51, 76–77, 142, 157
"Biba Frantzia!", 7–8, 11
Bidache, 51, 142. *See also* Bidaxune
Bidaxune, 51, 142, 147
Bilbao, 45, 86n30–33, 145. *See also* Bilbo *and* Bilbo-Bilbao
Bilbao, Juan Bautista, 45
Bilbo, 81–82, 145
Bilbo-Bilbao, 80–81, 83, 141
Bilbo-Bilbao Stock Exchange, 80–81
Biltzar (Assembly) of Lapurdi, 24
Biscay, 80, 155
Bismarck, Otto von, 13–14, 35
Bithiriña, 143, 147
Bizkaia, 45, 80–83

Bizkaia Provincial Council, 83
(the) Bolsheviks, 129
Bonaparte, Napoleon, 10, 57
Bonaparte, Louis-Napoléon, 68
Bonapartist, 10, 25–26
Le Bonnet Rouge, 71
Bordeaux, 38, 44, 52–53, 150
Bosphorus sea passage, 45
Bourg-et-Comin, 56, 58
Le Bouvet, 97, 129
Brest-Litovsk, 62
Brest-Litovsk armistice, 135
Brest-Litovsk peace treaty, 129
Brittany, 16, 18, 19, 75, 158
Broussain, Pierre, 20, 23n54
Brussels, 52
Bucharest, 99
Bucharest armistice, 135
Budapest, 131
Burgue-Erreiti, 144, 147
Bustince-Iriberry, 140, 145. *See also* Buztintze-Hiriberri
Bustinza, Evaristo, 45
Buztintze-Hiriberri, 140, 145, 147

Caillaux, Henriette, 27
Caillaux, Joseph, 27
Calais, 130
Californie, 57, 107
Calmette, Gaston, 27
Cambo, Chiquito de, 58. *See also* Kanbo, Chiquito de
Cambó, Francesc, 43
Cambrai, 132
Caminos de Hierro del Norte, 81
Cantabria, 44
Capbreton, 77
Cape Matapan, 99, 129
Caporetto, 110, 128, 132
Captain Miguras, 71
Carlists, 44, 68

Carnet B, 27–28
Carpathians, 61, 99
Catalan MP Francesc Cambó, 83. *See also* Cambó, Francesc
Catalans, 43–44
Catalonia, 18–19, 44, 70, 80, 83
Catholic Church, 10, 16, 24–26, 29, 44, 75–76, 92, 159
Caucasus Mountains, 62
Cazals, Rémy, 63n18, 115
censorship, 65, 84–85, 103
centralism, 18–19
Cerny, 108
Champagne, 61–62, 104, 108, 130, 132
Chancellor Bethmann-Hollweg, 14, 34, 36, 128
Chancellor Bismarck, 14. *See also* Bismark, Otto von
Chapitre forest, 104
Charleroi, 52–54, 65
Charo, Dominique, 54
Château Neuf, 39
Château-Thierry, 130
Château de Versailles, 135
Chemin des Dames, 56, 94, 103, 107–111, 128, 130, 132, 150, 157
chlorine, 61. *See also* poison gas
Churchill, Winston, 97–98
Cividale, 110
Clemenceau, Georges, 78, 128
clericalism, 25
Commandant Baron, 84
communists, 131, 159
Compañía Naviera Vascongada, 82
Compiègne, 135
Confédération Générale du Travail, 27. *See also* General Confederation of Labor
Congress of Oppressed Nations of Eastern Europe, 131
Constantinople, 96–97

convalescent homes, 77
Corbeaux forest, 103
El Correo del Norte, 83
Council of Ministers, 43
Count Pourtalès, 35
Corsica, 19, 129, 151, 158
Le Courrier de Bayonne, 77
Craonne, 56–57, 66, 107–109, 150
Craonnelle, 56–58, 108, 157
Crédito de Unión Minera, 82
Crépey, 51
Creute, 61, 107
Crimean War (1853–1856), 13
Croix de Guerre, 88, 94, 124
Cumières forest, 103

Danzig Corridor, 136
Dardanelles, 45, 96–98, 129
Dardanelles Strait, 96, 98
Dato, Eduardo, 43
Daudet, Léon, 10
Deba, 141, 146
Dehez, Jean-Baptiste, 51
Delay clinic, 77
development of capitalism, 14
disease, 99, 110, 151–152
Dibon, Pierre, 51
Donaixti-Ibarre, 143, 147
Donamartiri, 143, 147
Donazaharre, 144, 147
Donibane Garazi, 69–70, 93, 140, 147
Donibane Lohizune, 20, 29, 57, 68, 70, 79, 142, 147, 157
Donostia–San Sebastián, 42–43, 80, 141
Donoztiri, 143, 147
Dreyfus, Alfred, 26, 29n4
Dreyfus affair, 25, 29n4
Driant, Émile, 102
Duchess of Hohenberg, 31
Duchy of Italy, 13
Duhalde, Petri, 118

Duma, 128
Dunkirk, 130
Dupouy, Jean, 79
Durquet, 118

Eastern Front, 53–55, 61
Ebert, Friedrich, 137
economic sanctions, 135, 159
Eisner, Kurt, 133
Elissalde, Jean, 57, 63n1–2, 87–88, 95n4–6, 116
Elissamburu, Jean-Baptiste, 7, 9, 11, 12n7, 123
Elosu, Fernand, 27
Emmanuel II, Victor, 13
Emperor Franz Joseph, 31, 128
Epherre, Michel, 102
Erdozaintzi-Etxart, Bertrand, 102
Erratzu, 69, 141
Errenteria, 141, 146
Eskiula, 142, 147
Eskualduna, 10, 20, 29, 30n9, 30n25, 55, 71, 76, 78, 84–85, 87, 90–94, 95n8–9, 95n12, 95n23, 116–117, 124, 127n4
Espelette, 70, 143. *See also* Ezpeleta
Esterençuby, 69, 143. *See also* Ezterenzubi
Etchepare, Jean, 23n46, 63n24–25, 85n10–11, 87, 89, 95n7, 116, 137, 138n7
Etcheverry, Louis, 25
Etxalar, 141, 146
Etxarri, 144, 147
Etxeberri, Pierre, 65–66
Eupen, 136
Euskalduna, 81
Euskara, 15–16, 18, 20
Euzkadi, 45–46, 87, 89
Euzko Alderdi Jeltzalea, 20. *See also* Basque Nationalist Party
Excelsior-Cinéma, 76

Ezpeleta, 24, 70, 143
Ezterenzubi, 69, 143

Faxe, 52
federalism, 19, 22n36–37
Ferdinand, Franz, 31
Ferdinand, Sophie, 31. *See also* Duchess of Hohenberg
La Féria, 76
Ferry, Jules, 15–16, 25
Field Marshal von Hindenburg, 128
Le Figaro, 27
Fismes, 58
Flanders, 54, 128, 130, 132
Fleury, 104
Foch, Ferdinand, 132
Focsani armistice, 100
Foni, 110
Fontarrabia, 141
Fonteny, 52
Forges de l'Adour, 79
Fort Douaumont, 102, 104–105
fort at Ivangorod, 62
forts of Lemberg, 62
Fort Rupel, 99
Fort Seddul-Bahr, 98
Fort Thiaumont, 105
Fort de Vaux, 104–105
Fortis, Achile, 140
Fourmonon, 53
Fraize, 51
Franco, 154
Franco-Prussian War (1870), 5, 11n4
Francoists, 154
French Empire, 5, 9
French Foreign Legion, 44
French Military Justice Act, 65
French Ministry of Defense, 140–141
French nationalism, 9, 18–19
French Republic, 12n17, 24–25, 34. *See also* Republicans

French Revolution, 9, 24, 26, 28, 68, 155
French Socialist Party, 26
Freycenet, Louis Charles de, 43

Gabadi, 144, 147
La Gaceta del Norte, 83
Galicia, 53, 62, 80. *See also* Przemyśl
Gallipoli, 97–98
Gamarte, 145, 147
Gamere-Zihiga, 144, 147
Garat, Joseph, 27, 30n15, 30n24, 72n17, 73n20, 73n25, 73n31–33, 96
Gartzain, 141
Gaudin, Léon, 57
Gaudin, Pascal, 57
General Confederation of Labor, 27–28
General Fayolle, 110
General Gallieni, 53
General Joffre, 55n4, 56, 94, 102
General Nivelle, 94, 107–108, 110
General Pétain, 46, 103, 110
George, David Lloyd, 128
German Empire, 5, 9, 13
Getaria, 143, 147, 157
Gipuzkoa, 45, 68, 80
Gironde, 40
Gixune, 51, 143
Goiri, Luis Arana, 44, 83
Goiri, Sabino Arana, 20, 44
Goyenetche, Albert, 20
Gozée, 52
Grenade, Martin, 140
Grey, Edward 98
Grimm, Robert, 71
Grosrouvres, 51
Gruerie forest, 104
Guiche, 51, 143. *See also* Gixune
Guichenné, Léon, 93
Guipúzcoa, 45. *See also* Gipuzkoa
Gure Herria, 87

Haig, Douglas, 110
Haltsu, 144, 147
Hasparren, 140, 142. *See also* Hazparne
Hautes-Pyrénées, 40
Hazparne, 20, 140, 142
Heguy, Dominique, 140
Heleta, 142, 147
Hendaia, 70, 142, 147, 157
Hendaye, 70, 142. *See also* Hendaia
Hiriart-Urruty, Manex, 20, 72n3, 87, 91, 93, 95n13–14, 95n20, 95n22, 116
Hitler, 159
Holy Roman Empire, 9
Hosta, 140, 145. *See also* Hozta
Hozta, 140, 145
Hurtebise Farm, 56–57, 60, 107

Ibardin, 69
Ibarrola, 145, 147
Ilharre, 143, 146
Iholdi, 140, 143, 147
Iholdy, 140, 143. *See also* Iholdi
Industrial Revolution, 14
Inhabar, Nicolas, 140
Irabola, Matxin, 124, 126, 127n10
Iriart, Bernard, 140
Irisarri, 142, 147
Irun, 141, 145
Iruñea-Pamplona, 141, 146
Iruri, 145, 147
Irurita, 141
Ispoure, 65, 144. *See also* Izpura
Istanbul, 62, 96
Itsasu, 24, 142
Italian War (1859–1861), 13
Izpura, 65, 144

Jacobins, 18, 28, 155
Jauffret, François-Antoine, 25
Jaurès, Jean 28
Jestaze, 145, 147

Joffre, Joseph, 53, 102–103, 105. *See also* General Joffre
Le Journal de Bayonne, 116
Le Journal de Saint-Palais, 116
Judge Leoarat, 84
Jutsi, 140, 144, 147
Juxue, 140, 144. *See also* Jutsi

Kaïmaktchala, 99
Kaiser Wilhelm II, 14, 21n1, 34, 133
Kanbo, 77, 142
Kanbo, Chiquito de, 58, 117
Kienthal, 72
King Alfonso XIII, 43
King Constantine, 42, 99
King Louis XIV, 107
Kingdom of Bavaria, 13
Kingdom of Italy, 13
Kingdom of Prussia, 9
Kingdom of Sardinia, 13
Kingdom of the Two Sicilies, 13
Kirikiño, 45–46. *See also* Bustinza, Evaristo
Kragujevac, 131
Krakow, 61

Labetze-Bizkai, 144, 147
Labourd, 68. *See also* Lapurdi
Laida, 141, 146
Lakarri-Arhane-Sarrikotagaine, 143, 147
Lake Léon, 79
Lake Van, 62
Landais, 157
Landes, 24, 40, 158
Laon, 107–108
Lapurdi, 68–69, 146–147
Landes, 24, 40, 158
Larceveau, 102, 143. *See also* Larzabale
Larrañe, 147
Larresoro, 77, 144
Larressore, 77, 144. *See also* Larresoro

Larzabale, 102
Larzabale-Arroze-Zibitze, 143, 147
Lasa, 65, 145, 147
Lasse, 65, 145. *See also* Lasa
Latournerie, François, 51
Laudio, 141, 146
Law on the Provisional Deportation of Armenians, 62
Lay-Saint-Rémy, 51
Lazkao, 26
League of Nations, 136–137, 159
Lekorne, 142, 147
Lekuine, 145, 147
Lenin, Vladimir, 72, 129
Lévy, Louis Mardochée, 66
Lexantzü-Zünharre, 145, 147
Libourne, 40
Liège, 37, 51, 136
Lieutenant-Colonel Louis Gaussot, 157
Liginaga, 143, 146
Lille, 132
Limanowa-Łapanów, 61
Limburg, 87
Liverpool, 129
Łódź, 55
Lohitzüne-Oihergi, 144, 147
Lorriane, 5–6, 9–11, 19–20, 51, 136, 155
Lower Navarre, 25, 68, 69, 147
Ludwig III of Bavaria, 133
Lüküze Altzümarta, 144, 147
Lunéville, 51
Lusitania, 129
Luzaide, 68, 141, 146
Lycée Saint-Louis, 77

Madrid, 80
Maizy, 58, 66, 109
Makea, 143, 147
Malécarie, Antoine, 84
Malmedy, 136
Malvy, Louis, 29

Mangin, Charles, 132
Marchais-en-Brie, 54
Marítima de Nervión, 82
Marítima Unión company, 82
the Marne, 54, 130, 132, 150–151
Marseille, 98, 129
Martxueta, 143, 147
Martov, 71
Massif Central, 75
Masuria, 61
Matajur, 110
Maule, 68, 70, 115, 157
Maule-Lextarre, 142, 147
Mauléon 68, 142. *See also* Maule
Maurras, Charles, 10
Max, Karl, 36. *See also* Prince Lichnowsky
Medal of Remembrance, 118
Mémoires des Hommes website, 140–141
Mendigorria, 141, 146
Metz, 7
Meurthe-et-Moselle, 51
Meuse, 37, 103, 150, 151
Miarritze, 142, 147
Michaelis, Georg, 128
Milafranga, 87
Millerand, Alexandre 70
Minera Sierra Menera, 81
Ministry of War, 84
Miremont, Georges, 27
Mitikile-Larrori-Mendibile, 143, 147
monarchist, 25–26, 155
Mont-de-Marsan, 40, 150
Mont-le-Vignoble, 51
Montdidier, 132
Montori-Berroritze, 143, 147
Monument des Basques, 157
Moravia, 136
Mort-Homme, 103
"Mort pour la France", 156, 158

Moselle, 51–52
Moudros, 97–98
Moudros armistice, 133
Moulier, Jules, 63n3, 63n9, 67, 74, 85n1, 87, 90, 95n10, 116
Mount Kemmel, 130
Mulhouse, 51
mus, 58, 116
Muskildi, 143, 147

Nafarroa, 24, 68. *See also* Navarre
Nafarroa Beherea, 25. *See also* Lower Navarre
Napoleon III, 6, 9, 13, 25–26
National Assembly, 27, 93–94, 119
nationalism, 10, 12n14, 14–15, 18, 20, 22n28–29, 23n49, 27–28, 30n22, 41n10, 44, 82, 155
nationalist sentiment, 14
Navarre, 24, 67–69, 147. *See also* Erratzu
Nazi, 136
Nazism, 159
New York, 129
Nicholas II, 128
Northern Basque Country, 6, 9–10, 18, 20, 24–26, 29, 38, 40, 46, 68–69, 74–76, 78, 87, 90, 115–116, 119–120, 133, 140–141, 147, 150, 153, 154–156, 158–159
Nouvion forest, 53

Occitania, 18, 19
Offenstadt, Nicolas, 115–116, 127n3
Oise, 54, 151
Oragarre, 147
Order of the Division, 87
Orlando, Vittorio Emmanuele, 128
Oronoz, 141, 146
Ostankoa, 145, 147
Othart, Laurent. 140

Ottoman Empire, 13, 32–33, 37–38, 62, 96, 133
Oulches, 56, 66, 150, 157
Ourcq River, 54
Oxobi, 67, 74, 87, 90, 95n11, 116, 133. See also Moulier, Jules
Ozeraine-Erribareita, 147

pacifists, 27–28, 71, 155, 159
Pagola, 143, 147
Paissy, 108
Pan-Slavism, 34
Paris, 6, 29n4, 35, 40, 53–54, 61, 84, 92–94, 101, 129–131, 158
Paris Commune, 6, 68
Parois, 66
Pas-de-Calais, 54, 150–151
Pasaia, 80, 141, 146
Pasajes, 141, 146. See also Pasaia
Passchendaele, 110
Pau, 38–40, 140, 150
pelota, 21, 58, 76, 116–118
les pépères, 40
Pérès, Hubert, 158, 160n4
Pétain, Philippe, 94, 104, 110, 159. See also General Pétain
Petrograd, 128
Peytrain, Jean, 79
Piarres, 90
Piave, 131–132
Picardy, 54, 130
Piraeus, 99
plebiscite, 136
Poincaré, Raymond, 34, 53, 109
poison gas, 61, 153
Pont-à-Mousson, 51
Pont Saint-Esprit, 39
Pope Benedict XV, 92
Posnania, 136
Poudrière de Blancpignon, 79
Prague, 131

President Wilson, 129. See also Wilson, Woodrow
Press Office, 84
Prince Lichnowsky, 36
Prince Maximilian of Baden, 137
Princip, Gavrilo, 31
proletariat, 76
propaganda, 35, 45, 62, 66
Provence II, 99
Prussian kingdom, 5
Pyrenees, 67, 69–70, 72n12, 72n14–15, 72n18, 73n24, 73n26, 73n28, 88
Pyrénées-Atlantiques, 86n41, 141, 153
Przemyśl, 53, 61–62

Quatre Arbres Plateau, 57
Queen Elisabeth of Belgium 77
Queen Victoria, 43
Quinto Real, 69

Rapallo Conference, 132
the Reichstag, 131
Récicourt, 66
Reims, 109
Renteria, 141, 146. See also Errenteria
Republicans, 10, 12n17, 16, 25–26, 28, 71, 76, 155
Resurrección María Azkue, 44
Rethondes, 135
Rhine, 135
Rimavska Sobota, 131
Rochefort, 40, 52
La Rochelle, 40, 88
Rome, 13, 25, 131
Royaumieux, 51
Russian Empire, 13
Russian Revolution, 83, 100

Saarbrücken, 6
Saarland, 136
Saint-Esprit, 27, 76

180 | Index

Saint-Étiennede-Baïgorry, 69, 142. *See also* Baigorri
Saint-Gervais, 129
Saint-Jean-de-Luz, 29. *See also* Donibane Lohizune
Saint-Jean-Pied-de-Port, 39, 69, 101, 143. *See also* Donibane Garazi
Saint-Louis de Gonzague school, 77
Saint-Mihiel, 102
Saint-Nazaire, 130
Saint-Pée-sur-Nivelle, 124, 142, *See also* Senpere
Saint-Pierre, Jean, 55, 63n4–5, 63n7, 63n11–13, 63n16, 63n20, 72n2, 87–88, 93, 94n1, 95n2–3, 95n25, 116–117, 119, 127n5–6
Saint-Quentin, 130
Salaber, Dominique, 105
Salonika, 98–99, 101, 132
Sambre River, 52
San Daniele, 110
Sangla, Rémi, 105
Santa Grazi, 147
Santander, 42–43
Sara, 7, 24, 69, 143, 147
Sarajevo, 27, 31, 34, 36
Sare, 7, 143. *See also* Sara
Sarrikotapea, 144, 147
Sax, 13
Sazonov, Sergei, 35
Schlieffen, Alfred von, 35
Schlieffen plan, 35
Schleswig-Holstein region, 136
Second Battle of Ypres, 61
Second Empire, 6
Second International, 32
Second Reich, 13, 21n1
secularism, 20
Seine, 53
Senpere, 124, 142
Senpertarra, Matxin, 124. *See also* Irabola, Matxin

Séry-lès-Mézières, 53
Sestao, 141, 146
shipbuilding, 45, 80–82, 130
Siderúrgica del Mediterráneo, 81
Silesia, 136, 138
Socialist International, 71
socialists, 28, 32, 71, 76, 92, 137
Société d'Études Basques Eusko Ikaskuntza, 87
Société Nautique, 77
Socoa, 77. *See also* Zokoa
Soest, 7
Sohüta, 142, 147
Soissons, 53, 109, 130
the Somme, 102, 105–106, 109, 132, 150, 151
Sota y Aznar, 81
Sota, Ramón de la, 45, 81, 83
Souain, 62
Soule, 24, 41n32, 73n22, 73n29–30. *See also* Zuberoa
Southern Basque Country, 20, 26, 42, 44, 68–69, 71, 78, 80, 83, 120, 141, 154–155
Spartakists, 131
St. Petersburg, 34–35
submarine warfare, 78, 129
Le Suffren, 129

Tagliamento, 111
Tannenberg, 53
Tarbes, 40, 150
Tardets, 29. *See also* Atharratze
terroir, 19, 22n17–18, 22n20, 22n23, 22n25–26, 22n30
Teruel, 81
Thessaloniki, 62
Third Republic, 9, 15, 25
Thuin, 52
Tolosa, 141, 146
Toul, 51
toxic gas, 104

Treaty of Versailles, 136–137, 159
Triple Alliance, 33, 42, 98
Triple Entente, 32, 42–43
Trotsky, Leon, 72, 129
Tschirschky, Heinrich von, 34, 36
Tudela, 141, 146. *See also* Tutera
Tutera, 141, 146
Txirrita, 46

Udine, 110
Uhart, Arnaud, 140
Uhart, Michel, 140
Uhartehiri, 144, 147
Union Sacrée, 28
urbanization, 17–18, 155
Urdax, 141, 145. *See also* Urdazubi
Urdazubi, 141, 145
Urepel, 69, 145. *See also* Urepele
Urepele, 69, 145, 147
Urrugne, 69, 142. *See also* Urruña
Urruña, 69, 142, 147, 157
Ürrustoi-Larrebile, 145, 147
Uskub, 62, 98–99
Ustaritz, 70, 142. *See also* Uztaritze
Uztaritze, 70, 118, 142

Valcarlos, 68, 146. *See also* Luzaide
Vardar, 98
Vatican, 13, 92
Vauban, 101
Vauclerc, 57, 108
Veneto, 13
Venice, 111
Venizelos, Eleftherios, 99
Verdun, 46, 53, 63, 95n26, 101–106, 106n3, 107, 109, 148
Victoria-Eugenia of Battenberg, 43
Vienna, 32, 34, 36
Vigo-Almereyda, Miguel, 71
Villa Giusti armistice, 133
La-Ville-aux-Bois, 56
Ville-sur-Tourbe, 62

Villefranque, 87. *See also* Milafranga
Villers-sur-Fère, 109
Villiers, 53
Vistula River, 62
Viviers, 52
Vizcaya, 45, 86n30–33. *See also* Bizkaia
Voulpaix, 53

war of 1870, 7, 32–33
war of attrition, 55, 60, 148
War Council, 66
Warsaw, 55, 62
Wavrille forest, 102
Weimar Republic, 133, 137
Western Front, 35, 61, 97–98, 128–132
Westphalia, 7
Wilhelm I, 13
William I, 9
William II, 34
Wilson, Woodrow, 136
Winter Palace, 129
Wisła River, 62. *See also* Vistula River
Würtemberg, 13

Ybarnégaray, Jean, 26, 93–94, 96, 159
Ypres, 54–55, 110–111, 130, 132
Yser, 54

Zaldubi, Gratien Adema, 8–9
Zalla, 141, 146
Zaro, 146, 147
"Zazpi Euskal Herriek bat egin dezagun", 8
Zerbitzari, 57, 87–89, 104–105, 116, 119–120, 134. *See also* Elissalde, Jean
Ziburu, 143, 157
Zokoa, 79
Zuberoa, 24–25, 68–69, 147
Zugarramurdi, 141

www.ingramcontent.com/pod-product-compliance
Lightning Source LLC
Chambersburg PA
CBHW020738230426

43665CB00009B/486